MANNERS
A N D
CUSTOMS
IN THE BIBLE

Revised Edition

MANNERS
A N D
CUSTOMS
IN THE BIBLE

Revised Edition

VICTOR H. MATTHEWS

HENDRICKSON
PUBLISHERS

Copyright © 1988, 1991
Hendrickson Publishers, Inc.
P.O. Box 3473
Peabody, Massachusetts 01961-3473
Printed in the United States of America

Hardcover edition: ISBN 0-943575-77-X
Paperback edition: ISBN 0-943575-81-8

Twelfth Printing Revised Edition, March 2003

All Scripture quotations in the margins come from the New Revised
Standard Version, copyright © 1989, Division of Christian Education
of the National Council of the Churches of Christ in the United States
of America.

Library of Congress Cataloging-in-Publication Data

Matthews, Victor Harold.
    Manners and customs in the Bible   /   Victor H. Matthews. —
[Rev. ed.]
    Includes bibliographical references and index.
    ISBN 0-943575-77-X (hardcover). – ISBN 0-943575-81-8
(softcover)
    1. Jews – Social life and customs – To 70 A.D. 2. Palestine –
Social life and customs – To 70 A.D.   3. Bible – Antiquities.
I. Title.
DS112.M33 1988b
220.9′5 – dc20   91 – 27313
                                                                                           CIP

To Carol, Peter, and Samuel

TABLE OF CONTENTS

ILLUSTRATIONS

PREFACE TO THE REVISED EDITION

Votive tablet of Ur-Enlil found at Nippur. From M. Jastrow, The Civilization of Babylonia and Assyria.

Writing a biblical resource tool is a bit of a double-edged sword. There is so much that the author would like to include, based on the research done on the volume, but there is limited space in which to package it. In writing *Manners and Customs in the Bible,* I tried to answer in a readable and informative way the sort of questions I have heard from my students. The fact that the book in now going into its fourth printing, with a revised edition, suggests that many people have found it to be useful. In this newly revised edition, I have made some changes that, it would be hoped, will make it even more of a resource for the student of the biblical world.

Most obvious among the changes has been my attempt to make more effective use of the wide margins on each page. These margins were originally designed to provide space for personal notes on the text; however, we decided that it would be more helpful to add new illustrations and biblical quotations which complemented the discussion on these pages. In addition, there are also quotations from extrabiblical sources such as ancient Mesopotamia and Egypt and the Jewish historian Josephus. These quotations should whet the reader's appetite to consult the Bible or volumes of translated texts in order to read "the rest of the story."

In addition, the bibliographies for each chapter have been updated to reflect new works in each biblical period studied. There is a substantial amount of new scholarship being published, especially on the settlement of early Israel and the character of the monarchy. One other area which is receiving a great deal of attention is the social-scientific study of the biblical world. This is a cross-disciplinary approach which makes use of sociological and anthropological methods to delve into the culture described in the text. Ethno-archaeological research complements this approach adding the physical aspect to the reconstruction of ancient societies. I have utilized some of these methods in this volume, especially in chapters 1-3. However, for a more complete treatment of the subject I will direct you to my forthcoming Hendrickson publication, *Cultural Anthropology and World of the Old Testament,* co-authored with Don C. Benjamin of Rice University, which should be available in late 1992.

Let me encourage those that use this book to share the information you gain with others. Over the years I have discovered a tremendous hunger for knowledge about the world of the Bible. However, many people do not know where to turn, other than to the Bible itself. My hope is that through this volume they will gain the spark of curiosity to learn more and to read, with a more educated eye, the rich literature of ancient Israel.

PREFACE

One of the joys of studying the Bible is attempting to reconstruct the manners and customs of the peoples of ancient times. The gulf of thousands of years can be bridged, at least in part, by insights into their everyday life. These can be garnered through close examination of the biblical narratives and through the use of comparative written and physical remains from other ancient civilizations. The discoveries and interpretations of archaeologists and art historians, and modern anthropological research are also of prime importance to the reconstruction process.

In attempting to recreate the social world of ancient Israel there are several sources of information from which to draw. Written records from this period include the biblical text and a few extrabiblical documents which parallel but do not always corroborate the biblical narrative. Physical remains, however, are limited to what has been uncovered by archaeologists. These remains provide only a partial picture of life in ancient times — the garbage heaps, the ruins of conquered and/or abandoned cities, the bits and pieces of life that have almost miraculously survived the elements and the centuries. And finally, the social setting can be partially interpreted from the biblical text and inferred from analogous ancient and modern cultures. To be sure, not every aspect of life is available from the ancient sources. Preferences and individual tastes in cloth-

Winged bull with human face from Sargon's palace. Photo from M. Jastrow, The Civilization of Babylonia and Assyria. Pref-1

O LORD, how many are my
foes!
Many are rising against me;
many are saying to me,
"There is no help for you in
God."

Selah

But you, O LORD, are a shield
around me,
my glory, and the one who
lifts up my head.
I cry aloud to the LORD,
and he answers me from his
holy hill.

Selah

—Psa 3:1–4

ing, diet, and even worship practices are simply impossible to recreate due to our lack of information or understanding.

The biblical text itself contains a wealth of information on subjects ranging from civil and religious law to building codes and harvesting techniques. In the text can be found everything from the proper procedure for dealing with a delinquent son to the requirements for purifying a priest after he has come into contact with a corpse. The narratives specify the times, places, and manner in which to perform sacrifices to God as well as injunctions regarding the slaughtering of animals.

The sheer amount of data acquired through careful study of the Bible, while impressive, can also cause confusion. Technical terms, such as "selah" in Psalms, point out that some of these writings were to be used for community worship and as a guide for religious professionals in antiquity. Words or jargon associated with professional groups, in antiquity or the present, often require additional explanation for the reader. Unfortunately, the meaning of some of these biblical terms is still a mystery that requires further research and the careful use of extrabiblical materials. For instance, the poetic texts found at the ancient seaport city of Ugarit (dating to between 1600–1200 BC) are similar in style and vocabulary to the Psalms and the epic sections of the biblical text. Comparative study of these texts has in some cases provided the key to identifying the meaning of a word which has long remained unknown.

Occasionally, the text includes the smallest and seemingly most insignificant details, monotonously droning on with a series of "begats" or the dimensions of the doorway of the temple. In other cases, the narrative may skip over the entire reign of a king, dismissing him with the phrase "he did what was evil in the sight of the

Lord." The narrator then summarizes the remainder of the king's life with the tantalizing footnote, "Now the rest of the acts of _____ which he did, are they not written in the Book of the Chronicles of the Kings of Israel?" As this lost work and others, like the Book of Jashar, demonstrate, a great deal of information was available to the ancient writers which we will never be able to consult. These citations of lost works are a ready reminder that we have only an editorialized version of events from which to draw a picture of life in biblical times.

The book of Judges is another section of the biblical text in which large segments of the narrative appear to have been edited out — perhaps because the stories were so well known to contemporary readers. For the modern reader, however, there are many questions about the activities of the judges and people of this time period left unanswered. For example, why is this society so violent and accepting of violence? Why do the judges have to rely on primitive weapons like oxgoads and animal bones? Why is it that obedience to the laws of hospitality is judged more important than the life of the host's virgin daughter in Judges 19? Because these things are so foreign to today's world, it is sometimes only through the use of comparative materials from nonbiblical sources, such as the texts from the city of Ugarit or the cities of Mesopotamia, that

Cuneiform tablets with cylinder seal impressions. Photo courtesy of Southwest Missouri State University. Pref-2

a better understanding of life in ancient times can be obtained.

The researcher, however, can too easily fall into a trap when using comparative materials or the findings of archaeologists. Each of these sources of information provides a slightly different picture of life in the biblical period than is found in the biblical text. As a result, care must be taken to prevent overly enthusiastic attempts to match the biblical narrative with seemingly parallel information.

The perspective of many extrabiblical writings is secular, with no attempt being made to create a religious framework for them. Overreliance on parallels can therefore lead to incorrect interpretations and wishful thinking. For instance, in the ancient letters from the Mesopotamian city of Nuzi (c. 16th–15th century BC) we find family customs regarding marriage preference and the adoption of an heir. At least in a superficial way these customs resemble those reflected in the stories told about Abraham, Isaac, and Jacob in Genesis. However, these Nuzi texts are family legal documents. There are no overtones of adherence to a covenant with God or a concern to maintain the cultural purity of a chosen people as there are in Genesis. Without more complete evidence caution must therefore be the watchword when using parallel materials to explain or clarify the biblical narratives.

Archaeological evidence provides the best information on life in ancient times. When careful methods are applied to the excavation of ancient city and village sites, information slowly emerges from the ground which can aid our understanding of the people of the past. Careful methods include systematic recording of finds — photographic and written records — and the sharing of this material with a wide range of experts who can draw a more complete conclusion on life in the biblical period than the archaeologist alone. So, for

Modern bedouin; in the background, the city of Jerusalem. Photo by Ralph Harris. Pref-3

instance, the carbonized remains found in storage jars and on the floors of excavated threshing floors, when examined by teams of microbiologists, botanists, and paleobotanists, can lead to the discovery of what ancient human beings regularly had in their diets. Their general level of health can be surmised, and the level of their methods of agriculture and animal husbandry can be at least partially ascertained.

At the same time, to expect these discoveries to conclusively "prove the truth of the Bible" is unreasonable. The findings of archaeologists are only mute evidence of life in the ancient past. In other words, to say, as John Garstang did earlier in this century, that a particular wall found in the excavations at Jericho was the one that fell to the trumpet blasts of Joshua without examining all of the surrounding evidence (pottery, building styles, depth within the mound) is unfair to the student and to the text as well. Improved methods of excavation later proved Garstang to be incorrect even in his identification of the stratigraphic level of Joshua's Jericho, and this mistake led to controversy and a misunderstanding of the proper role of archaeological research in relation to the study of the Bible.

Finds must first be accepted for what they are in the context of the mound as a whole. The sites of ancient Palestinian cities are layered, with each level representing a different phase in the life history of the city. Since objects found lower in the mound can generally be assumed to be older than those found closer to the surface, a chronology of the various levels or strata can thus be developed.

Some confusion of the strata does occur, however, due to earthquake activity and the digging of pits and foundations by later inhabitants of the site. To overcome this obstacle and to establish a relative chronology for each city site, pottery types and other artifacts from each layer are examined. They are then compared with finds from the same levels in several similar sites. Carbon 14 dating is also used to aid in the process as well as other scientific dating methods.

Due to the limitations of time and money, archaeologists seldom uncover an entire mound. They carefully map out squares for excavation or dig exploratory shafts in those portions of the mound which surveys have shown to contain the most important structures (temples, palaces, gates) or the most representative objects of interest.

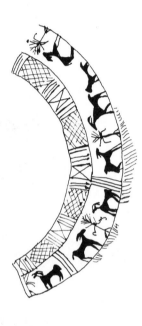

A Canaanite vase decorated with antelope grazing. Found near Ziklag. Pref-A

The most recently developed archaeological techniques do try to obtain a broader perspective on the entire mound, but it is unlikely that every shovel full of dirt will be turned or every object uncovered. Magnifying the difficulties of obtaining a complete occupational picture is the fact that many sites were excavated before modern methods were developed. This means that a great deal of valuable information has been lost forever. Archaeology is a destructive process (each level must be recorded and then removed to get to the level below it) and what has been removed can never be replaced. As a result, we learn but we do not learn all there is to know about life in these ancient cities through archaeology. Thus, responsible archaeologists today intentionally leave some portions of the mound untouched for later generations and their more advanced excavation methods.

To complete this cautionary survey of aids to the reconstruction of the biblical period, it should be noted that modern anthropological research can be of great value to the student of the Bible. Up until the beginning of the 20th century, tribal peoples continued to live in the Near East in much the same way that their ancestors had done thousands of years ago. Even in more recent times there are tribal peoples studied by anthropologists and ethnologists, whose manners and customs are very similar to those found in the biblical text. They still engage in seasonal migration with their flocks and herds in much the same way as that portrayed in the patriarchal narratives. Their relations with villages and cities are still marked with suspicion on the part of both parties just as when Abraham deceived Abimelech of Gerar in Genesis 20 by pretending that his wife was his sister.

Abraham said of his wife Sarah, "She is my sister." And King Abimelech of Gerar sent and took Sarah. —Gen 20:2

In doing comparative work, however, it should be understood that no parallel is likely to be totally exact. Customs and traditions can remain unchanged for centuries, but every group of people, even in the same area and with the same basic economy, is different in some way from its predecessors in the region. Therefore it is necessary to qualify most statements made in comparing ancient and modern peoples.

Having noted possible sources of information for our study and recognizing their potential for imprecision, let us now begin our reconstruction of the manners and customs of the peoples of the biblical period.

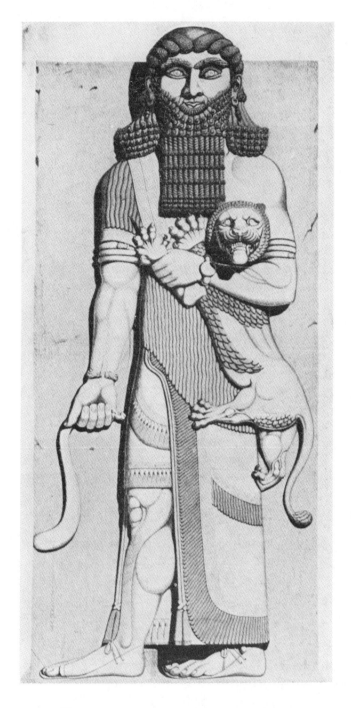

Gilgamesh, the hero of the Babylonian epic. Photo from M. Jastrow, The Civilization of Babylonia and Assyria. Intro-1

INTRODUCTORY
STATEMENT TO READERS

Before exploring the social world of ancient Israel, a few preliminary questions must be raised: First, why should such an attempt be made at all? Is not the biblical text sufficient to answer any question which may arise on this subject? Would not a careful reading of the text supply all the information anyone would need? Second, is it really necessary to write yet another book to serve as an aid in the reading of the biblical material?

The biblical text is in fact a storehouse of useful information. It describes many aspects of everyday life in ancient times, written in many cases from the perspective of the people of that period. Questions, such as: What did they eat? What did they wear? and How did they worship? can be partially answered by simply reading the Scriptures. Having a mass of information and being able to relate it to our own times and situation is, however, not always an easy task. After all, in many cases our interest in ancient times is sparked by our desire to understand the roots of our own culture. And, in the case of the biblical world, our concerns are expanded to include how God established his covenant with his people and how they lived under that covenant.

The first place to start in this study of biblical manners and customs is the environment. Under what conditions do the people live? What physical, economic, and social demands do geography, climate, physical resources, and neighboring groups place on the people? How much of what a culture says about itself can be traced to borrowings from other cultures or to an insulated or prejudiced attitude? In the case of ancient Israel, all of these questions must be raised; the answers may vary according to time period and level of cultural development. Israel did change its social attitude and customs over the two millennia of its existence before the Christian era.

With this in mind this volume is designed to be useful to both the lay person and the scholar in their study of the Bible. The biblical material is presented in chronological order, with chapters on each of the major periods of biblical history: Patriarchal, Settlement, Monarchy, Post-Exilic, and Intertestamental/New Testament. This kind of arrangement allows the peoples of the Bible to be examined according to stages of social development, starting with the pastoral nomadic culture of the patriarchs and concluding with the subjugated urban-based culture of Judea and Samaria in Roman times.

Each chapter provides a basic introduction to the historical and physical setting of the time period and sketches the basic elements of its social world. This will be accomplished through the examination of specific scenes in the biblical text with an eye toward what they can reveal about the everyday life of the peoples in the time of the Bible. Following the historical sketch are selected units dealing with specific social customs. These in turn are divided into sub-headings using examples from the biblical text, information from modern anthropological data, and archaeology.

Additional aids in this volume, which will help to identify particular topics and examples, include a full subject index, a biblical passage index, and an index of extrabiblical sources. The table of contents is as exhaustive as possible in listing the units and comparative materials

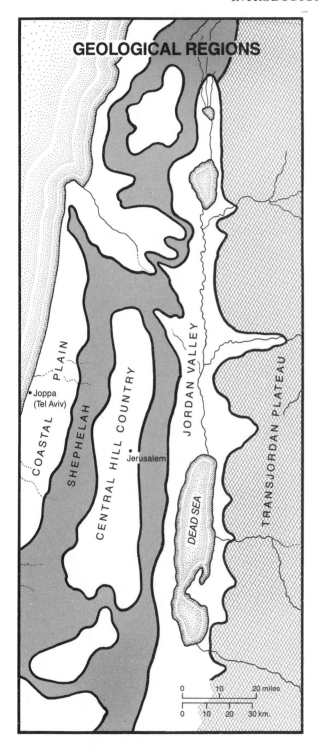

GEOLOGICAL REGIONS

Joppa
(Tel Aviv)

COASTAL PLAIN

SHEPHELAH

CENTRAL HILL COUNTRY

Jerusalem

JORDAN VALLEY

DEAD SEA

TRANS-JORDAN PLATEAU

0   10   20 miles
0   10   20   30 km.

*Geological regions of Palestine.
Adapted with permission from
InterVarsity Press.*   Intro-A

found in each chapter. Footnotes and citations, other than to the Bible or certain extrabiblical texts, have been omitted. However, at the end of each chapter is a select bibliography containing the major works consulted in writing the chapter as well as suggested additional readings.

A word now needs to be said about the selection of material. It will not be possible in this volume to examine every piece of information, every example, or every event in the biblical text as it relates to the social world of ancient Israel. As a result, a selection process was devised to give the clearest picture of everyday events, to avoid repetition, and to provide examples, using comparative materials, where events or situations are not fully understood.

HISTORICAL GEOGRAPHY OF BIBLE LANDS

Before moving on to the first chapter in the history of ancient Israel, it is necessary to sketch out the geographical character of the area in which this ancient people was shaped. Palestine lies in the midst of the so-called Fertile Crescent, which includes the major cultures of Egypt to the west and Mesopotamia to the east. Both of these river valley cultures developed high civilizations around 3000 BC. Major cities, with huge palace complexes and temples, as well as the large-scale commercial activity needed to support them, are hallmarks of their achievements. Very early in their history the Egyptian and Mesopotamian city-states established trade contacts, and succeeding periods saw a growth in these connections as well as in competition for ultimate supremacy in the region.

Travel to the south of the Tigris-Euphrates river valley of Mesopotamia was hampered by the Arabian desert, and sea travel to Egypt was

limited to the Mediterranean coast or the southern route down the Red Sea and around the
Arabian peninsula to the Persian Gulf. The
northern maritime trade routes were controlled
in most periods by middleman states like Byblos,
Ugarit, and the Phoenician ports of Tyre and
Sidon.

All of these geographical factors made the area
inhabited by the Israelites a crossroads from the
beginnings of civilization in this region. International trade routes and international highways,
such as the Transjordanian King's Highway,
connected the major population centers while
running directly through Palestine. Palestine's
position as a crossroads brought cultural contact
and trading opportunities. This also turned it
into a center of conflict between the superpowers
as they vied for control of the ancient Near East.
Palestine thus became both a beneficiary and a
victim of its geographical placement.

Although Palestine is a relatively small land
(350 miles long and 60 miles wide at its broadest
point), several spectacular geographical features
dominate the terrain and affect the people who
live there. Most prominent among them are the
Jordan Rift and the central hill country which
run north-south in tandem. The Mediterranean
coastal plain lacks deep water harbors and is thus
of less importance to the economy of the people.
However, the Shephelah, which is located between the coast and the hill country, was heavily
populated in ancient times, containing the city-
states of the Philistines. The Judean wilderness
and the Negeb desert have the harshest environ-
ments in Palestine. Still, they too have featured
prominently in the history of the land as the
home of pastoral nomadic tribes and the Qumran community.

The Jordan Rift is part of a massive fissure in
the earth which runs from just north of the Sea
of Galilee down into Africa. Within Palestine,

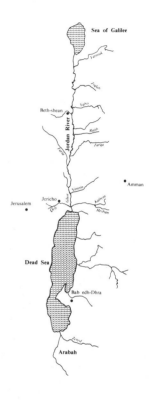

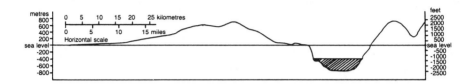

Cross-section of Holy Land elevations. Adapted with permission from InterVarsity Press.   Intro-D

the rift contains the Jordan River valley and is marked by a swift drop in elevation in that 70-mile span of over 1,500 feet. The river meanders south along its course toward the Dead Sea, providing water for crops and livestock. The further south the Jordan flows the more saline it becomes, thereby dividing the country agriculturally with wheat being planted in the north and the more salt resistant barley in the south. What little water does finally reach the Dead Sea is so clogged with brine that plant life along its banks is limited to poplars and the tamarisk tree.

Paralleling the Jordan Valley and bisecting the country north and south is the central hill country. While it is not a precipitous range of hills, the swift plunge eastward into the Jordan Rift (an area known as the "slopes") causes a spectacular drop in elevation. Jerusalem and Jericho serve as one example of the differences in elevation that occur within a relatively short distance in this region. Lying in the southern portion of the hill country, Jerusalem has an elevation of over 2,500 feet above sea level. However, Jericho, just 15 miles to the east, in an oasis near the Jordan, has an elevation of 1,275 feet below sea level. Such massive shifts in the earth's surface make travel difficult and tend to cut off direct communication and cultural interaction.

Three distinctive areas further divide the central hill country. In the north the Galilee region enjoys the advantages of the highest annual rainfall in the country and the most fertile soil. Samaria was located in the central portion of the hill country, with its important population centers at Megiddo, Shechem, and Bethel. This area supported wheat farming along with fruit and olive orchards. The southernmost section of the hill country, known as Judea, was dominated by the city of Jerusalem. Irrigation farming was common here as well as terraced agriculture on the slopes of the hills. Further south was the most uncertain and fragile environment in Palestine, with low annual rainfall in the areas bordering on this wilderness and the Negeb desert.

Ancient Palestine had no deep water harbors. This prevented large-scale sea trade, and made the region more dependent on the ships and merchants of Phoenicia. Immediately inland from the coast, however, is a plain which gradually merges to the east with a hilly region known as the Shephelah. Settlement was relatively heavy in this area (especially after the coming of the Philistines), and a major highway, the Via Maris, ran along the coast bringing trade as well as the armies of conquering nations.

Because of the dominating geologic character of the central hill range and the Jordan Rift, the climate of Palestine is also influenced by a north-south pattern. Temperatures follow a basically Mediterranean range, although snow does fall on the peaks of the mountains and occasionally in Jerusalem. Average annual rainfall amounts (concentrated in the months from November to March) range from as much as 45 inches in the Upper Galilee region to 8 inches in the Negeb desert around Beer-sheba and Arad. There are also years when these latter areas have no rainfall at all.

It is the scarcity of water which makes the Negeb suitable only for pastoral activity and sporadic, terrace-based agriculture. Rainfall also declines from west to east with the hill country blocking the path of storms moving in from the Mediterranean. The result is the creation of an extremely arid region known as the Judean wilderness. In this area rain may not come for years and this barrenness has made it synonymous with pain, trial, and death. The southern portion of the Transjordanian plateau, east of the Jordan River, also tends to be semi-arid, especially in the kingdoms of Edom and southern Moab.

Transjordan, while not within the land of Palestine, contained several kingdoms which had dealings with the Israelites. Running from north to south they were Bashan, Gilead, Ammon, Moab, and Edom. In some periods they were adversaries of the Israelite tribes, while in others they were vassal states of Israel or its enemies. These kingdoms were also a part of the Jordan ecosystem, drawing water from the river and its tributaries and sharing in its climatic shifts. A major trade route, the King's Highway, ran from Egypt through Transjordan and eventually on to Mesopotamia.

Each of the regions and geographical features described above figured into the development of the various cultures that inhabited Palestine. They will be referred to repeatedly in the text of this volume and thus it is advisable to become familiar with them and their place on the map in order to fully understand the history and social life of the Israelites.

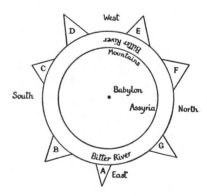

Babylonian map of the world, ca. 2000 B.C. The design was found on a clay tablet. Intro-E

1

PATRIARCHAL PERIOD

HISTORICAL INTRODUCTION

Abraham and the other patriarchs are portrayed as traveling throughout the regions of Palestine and west into Egypt with their flocks and herds. Along the way they engage in the normal pursuits of pastoral nomadic peoples seeking pasturage and interacting with the settled population. The efforts of historians and the excavations of archaeologists have not yet provided clear evidence for the historical reality of the patriarchs. This has led some scholars to argue that the narratives are literary recreations of tribal history compiled by bureaucrats during the monarchy period to provide the nation of Israel with a claim to Canaan. The patriarchs, according to this view, were either folk heroes or composites of many tribal leaders of the nation's past.

While the history of this period is hazy, the episodes in the patriarchal narratives contain quite exact and poignant memories of itinerant herders and their families. The attention to detail and the reinforcement of certain customs suggest that this material is more than a literary attempt to recreate an ancient period in the nation's history. Certainly there are some anachronisms, and the evidence of later editing of the text is clear in many places. Nevertheless, the narratives give the overwhelming impression of a time when the Hebrews were new to the land and still depended on the tribe, not the nation, for their identity.

The exact date of the period of the patriarchs is still uncertain. Ancient cuneiform tablets found at the northern Mesopotamian city of Mari (18th century BC) do contain descriptions of tribal groups whose activities and interactions with the urban community are surprisingly similar to those of the biblical patriarchs. Parallel information like this, however, must be used with care when drawing comparisons with the Bible. The similarities in social condition and economic pursuits, though, make it possible to at least suggest this time period as the setting for the stories of the patriarchs.

The 18th–17th centuries BC are a time of flux and development in the culture of Mesopotamia. Under the leadership of Hammurabi and his descendants, Babylon conquered all of the city-states and kingdoms of the land. They subjected the inhabitants of the entire Tigris-Euphrates valley to centralized rule and placed them under the benefits and constraints of Babylonian law. After 1600, the Babylonian empire went into decline and was eventually replaced by a group of smaller states, including the Kassites in the south and the Mitanni in north-central Mesopotamia.

Egypt, during the period from 2000 to 1800, experienced some internal disorder. This is demonstrated in the epic narrative of Sinuhe, a political refugee who fled to Palestine to escape being implicated in the murder of a pharaoh (*ANET*, pp. 18–22). In the 18th century BC, Egypt was invaded by the Hyksos raiders, and thus it had little time to deal with its political and economic contacts in Palestine. These foreign invaders set themselves up as pharaohs in their Delta region capital at Avaris.

The result of Babylon's rise and fall as an empire builder in Mesopotamia and Egypt's internal problems was relative freedom for the peoples of Canaan. For a time, until the rise of the New Kingdom in Egypt (16th century BC) and its aggressive pharaohs, the nation of Pales-

Hammurabi of Babylon receives the law from the sungod Shamash.
1-B

tine controlled its own fate and had only minimal concern for the actions and desires of the
·superpower nations. New peoples, like Abraham's
household, entered and settled in the underpopulated regions of Palestine and Transjordan. New
opportunities arose for building a life in other
lands away from the conflict.

With this historical background in mind, this
chapter examines the basic economy and social
life of pastoral nomadic peoples in the ancient
Near East. Individual aspects of existence are
highlighted, and special regard is given to the patriarchal narratives, archaeological discoveries,
and the parallel written material from Mesopotamia and Egypt.

I. PHYSICAL APPEARANCE
OF THE PEOPLE

What did the patriarchs and their wives look like?

The patriarchs and their families were Semites, the dominant ethnic group in Mesopotamia
and much of Syro-Palestine. Physically, Semites
in the ancient Near East had black hair, were
short in stature (averaging about 5 feet tall for
males), with a swarthy complexion burned even
darker by the sun, and a prominent, flat nose.
The examination of burial remains and a few surviving paintings, such as those found in the 19th
century Egyptian tomb at Beni-Hasan, provide
us with this picture, since there are few biblical
descriptions of an individual's features.

In Mesopotamia men generally wore beards,
carefully curled and squared off at the bottom.
The Semites portrayed in the Beni-Hasan painting, however, have short, pointed beards with no
moustache. This may represent a more functional style for travel and thus may have been a
style adopted by Abraham after his departure
from Haran. Hair was often worn shoulder

Bedouin girl carrying water jar.
Photo by Ralph Harris.   1-1

length with a band of cloth or beads to hold it in place. Women's coiffures tended to be fairly simple. Their long hair was sometimes bound up with beaded ropes or intertwined with combs of bone, gold, or silver. On the road or in the pastoral encampment, however, such attention to fashion would not be possible or desirable.

In Mesopotamia and other regions where the climate was dry, the complexion could be easily damaged. As a result, meticulous attention was given to skin care. Both men and women regularly oiled their skin and hair. This gave the body a glossy appearance and also killed hair lice and other parasites.

Clothing for pastoralists, by necessity, was primarily functional, although not that much different from the clothing worn by artisans and other commoners. Sturdy leather sandals protected the feet of both sexes. They enclosed the heel and were fastened to the ankle by a thong which passed between the first and second toes.

Throughout the biblical period, men wore the *kethoneth,* a knee-length, wool tunic with half-sleeves. This was held at the waist with a belt. An over-robe or mantle (*simlah*) was also worn as protection against the sun and during storms. In the exodus account it was used to carry bread dough and kneading bowls (Ex 12:34). A girdle (*ezor*), or loincloth, was also worn in later periods (Isa 20:2; Jer 13:2; Job 12:18). Women wore a similar tunic and robe which concealed the figure, although some representations in art (as in the Beni-Hasan tomb paintings) portray them with the right shoulder bare.

There was also a particular fashion for widows, described in Isa 58:5 and Jer 6:26 as sackcloth. From the fact that Tamar removed her widow's garb and wore a veil in Gen 38:14 to disguise herself as a harlot, it might be assumed that in this period women went unveiled. The issue is clouded somewhat by the action of Rebekah in Gen 24:65. In this passage she put her veil on in expectation of meeting her future husband Isaac for the first time. Her act of modesty is more in line with Mesopotamian custom. The Middle Assyrian law code #40 (*ANET,* p. 183, dated to c. 1100 BC) required that harlots appear unveiled in public on pain of death. From these two circumstances it can thus be surmised that Tamar was following Canaanite custom (see the veiled sacred prostitutes of the Canaanite goddess Asherah in 2 Kgs 23:7) when she played the role of a veiled harlot.

Jewelry, then, as now, was a common adornment for both men and women. Abraham's servant in Gen 24:47 gave Rebekah a nose ring and arm bracelets, as well as unspecified ornaments of gold and silver as bridal presents (v 53). Joseph, when he rose to his position as advisor to

She put off her widow's garments, put on a veil, wrapped herself up, and sat down at the entrance to Enaim, which is on the road to Timnah. She saw that Shelah was grown up, yet she had not been given to him in marriage. —Gen 38:14

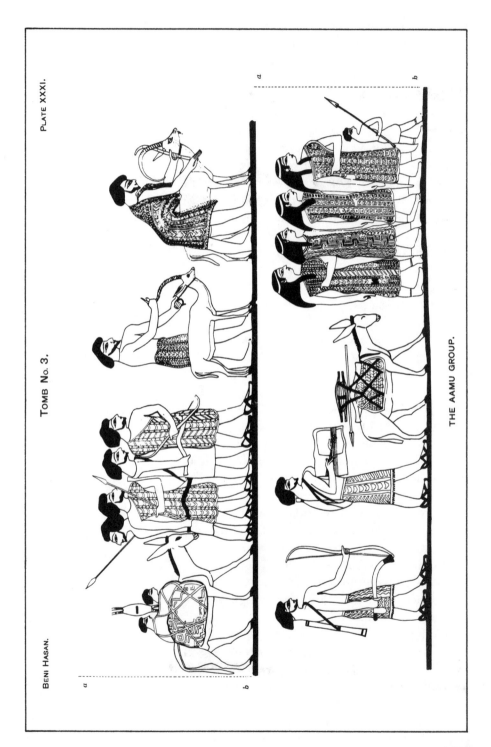

PLATE XXXI.

TOMB No. 3.

BENI HASAN.

THE AAMU GROUP.

the pharaoh, was given a gold chain to wear around his neck and a signet ring as a symbol of his power and authority (Gen 41:42). After the escape from Egypt, Aaron fashioned a golden calf for the people out of their earrings (Ex 32:2–3).

II. SOCIAL AND CULTURAL PROBLEMS OF IMMIGRANTS

What sorts of problems did the patriarchs face on their entrance into Canaan?

The earliest picture of the patriarchs in the text is as inhabitants of Ur of the Chaldees in southern Mesopotamia. Abram and his father Terah planned a move to Canaan, but they stopped in Haran, a city on the upper reaches of the Euphrates and Balikh rivers. There they settled for a while and Terah died (Gen 11:30–32). Since his origins were in Mesopotamia, that was the seat of Abram's cultural heritage. During this period of his life, he undoubtedly worshipped the Mesopotamian gods and he was intimately familiar with Mesopotamian law and social customs.

Abram's household was faced with a new challenge, however, when he led them from Haran and immigrated to Canaan. From this point on (Gen 12:1–4), they are portrayed in the text as moving from campsite to campsite and from pasturage to pasturage while living in goat-hair tents. According to the biblical narrative, Abram once again left his home and became an immigrant for theological reasons—God instructed him to go to a land which he would show him. Even his name change to Abraham (Gen 17:5) was designed to emphasize his new status and the covenant with his God. Whatever the reason for his departure from Haran, however, the basic psychology of being an immigrant, a stranger in a foreign land, affects nearly all of his and the

No longer shall your name be Abram, but your name shall be Abraham; for I have made you the ancestor of a multitude of nations. —Gen 17:5

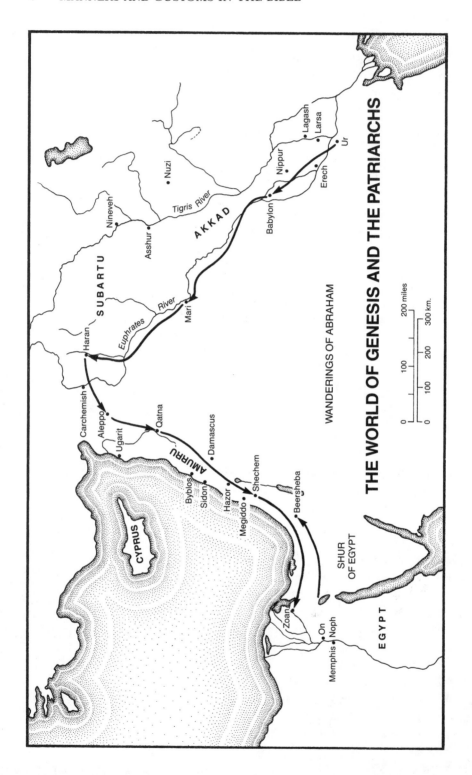

other patriarchs' actions during this period of Israel's history.

Abraham left Haran, a northern Mesopotamian city that was controlled in the 18th century BC by the king of Mari. The journey to Canaan covered several hundred miles. His route, although not described in the biblical text, probably followed the Via Maris, the international trade highway from Mesopotamia, through Damascus and Hazor and then down the coast of Palestine to Egypt.

In preparing for his trek he had to equip his group for survival as new immigrants in the new land. What was required of Abraham and his family was an adjustment of lifestyle from an urban based existence to the constant travel of pastoral nomads. A change in perspective also confronted them in this undertaking. They had to accept the shift from being "part of the group" to being "outsiders."

There were undoubtedly language problems, although they are not mentioned in the narratives, and even when they did learn the local dialect their accent would have marked them as strangers. Over the years, they had to depend upon their own skills as herdsmen and on the produce of their flocks and herds. Life was dominated by the search for forage and water for sheep and goats and by the attempt to draw as little hostile attention to their group as possible. Abraham's ability to interact as an intermediary with the local chieftains and village elders was therefore essential to the acceptance of his household into the land and its ultimate survival.

The process of having to walk a social and economic tightrope caused some tensions between Abraham's immigrant group and the settled communities. Each newly arrived household would put additional strain on the available natural resources of the land. As a result, the attempt by immigrants to acclimate themselves to the new social and economic environment required a willingness to operate within the rules set by the people who already lived there. This could well explain why so much attention is given in the biblical text to negotiations between the patriarchs and the local leaders.

Another difficulty faced by every immigrant group arriving in a new land is legal helplessness. Immigrants are seldom familiar with the laws of the land and very often are not given the legal protections guaranteed to citizens. This can lead the immigrants to use deception as a defense mechanism. The morality of such a deception did not present a problem for the patriarchs since they assumed that their survival and that of their group had priority over providing a potential enemy with all the facts.

A. WIFE-SISTER STRATAGEM

Shortly after their arrival in Canaan, Abraham and Sarah were forced to go to Egypt to escape a famine (Gen 12). Since they were new arrivals in Palestine, it would have been difficult for them to obtain food from the local inhabitants. This meant a further trek to Egypt where food could be purchased and transients were tolerated and occasionally used as temporary sources of cheap labor.

In addition to his own life, Abraham's one irreplaceable possession was his wife. As they entered Egypt, he feared that she might be taken from him and added to the pharaoh's harem. He was also afraid that the Egyptian king might consider it easier to kill or otherwise do away with him as her husband. Therefore, Abraham devised a scheme in which Sarah claimed to be his sister. This removed personal danger to him and resulted, when she was taken into the pharaoh's harem, in the enrichment of Abraham's household.

While the story has an underlying theme of a contest between the god/king of Egypt and Abraham's God, Yahweh, it also contains elements of immigrant psychology. This is seen in the other two examples of the wife-sister motif (Gen 20 and 26) as well. In these instances, the threatening authority figure is Abimelech of Gerar. As in the previous case, he was taken in by the deception. He added significantly to the household and herds of his visitor (first Abraham's and later Isaac's); and, like the pharaoh in Genesis 12, he eventually returned the patriarch's wife unharmed after God intervened.

B. THE PURCHASE OF MACHPELAH: GENESIS 23

Another example in which Abraham found himself, as an immigrant, constrained to obey the legal traditions of the people of Canaan is contained in the story of his purchase of the cave of Machpelah as a burial site for Sarah. His encampment at that time was near the city of Hebron in southern Canaan. In order to make the purchase, Abraham had to go to Hebron and engage in a predetermined set of procedures, all of which favored the settled community over the pastoral nomads. First, he went to the city gate, where much of the city's business and legal activities were conducted. Here he requested the elders to serve as witnesses and advocates for him (a non-citizen) in his attempt to purchase the cave.

And Sarah died at Kiriath-arba (that is, Hebron) in the land of Canaan; and Abraham went in to mourn for Sarah and to weep for her. —Gen 23:2

The owner, Ephron the Hittite, and Abraham then engaged in a legal dialogue bargaining over the price and the exact parcel to be purchased. Abraham had originally only wanted the cave, but eventually he was also forced to pay for an adjoining field and its trees.

The dialogue is interesting and almost comical. Ephron first offered the cave to Abraham as a gift. This gambit was designed to force the buyer into being equally gracious by asking the

An ancient Philistine anthropoid coffin. Photo by LaMoine DeVries. 1-2

owner to set his own price. Once this had been done all that remained was for Abraham to count out the 400 shekels of silver, an exorbitantly high price (compare Jacob's purchase of land in Gen 33:19), and have the transaction duly witnessed by the elders.

Two pieces of information regarding this purchase are worth noting. To begin with, this was the first piece of land owned outright by a Hebrew. God had promised the land to Abraham and his descendants, but now the patriarch had obtained legal title to a portion of it. This claim was then extended in later periods to the entire region. Secondly, it was rather unusual for land to be sold outright in this manner. Land was considered sacred, entrusted by the god/gods to the ruler, and he, in turn, entrusted it to individuals. In some cases its sale could even be considered a crime against the heirs of the owner (see Naboth's reaction to Ahab's request to purchase his vineyard in 1 Kgs 21:3). One way in which this customary restriction was sometimes avoided was by having the purchaser adopted into the family of the owner (as is found in the 15th century BC texts from the eastern Mesopotamian city of Nuzi).

The fact that Ephron was willing to make the sale here may be due to the fact that Abraham specifically wished to use it for his wife's burial and not as a base of operations that could threaten the local people or their economy. An even more telling explanation for the sale may be found in the title given to Abraham by the city elders, "a mighty prince among us" (v 6). Rather than being a potential threat to the peace of the area like other nomadic groups, Abraham's was seen as an asset. This did not, however, prevent his being taken advantage of in the bargaining.

C. BURIAL CUSTOMS

The choice of a cave near Hebron also brings up the question of the forms of burial in this period. Nomadic groups utilize a variety of burial types. These include rock cairns in which the body is interred within a mound of stones along their line of march, as in the case of Rachel's

A pair of tomb entrances. Photo by Ralph Harris. 1-3

death in Gen 35:19–20. Similarly, some are buried near distinctive landmarks or trees, which are then given a new name to mark the event (see the burial of Deborah, Rebekah's nurse, under an oak near Bethel in Gen 36:8).

Abraham's purchase of the cave at Machpelah initiated its use for both primary and secondary burial. Several members of his family in subsequent generations were buried here, and, in some cases, this involved the transport of the remains to the cave for burial (see Gen 50:12–13 for the burial of Jacob). Archaeologists have discovered many tombs in Palestine dated to the Late Bronze period (1500–1200 BC) in which burial space was utilized over and over. The remains of previous burials were simply shoved to the rear of the cave or placed in ossuary jars along with the possessions that were left with the bodies.

D. THE RAPE OF DINAH

Another case in which the tensions between nomadic groups and the settled population is quite evident occurs in Genesis 34. This episode involves a request by a local prince to marry Jacob's daughter Dinah. Jacob had settled his household near the city of Shechem. He purchased a piece of land as a base of operations for his herds and appeared to be on the road to settling down permanently. This process of sedentarization occurred among pastoralists occasionally, especially those who were wealthy and had holdings both among the tribes and in towns.

Jacob's daughter, not showing the caution usually expected of tribal women, left the encampment and was raped by the son of Hamor the king of Shechem. Middle Assyrian law codes, which date to the period of the 18th century BC, provide a parallel to this case. According to this legal code, an unbetrothed virgin could be ob-

Now Dinah the daughter of Leah, whom she had borne to Jacob, went out to visit the women of the region. When Shechem son of Hamor the Hivite, prince of the region, saw her, he seized her and lay with her by force. —Gen 34:1–2

tained as a wife through forcible sexual relations. The man involved was obligated to marry the woman he had abused, and the king's son in this case requested to do just that. He negotiated with Jacob's sons (since the patriarch was absent at the time) and they stated that the entire male population of Shechem had to conform to the tribal custom of circumcision before the marriage could take place.

Will not their livestock, their property, and all their animals be ours? Only let us agree with them, and they will live among us. —Gen 34:23

The request for such a drastic act can probably be seen as an attempt on the part of the brothers to discourage this marriage. It also signals the difference in social custom and lifestyle between the two peoples. Hamor and his son, like the elders of Hebron (Gen 23:6), cited the wealth of the pastoral group and the resulting benefits this would have for the city of Shechem. Their argument was persuasive and the citizens of Shechem agreed to go along with the demand to be circumcised.

Having undergone this painful procedure, the men of Shechem were then easy prey for the raid by Jacob's sons three days later. A massacre ensued and the women and children were taken away as slaves by the Hebrews. Raids of this type were not uncommon, although they seldom resulted in the total annihilation of a city's population. Usually they only involved the stealing of animals or women (see the capture of the dancers of Shiloh in Jdg 21:19 – 23).

The justification given for this act was to obtain revenge on Shechem for the rape of Dinah. Unfortunately, it also magnified Jacob's fear that the stigma of "immigrant" would once more haunt the group. The patriarchs had worked for generations to be accepted by the local population. An act such as this could once again arouse suspicions and hostilities that had been dormant for years. The story thus demonstrates the antagonism between settled and nomadic groups which was always under the surface.

Ancient bedouins lived in tents, perhaps similar to this one. Photo by Ralph Harris.   1-4

III. HERDING PRACTICES

What was it like to be a pastoral nomad?

One reality of pastoral life is that occasionally the herd becomes too large for its grazing area. In this instance it had to be partially sold off or the group had to divide, with each segment seeking pasturage in different areas. In Genesis 13, Abraham's herds had significantly increased during his stay in Egypt. When he and his nephew Lot returned to Canaan they discovered that the region would not support their entire herd. As a result, the herdsmen were at the point of coming to blows. The solution was for Lot to choose the specific area in which his portion of the herds would graze and Abraham would then choose another.

An alternative would have been to graze the herds over a larger area. For instance, in Genesis 37, Jacob's sons are said to have taken their father's herds north from Hebron to Dothan. This sort of movement is known as transhumance. Jacob maintained a base camp from which his sons took the herds to seek pasturage in the hill country to the north; they returned when the seasons changed. Jacob's sending of Joseph in search of his brothers may reflect that they were late in returning or that the normal communication links (travelers or other herdsmen) had been broken.

One additional aspect of this story worth noting is that during the search for his brothers Joseph met a man near Shechem. They met in a field that had been grazed over. The practice of allowing herds of cattle, sheep, and goats to graze in harvested fields was very common in ancient times. It provided good forage for the animals and fertilized the field in preparation for the next planting season.

GENESIS 20 AND 26: WATER RIGHTS

For a herding group to survive, access to water is essential. Sheep cannot go for more then three or four days without water. Because of this, knowledge of wells and springs is among the most valuable and guarded pieces of tribal information. This knowledge and the right to use water resources is only shared with close kin and allied groups. An example of the importance which water held for pastoralists is found in Genesis 29 where several groups of herdsmen are gathered around a well near Haran. No one dared water his sheep until all of the herdsmen had assembled. An accusation that one was getting more than his fair share might have led to armed conflict. Similarly, in Ex 2:16–17, shepherds drove Jethro's daughters away from a well. Moses intervened, serving as a male representative for their herding group, so that their animals could be watered.

In Genesis 20 and 26 the patriarchs have to negotiate with Abimelech, the king of Gerar, for usage of wells in his region. They obtained the right to do so as a result of the wife-sister deception, but the embarrassment caused by this incident did not prevent eventual friction between the herders and the people of Gerar who also needed the water for their own herds and fields. Gradually, as the men of Gerar confiscated his wells, Isaac and his herds were driven further south toward Beer-sheba. Once they left the immediate region of Gerar, however, they were left alone, and the wells that they subsequently dug were theirs to name and use.

What this narrative tells us is that there were specific zones designated for use by the urban-based communities. Within these zones, outsiders were only grudgingly given water rights and grazing resources. When the leaders of a city or village felt that the pastoral nomads were threatening the welfare of their economy, it was almost a certainty that the newcomers would be forced to leave.

A shepherd waters his flock. Photo from Elmendorf, A Camera Crusade through the Holy Land.   1-5

IV. FOOD PREPARATION
AND DIET

What did the patriarchs and their families eat?

The patriarchal narratives provide only occasional references to food and food preparation: Melchizedek, king of Salem (Gen 14:18), offered Abram the Hebrew bread and wine in welcoming him and offering a blessing; Abraham ordered Sarah to prepare a meal consisting of bread made in the form of cakes, milk and curds, and roasted calf for his three visitors (Gen 18:6 – 8); Jacob offered a red lentil soup to his brother Esau in exchange for his birthright (Gen 25:34); and, freshly killed game was apparently a favorite dish of Isaac's (Gen 27:7). This diet was spiced with a variety of fruits and nuts, considered such a delicacy that they were offered along with myrrh and balm as presents to the pharaoh's representative in Gen 43:11.

Few archaeological remains exist of the foodstuffs consumed by people in biblical times. Archaeologists, using new filtration methods, including a botanical analysis, have, however, discovered the contents of ancient granaries from the settlement and monarchy periods. These underground silos contained the carbonized remains of the agricultural produce of that time: wheat and barley, as well as date and grape seeds.

The cuneiform documents found at the site of ancient Babylon contain menus of the food prepared for the king and his court. These include elaborate lists of breads, meats, and desserts, few of which would have been on the menu of the pastoral nomadic tribesmen. These people, like the patriarchs, lived off their herds and the products (milk, and meat) of the sheep and goats that they tended.

Since bread was a staple of life for all peoples in the ancient Near East, seasonal agriculture was sometimes practiced by pastoralists (as is shown in Isaac's sowing and reaping in Gerar in Gen 26:12). For the most part, however, grain had to be purchased from villages along the migration route. Because the pastoralists were often on the move, permanent ovens to bake their bread would have been impractical. Therefore, like their modern descendants, ancient nomadic peoples baked their bread in small, thin cakes on a heated stone or a metal griddle.

Isaac sowed seed in that land, and in the same year reaped a hundredfold. The LORD blessed him, . . . — Gen 26:12

The diet of ancient, as well as modern, pastoralists primarily consisted of various breads, milk and curds, and fruits and nuts gathered along the line of march or purchased from villagers. The consumption of meat, since it involved reducing the size of the herd, occurred for the most part only on important occasions — such as when visitors were being hosted and the generosity of the host was being demonstrated. A feast like the one Abraham prepared for his guests in Genesis 18, can therefore be compared to a text from the ancient seaport city of Ugarit (*ANET,* p. 146; dated to c. 1600–1200 BC). In this epic poem the legendary King Keret ordered his wife Hurriya to have "a lamb from the flock" slaughtered to feed his guests.

The physical effects of such a heavily carbohydrate diet and the periods of famine common to this region (Gen 12 and 26) would have caused some health problems for the people. It can be speculated that some of the difficulties and illnesses caused by a poor or unbalanced diet may have been offset by eating figs and dates and using cooking oil made from dates and olives.

V. MARRIAGE CUSTOMS

What were the basic marriage customs of the patriarchs?
Marriage customs among pastoral nomadic groups are often designed to maintain the social continuity as well as the perpetuation of the

group. As a result, marriage contracts are arranged by the father or oldest male kin to benefit the individual family and to ensure that the children will be brought up in such a way as to be a credit to the group as a whole. This means that marriage with non-nomadic peoples or with people outside the kinship group is generally discouraged. Betrothals may be made while the couple are still children and they may have never met before the wedding ceremony. Girls were usually married as soon as they reached puberty, while boys often waited until they received their inheritance or had earned enough to establish their own household.

Let the girl to whom I shall say, "Please offer your jar that I may drink," and who shall say, "Drink, and I will water your camels"—let her be the one whom you have appointed for your servant Isaac. By this I shall know that you have shown steadfast love to my master.
—Gen 24:14

A. MARRIAGE WITHIN THE GROUP

Marriage customs are highlighted in the biblical text on several occasions. The first instance recounts Abraham's insistence in Genesis 24 that his servant return to Haran to obtain a bride for Isaac. The servant was equipped with a suitable array of gifts for the bride's family and journeyed back to Mesopotamia using camels (an expensive and little-used beast of burden in the period before 1200 BC) to carry his goods.

When he arrived in the vicinity of Haran, the servant went to the most likely place to view the local girls, the well. At least twice a day the women of the villages and surrounding encampments came here to obtain water for cooking and washing purposes or to water their animals. The servant showed his knowledge of everyday activity by seeking a suitable bride for his master's son in this place.

The test which the servant used to find a proper wife for Isaac is a signal to the reader of the values expected of the wife in this society. This was so important that the narrative has him repeat the description of the test three times for emphasis. His plan was to let the bride demonstrate her wisdom by offering him and his camels a drink. Such attention to the laws of hospitality could be expected with respect to the man, but only a truly wise woman could be expected also to have concern for another man's animals. If she knew the value of property before marriage, it could be expected that she would be a suitable mistress of his master's household afterwards (see also Prov 31:10–31.

The actual negotiations (Gen 24:34–50) that led to Rebekah's becoming Isaac's wife were carried out with her brother Laban and father Bethuel. Her father, however, played a secondary role in these negotiations to Laban. Her brother was quite impressed by the wealth of the servant's gifts to Rebekah and certainly planned to get as good a price as he could for her. The servant, however, demonstrated his own shrewdness by refusing to accept the hospitality of Laban's house before beginning the negotiations. He did not wish to be unfavorably obligated to Laban, and thus it was only after the bargain was struck that he willingly entered the house and ate a meal (24:33).

And they called Rebekah, and said to her, "Will you go with this man?" She said, "I will."
— Gen 24:58

While Rebekah had no direct role in the negotiations that sent her away from her family and home forever, she was consulted before the departure (24:57–59). Laban undoubtedly hoped to detain the servant and thus obtain even more gifts. It was Rebekah's willingness to leave that allowed the servant to depart gracefully without further delay or expense. This may again be evidence of the change in loyalties of a woman who must now be concerned with the wealth of her new household.

A similar case of endogamy, marriage within the kinship or social group, is found in Jacob's return to Haran to obtain a bride. His brother Esau had broken with custom and married two "Hittite" girls (Gen 26:34–35). This disappointed his parents. It also fits into a literary and theological motif designed to show how Esau dis-

qualified himself as Isaac's heir. Jacob, on the other hand, is shown to be the upholder of tradition and thus a proper heir when he obediently travels to Paddan-aram and asks Laban for one of his daughters as his wife (Gen 27:46 – 28:5).

Again the initial scene centers on the well where Jacob meets Rachel. However, in this case Jacob demonstrated his worthiness to his future bride by removing the stone from the top of the well and watering her sheep (Gen 29:1 – 10). This showed his wisdom as a herdsman, a talent he later used to pay for his bride. His meeting with Laban was cordial enough, but it swiftly became evident to the crafty Laban that Jacob was only a poor relation. As a result, Jacob had to assume the role of an itinerant herdsman. He was part of the surplus labor pool of young men who contracted themselves to work for wealthy herding leaders. His bride price was to be seven years of labor in exchange for Rachel as his wife. Laban's deception, exchanging Rachel's sister Leah on the wedding night, ensured an additional seven

The community well was a traditional gathering place. Photo from Elmendorf, A Camera Crusade through the Holy Land.   1-6

years of labor. Yet another seven years were expended as Jacob worked for a percentage of the herd as a way of building up his own fortunes. Labor contracts such as this are commonly found among the business documents unearthed in the remains of ancient Mesopotamian cities.

B. CUSTOMS OF INHERITANCE

The primary purpose of a marriage in biblical times, aside from the possible monetary gain involved in marrying into a rich or influential family, was to produce an heir. In each cycle of stories about the major patriarchs there is a common theme of obtaining a male heir for the family and for the covenant with God. The wives of the patriarchs were often barren for long periods as a way of heightening the suspense of the birth of the heir. For instance, after Rebekah finally gave birth to twins, following 40 years of marriage to Isaac, a contest for supremacy ensued between her sons Jacob and Esau. This was resolved when the younger twin, Jacob, obtained the blessing and heirship from his father by means of a deception. The narrative justifies his actions by pointing out that he had concerned himself with the family's flocks and had obeyed his parents with regard to tribal marriage customs.

Then she said, "Here is my maid Bilhah; go in to her, that she may bear upon my knees and that I too may have children through her." — Gen 30:3

On occasion, when the wife of the patriarch was unable to produce a male heir, concubines or slave women were used as surrogate mothers, and their children then became the legal offspring of the primary wife. This was the case with Hagar, the maid of Sarah and mother of Ishmael (Gen 16:2–4). Similarly in Gen 30:3, Rachel's maid Bilhah bore children to Jacob on Rachel's knees to mimic Rachel's giving birth to them herself. Subsequently, both Sarah and Rachel bore their own children, much as women today who adopt a child then bear a child of their own.

Another example of marriage customs which also centers on the production of an heir in the period of Israel's tribal history appears in Genesis 38. In this passage, Judah, one of Jacob's sons, married and had three sons. He arranged a marriage for his oldest son, Er, to a girl named Tamar. Er died before fathering a son and thus the law of levirate marriage came into play (see Dt 25:5 – 6). Since the dead man had no heir, it became the obligation of his brother or closest male kin to marry or at least impregnate the widow. The male child born of this union would then be the legal heir of the dead man.

When brothers reside together, and one of them dies and has no son, the wife of the deceased shall not be married outside the family to a stranger. Her husband's brother shall go in to her, taking her in marriage, and performing the duty of a husband's brother to her, . . .   – Deut 25:5

Thus Judah gave his second son, Onan, to Tamar as a husband. Onan refused to fulfill his obligation, using a method of birth control to prevent Tamar from conceiving. For this action he was struck down by God and the levirate obligation then fell to the third son, Shelah. At that point he was too young for marriage. Therefore Judah, who had already lost two sons as a result of this unlucky marriage, promised to send Shelah to Tamar when he was of age.

Time passed, Tamar sat in her father's house, and Judah delayed the marriage fearing he also would be left without an heir. Finally, Tamar felt she had to take matters into her own hands in order to obtain what was due her according to the law. Wearing a veil, she disguised herself as a prostitute and sat beside the road at the entrance to Enaim. Judah attempted to hire her by offering a kid from the flock. He did not have the animal with him, however, so he gave her his cylinder seal and staff as pledge of later payment. These were very important items to Judah. The seal was used to inscribe his name on clay tablets and personal property, and he carried the staff while walking and working the sheep. He must have assumed that he would get them back shortly. However, the supposed harlot had mysteriously disappeared by the time Judah's ser-

vant returned with the kid and Judah was forced
to shrug it off. Tamar, on the other hand, had gotten what she wanted and returned home.

Three months later, when it became evident
that Tamar was pregnant, Judah initially, and
perhaps with a sense of relief, ordered that she
be burned. However, he had given her his cylinder seal and staff as a pledge when he did not
have the payment for her services as a harlot.
Tamar quickly produced these as evidence to
identify the father of her child. This forced Judah to admit his failure to adhere to custom and
Tamar was cleared of the charge of adultery and
subsequently gave birth to twins.

VI. RELIGIOUS PRACTICES

In what ways did the patriarchs worship God?

From their first days in Canaan, the patriarchs
initiated a system of sacrifice marking their and
Yahweh's entrance into the land. At each stop-
ping place a rough stone altar was built for offerings to be made to God (Gen 12:7 – 8 and 13:18).
Each of these altar sites — Shechem, Bethel, and Hebron — subsequently became important in the history of Israel. The first of these cities has yielded
evidence to archaeologists of significant religious
activity prior to the time of the patriarchs. Such
evidence adds strength to the assertion that Abraham's altars signaled the introduction of Yahweh
worship into Canaan. The fact that they were
built near Canaanite worship centers adds even
more weight to this theory.

A similar use of a marker/altar is found in Gen
31:43 – 54, where we read that Jacob and Laban
commemorated a treaty between them by building a pillar of heaped stones, eating a meal together, and making a sacrifice. The pillar served
as a boundary marker between their two spheres
of influence. The meal was an example of the use

of hospitality traditions to mark their peaceful intentions and the sacrifice invoked God to be a witness to their transaction.

In none of the above cases, however, are the details of sacrifice spelled out. The text seems to assume that readers are already familiar with the procedure. The only instance in the patriarchal narratives where sacrifice is described in greater detail is found in the story of the "sacrifice of Isaac" (Gen 22). Here Abraham was told by God to offer his son as a burnt offering. The unquestioning response of the patriarch included gathering wood, traveling to a sacred site, building an altar on a mountain (high place), and providing a knife with which to slay the boy.

This story is described as a test of Abraham's faith, but it may also be an explanation of why the Israelites did not practice human sacrifice like the other peoples of Canaan. Just as Abraham was about to plunge the knife into Isaac, God called to him to stop and provided a substitute sacrifice, a ram. It seems from the story that Abraham was familiar with human sacrifice and was probably not surprised that Yahweh might demand such an offering. One point made by the text, however, is that this God, unlike those of the Canaanites, found animal sacrifices more acceptable.

While not often thought of today as a sacrificial act, circumcision, as practiced by the Hebrews, was just as much a sacrifice as the slaughtering of a sheep on the altar. The removal of the male foreskin was a mark of the covenant with Yahweh and evidenced a physical distinction from the uncircumcised men of the cities of Canaan. The practice, also common among the Egyptians, was instituted in Gen 17:9–14 and required that every male at least eight days old (and thus viable) undergo this painful procedure.

You shall circumcise the flesh of your foreskins, and it shall be a sign of the covenant between me and you. —Gen 17:11

As noted above, circumcision was required of the men of Shechem before the king's son could marry Jacob's daughter Dinah and thus become members of the tribe (Gen 34:15). Yahweh demanded that Moses circumcise his son before he returned for Egypt (Ex 4:25). In this case Moses had failed to conform to custom and thus the people's liberation could not begin until this was rectified. Zipporah, Moses's wife and the daughter of the Midianite herdsman Jethro, performed the circumcision. She used a flint knife to cut off her son's foreskin and then touched it to Moses' feet (a euphemism for his genitals), declaring him to be "a bridegroom of blood." This act, a parallel to the ritual of placing the blood of the sacrificial lamb on the doorpost before the Passover in Ex 12:22, signaled the renewal of the covenant pact. It marked the beginning of a new contractual arrangement with Yahweh that was again repeated when the Israelite males were circumcised prior to the conquest of Canaan (Jos 5:2).

But Zipporah took a flint and cut off her son's foreskin, and touched Moses' feet with it, and said, "Truly you are a bridegroom of blood to me!"

— Exod 4:25

VII. LEGAL CUSTOMS

In what ways did law and legal tradition shape the manners and customs of the patriarchal groups?

The one overriding legal custom among pastoral nomadic peoples is that of hospitality. Once it has been offered and accepted, no hostilities are possible until the parties separate and a mutually agreed upon period of time has passed. Thus hospitality is not offered or accepted lightly, since it places obligations on both parties. While it most often appears in the biblical text in cases involving individuals, it also has national and international implications in the ratification of treaties and other contracts.

Several examples of the principle of hospitality have already been mentioned — in the negotiation between Abraham's servant and Laban and in the treaty ceremony marking the separation of

Jacob and Laban. Two quite graphic examples are also to be found in Genesis 18 and 19. These stories are parallel accounts with one of the chief similarities being the manner in which the laws of hospitality are exercised and defended.

In Genesis 18, Abraham was visited by three "men" as he sat at the door of his tent "in the heat of the day." While the text does not at first say that these visitors are from God, it seems unlikely that Abraham would have rushed out to meet just any group of strangers offering them the hospitality of his encampment. Nevertheless, his welcoming statement sounds like a formula:

> My Lord, if I have found favor in your sight, do not pass by your servant. Let a little water be brought, and wash your feet, and rest yourselves under the tree, while I fetch a morsel of bread, that you may refresh yourselves, and after that you may pass on — since you have come to your servant (vv 3 – 5; RSV).

Each of these comforts would have been welcome to the traveler and there is a note of due respect in Abraham's address that is pleasing to anyone's ear.

The visitors' acceptance of Abraham's hospitality then obligated them to express good wishes to him and his family. Their statements included the prediction that Sarah would bear a child within a year. Acceptance of Abraham's food and attention also seemed to put the patriarch on a more nearly equal footing with God when they later (vv 22 – 32) debated over the destruction of Sodom and Gomorrah. Men who eat together in peace can thus be said to be equals while they enjoy each other's hospitality.

Genesis 19 records the visit of the angels to Sodom. In this text it is Lot, Abraham's nephew, who is sitting in the gate of the city, the physical and legal equivalent of the doorway of Abraham's tent. He also went out to meet them as they approached and made a statement similar to that of his uncle: "My lords, turn aside, I pray you, to your servant's house and spend the night, and wash your feet; then you may rise up early and go on your way" (v 2).

Once they had eaten with him, Lot was forced to demonstrate just how seriously the obligations attached to hospitality customs were taken. During the night "all the men of Sodom" came to his door and demanded that the two visitors be sent out to them to be sexually assaulted. Lot's sense of duty to protect his guests was so strong, however, that he offered to send his two virgin daughters out to the mob to satisfy their appetite for violence. The daughters were technically his property, and he could dispose of them as he wished, but this would involve both a financial and a personal sacrifice. He was saved from taking this action when the angels blinded the crowd and his family was able to escape.

EXECUTION OF JUSTICE

In pastoral nomadic groups the father is the absolute master of his own family and has complete legal control over them. He arranges marriages, conducts all business transactions, and serves as the sole source of justice in legal matters involving his family. The principle of *pater familias,* in which the father has the power of life and death over his household, thus applies.

One example of this principle has already been mentioned. When Judah discovered that Tamar was pregnant and apparently guilty of adultery (Gen 38:24), he immediately, without trial, ordered her to be burned. This was his right as head of the household.

The father's full legal control is portrayed in another case (Gen 16:5–6). In this text Sarah stated correctly that the verbal abuse which she had received from her servant Hagar was due to Abraham's impregnating her. She had been used as a surrogate mother in an attempt to produce

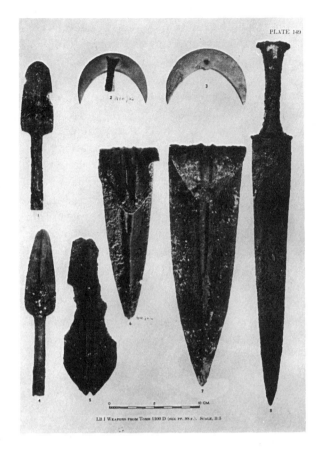

Ancient weapons. Courtesy of the Oriental Institute of the University of Chicago. 1-7

an heir, but now the servant had become con-
temptuous of her barren mistress. Abraham settled the matter by simply turning all punishment
of the insolent servant over to Sarah.

VIII. WEAPONS AND WARFARE

*What were the methods of warfare practiced by the
patriarchs?*
Since they had limited resources and manpower, war for the patriarchs generally took
the form of raids or small-scale battles. The
instances in which combat are mentioned in the
text point to the use of surprise attacks (Jacob's
sons against Shechem in Gen 34:25) or night as-

saults, such as Abraham's rescue mission in Gen 14:15. The latter contains the largest group of men assembled for a battle by a patriarchal figure in this period. Abraham divided his forces and attacked the camp of Chedorlaomer and his allies with 318 "trained men, born in his house."

The raid on Shechem contains the only specific mention of weapons in the patriarchal narratives. The sons of Jacob took swords and killed the male inhabitants of that city. The type of swords used during this period were sickle-shaped blades. This style of sword probably evolved from the duck-bill axe which was the most common weapon of the time. Axes of this type, with curved shafts and a narrow-edged blade were designed as an effective armor-piercing instrument. They are depicted in the hands of Semitic caravaneers in the Egyptian Beni-Hasan tomb paintings from the 19th century BC.

2

EXODUS-SETTLEMENT
PERIOD

*Horned altar. Photo by
V. Matthews.* 2-1

HISTORICAL INTRODUCTION

The second major historical era described in
the biblical text is the period of the Exodus-
Settlement. This period includes the escape from
Egypt, the wilderness wanderings, the conquest,
and the judges period. There is a great diversity
of lifestyles during this period. The manners and
customs can be described as in transition from
pastoral nomadic wandering after the flight from
Egypt to a sedentary existence in the village culture of Palestine. New patterns were set for the
refugee groups (including both the Israelites and
others from the northern areas of the Near East),
and adjustments were made to accommodate to
life within the Canaanite cultural sphere. Lacking the strength to capture walled cities, the Israelite tribes settled primarily in the hill country of
central Palestine.

Establishing a clear historical setting for this
period is not easy. The biblical account (1 Kgs 6:1)
places the exodus in the 15th century BC. The
strength of the Egyptian presence in Canaan during this period and other chronological difficulties (including the exact length of the Middle
Bronze Age and the circumstances of the transition into the Late Bronze Age) make this date
problematic.

Extrabiblical sources which could indicate a
clear date for exodus-settlement period are scarce;
the evidence of archaeology is incomplete and

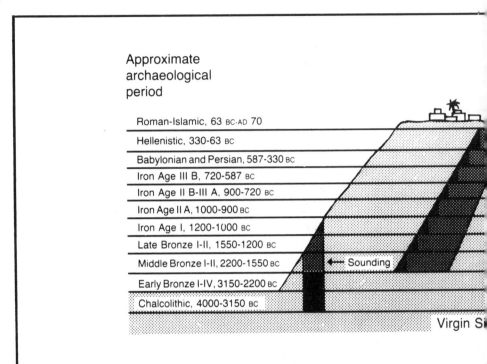

Approximate
archaeological
period

Roman-Islamic, 63 BC-AD 70	
Hellenistic, 330-63 BC	
Babylonian and Persian, 587-330 BC	
Iron Age III B, 720-587 BC	
Iron Age II B-III A, 900-720 BC	
Iron Age II A, 1000-900 BC	
Iron Age I, 1200-1000 BC	
Late Bronze I-II, 1550-1200 BC	
Middle Bronze I-II, 2200-1550 BC	◄─── Sounding
Early Bronze I-IV, 3150-2200 BC	
Chalcolithic, 4000-3150 BC	

Virgin S[i]

Cross-section of a tell. Adapted with permission from InterVarsity Press. 2-A

in some cases contradictory. Egyptian sources do not provide any mention of the exodus, although there is evidence of the use of forced labor gangs to construct the Egyptian storehouse cities of Pithom and Rameses in the time of Seti I and Rameses II (c. 1300–1250 BC). This fits the description of the Israelite slaves who built these cities or others of similar name recorded in Ex 1:11.

The settlement of so-called 'Apiru tribes in the Delta region is also mentioned in Egyptian texts. The label 'Apiru or Habiru appears to be a generic term for stateless people or tribal groups who lived on the fringes of the settled areas of the ancient Near East. They sometimes served as surplus labor or as mercenaries, but they appear in texts from several different historical periods (from 2000 to 1200 BC) and several different areas as brigands and raiders. While there is no direct linguistic connection between Habiru and Hebrew, the description of a people without

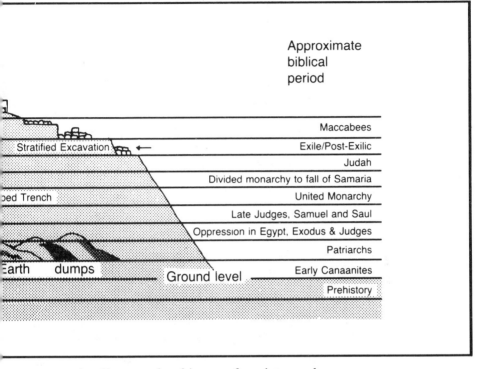

Approximate
biblical
period

Maccabees

Stratified Excavation   Exile/Post-Exilic

Judah

Divided monarchy to fall of Samaria

ʒed Trench   United Monarchy

Late Judges, Samuel and Saul

Oppression in Egypt, Exodus & Judges

Patriarchs

Earth   dumps   Ground level   Early Canaanites

Prehistory

roots who live on the fringes of society and sometimes infiltrate themselves into poorly defended areas does fit the biblical description of the Israelites.

The only documentary evidence from Egypt of Israel as a people is found in a victory stele of Pharaoh Merneptah dating to c. 1225 BC. This inscription lists the peoples and cities which the pharaoh conquered in an expedition into Palestine. In one line it states that Israel (specified in the text as a people, not a nation) was laid waste. This follows a pattern of systematic destruction by the pharaoh's armies of the area. There is a difficulty with this interpretation, however. The language of the inscription is typical of many other similar victory announcements, and the inclusion of Israel may reflect knowledge of its existence, but no actual contact with it. The pharaoh may just be boasting that he has subdued all of the peoples in the area. Still, it is the first extrabiblical mention of the name Israel and thus provides us with the best available evidence of its existence in the 13th century BC.

Evidence for the conquest period, as described in the book of Joshua, is just as problematic. The only discussion of this holy war is found in the biblical text. Archaeological investigations of the major sites said to have been destroyed by the Israelites have provided mixed results. Jericho, the first city listed as being conquered by the Hebrews, has been extensively excavated three times in this century, with the most scientific investigations being done by John Garstang and Kathleen Kenyon. Despite some early claims by Garstang that he had found the remains of the walls of Joshua's Jericho, it has generally been determined that the level he identified with the conquest actually is to be dated to the third millennium BC. Kenyon was able to demonstrate that those levels within the mound that correspond to the 14th and 13th centuries are too badly eroded to provide explicit evidence of destruction.

Ai from a distance. Photo by LaMoine DeVries.   2-2

Ai has also proven to be a puzzle. Excavations at this site (1965–1975) by Joseph Callaway demonstrated that the mound was unoccupied from 2400 to 1200 BC. It is possible that it was used as a military outpost by the nearby city of Bethel, which does show evidence of destruction in the 13th century, but there was no settlement at Ai such as that described in Joshua. Its name, which means "the ruin," may have also caused it to be added to Joshua's list of conquests.

The ruins of Hazor, one of the principal cities conquered by Joshua. Photo by Ralph Harris.   2-3

Other cities, including Hazor, Lachish, and Tell beit Mirsim, do have destruction levels which date to the 13th century. However, it is unclear whether their destruction is the result of any effort by the Israelites. They could just as easily be seen as evidence of the expedition of Merneptah as he tried to reestablish Egyptian control over Palestine or of the conquests of the Sea Peoples who raided much of the Near East around 1200 BC. Another site, Tell deir-'Alla, possibly to be identified as Succoth, was destroyed in this period (although a little after 1200 BC), but its demise is to be attributed to an earthquake.

With so many conflicting pieces of information, it is best to take a cautious view of the Israelite conquest of Canaan. Several theories have tried to explain the disparities between the archaeological evidence and the description of a nearly total victory sweep by the Israelites in Joshua 1–12. One possible explanation is that the text in Joshua is not as interested in historical details as it is in making the theological point that the victory was engineered by the divine warrior, Yahweh. Each battle is won because of the direct intervention of God. For instance, the fall of Jericho is not based on a conventional siege of the city by the Israelites, but rather on the opening given their forces when God destroyed the city walls.

A certain selectivity may also be evident in the conquest account. There is no clear indication of the amount of time the conquest took to complete. Possibly some cities fell to one wave of migrants while others succumbed to later attacks. The Israelite tribes may have entered Canaan over a fairly long period of time with each successive wave adding to their numbers and victories. Other migrating groups or even Canaanite villages (Gibeonites in Jos 9:3–15) may have joined forces with the Israelite tribes as they began to settle in the hill country. This could have in turn undermined the authority and strength of the Canaanite culture and eventually allowed the Israelites to dominate some areas, while engaging in a minimal amount of armed conflict.

The tribes of Israelites can be seen as assimilating themselves into the Canaanite culture after settling initially in the underpopulated areas of the hill country. As they learned the technology and social skills of the Canaanites, they gradually and, for the most part, peacefully merged into the dominant culture. Over time the Israel-

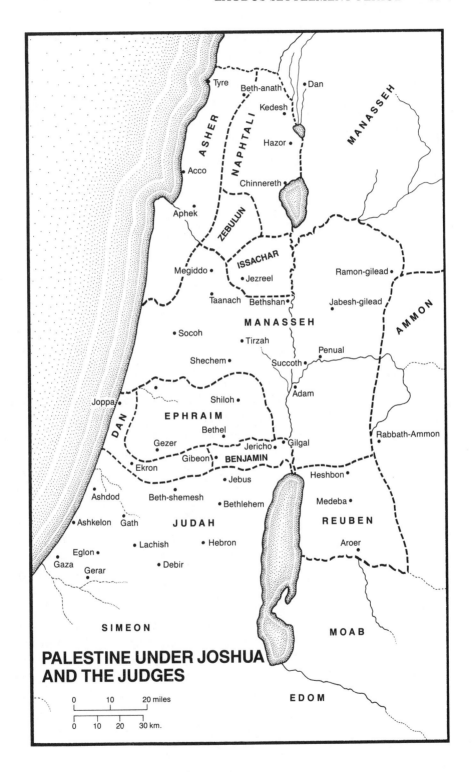

PALESTINE UNDER JOSHUA AND THE JUDGES

The LORD was with Judah, and he took possession of the hill country, but could not drive out the inhabitants of the plain, because they had chariots of iron.

—Judg 1:19

ites came to control larger areas and some cities with only the Philistine city-states in the south central plains of Palestine providing a major opposing force by the time of King David.

This explanation of a gradual infiltration by waves of migrants seems to fit the description in Judges 1–2. These chapters discuss the conquest attempt and list those cities and regions that the Israelite tribes were not able to conquer. Forced entry into central Canaan by Judah and the Joseph tribes of Ephraim and Manasseh can then be seen in the destruction of cities like Lachish and Bethel. The lack of evidence at other sites, like Ai, could be attributed to a later chronicling of the events or to overly enthusiastic battle reports.

However it happened, it is apparent that groups of Israelites did eventually settle in Canaan and in portions of the Transjordanian areas of Moab and Gilead. Engaging in a mixed economy of agriculture and herding, most of the Israelites would have lived in small, unwalled villages. Life, as described in Judges, was somewhat uncertain. Villages had to endure fairly frequent raids by Philistine and other Canaanite groups who took advantage of their technological superiority in weapons to harass the Hebrews. For most of this period, social and political organization remained on the tribal and village elder level. Direct contact with the urban-based cultures of Canaan and the need for a centralized political system eventually led the Israelites to adopt a monarchy and a more sophisticated religious system with a priestly organization.

In the following units the manners and customs of this era will be sketched out, indicating the shift from a stateless people to a loosely organized group of settled tribes and villages. This transition required some basic changes in social life and eventually formed the basis of the covenantal community.

I. VILLAGE LIFE

What was life like in Israelite villages during the settlement period?

The tribal allotments found in Joshua 15–17, which list the areas of Canaan assigned to the tribes of Israel, include both a list of towns and adjacent villages or "encampments." These latter settlements, sometimes referred to as "daughters" (Num 21:25, 32), contained the vast majority of the population during the early settlement period (c. 1200–1050 BC). The "iron chariots" of the Philistines and Canaanites are said to be responsible for bottling up the Israelites in the inhospitable, underpopulated regions of the country. This was the case even though, as the biblical writer says, "the hill country is not enough" (Jos 17:16) to support the needs of the people as the population expanded. Very likely, the higher technology and tighter political organization of the Canaanites held the new immigrants in check for some time.

A recent archaeological survey was done of those Israelite settlements in the hill country which date to the period after 1200 BC. The archaeologists discovered that of 114 sites located, 97 are new settlements. The rest are built on the ruins of abandoned ancient cities, such as Ai and Gibeon. In the period before 1200 BC, known as the Late Bronze Age, only 23 sites were located in this same area of the hill country. These findings suggest rapid population growth as the Israelites and other settlers entered the highlands of central Palestine at the beginning of the Iron Age.

Depending on their inaccessibility and poverty for protection, the small villages built by the new settlers were unwalled. Extended family groups were housed in multiple family compounds. These complexes may have been styled after the settlements in which the Hebrews lived while in Egypt or perhaps after the nomadic encampments of the wilderness period. Villages in the hill country consisted of closely packed rows or clusters of 15–20 dwellings which could house perhaps 100–150 people. The primary building materials were rocks and sun-dried, mud brick. Situated as they were on the hill tops, these villages seldom covered an area of more than about five acres.

Life in the village centered around agricultural pursuits and the maintenance of small herds of sheep and goats. Some domestic industries, such as the making of pottery, garments, and tools, were necessary for every household. Each settlement was isolated and therefore strove to be as self-sufficient as possible with regard to the basic necessities of life. Some natural resources were available nearby, such as clay for pots and copper deposits (Dt 8:9). More advanced technology and styles of workmanship, as well as some raw materials, could only be obtained from traveling craftsmen or in the larger cities of Canaan. For instance, 1 Sam 13:19 states:

> there was no smith to be found throughout the land of Israel. . . . every one of the Israelites went down to the Philistines to sharpen his plowshare, his mattock, his axe, or his sickle.

He dug it and cleared it of stones, and planted it with choice vines; he built a watchtower in the midst of it, and hewed out a wine vat in it; he expected it to yield grapes, but it yielded wild grapes. And now, inhabitants of Jerusalem and people of Judah, judge between me and my vineyard. What more was there to do for my vineyard that I have not done in it? When I expected it to yield grapes, why did it yield wild grapes? And now I will tell you what I will do to my vineyard. I will remove its hedge, and it shall be devoured; I will break down its wall, and it shall be trampled down.
—Isa. 5:2–5

Adjoining fields provided food for the villagers and commanded the bulk of their work day. Because there is little level ground in the hill country, a great deal of labor went into the building and maintaining of stone terraces on the slopes (see Isa 5:2–5). Vines and some cereals were cultivated on these artificially constructed plots. The flatter areas of the plains did allow for more conventional farming methods, but they were not settled by large groups of Israelites until the monarchy period. The uncertainties of rainfall in the hill country, hungry birds, and insects also plagued the farmers and severely cut into their harvest.

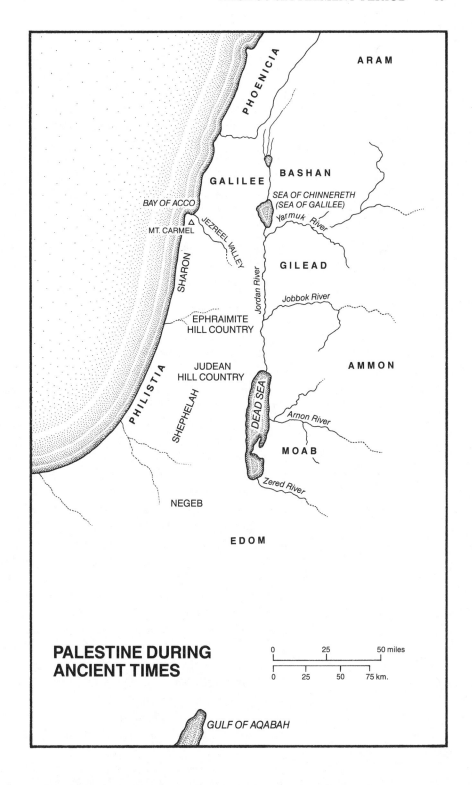

PHOENICIA

ARAM

BASHAN

GALILEE

SEA OF CHINNERETH
(SEA OF GALILEE)

BAY OF ACCO

Yarmuk River

MT. CARMEL

JEZREEL VALLEY

SHARON

GILEAD

Jordan River

Jobbok River

EPHRAIMITE
HILL COUNTRY

PHILISTIA

JUDEAN
HILL COUNTRY

AMMON

DEAD SEA

SHEPHELAH

Arnon River

MOAB

Zered River

NEGEB

EDOM

**PALESTINE DURING
ANCIENT TIMES**

0   25   50 miles

0   25   50   75 km.

GULF OF AQABAH

Each village had flocks of sheep and goats that were pastured some distance from the settlement. The herdsmen sometimes kept the animals up in the higher elevations for a season, but it was also quite common to bring them back to the village for the night. The open "square" in larger settlements was sometimes used to shelter the flocks. However, primitive enclosures were more often used to prevent the animals from wandering away and some homes were constructed with a lower, stable level in which the animals could be housed. During the winter, the body heat of the animals below the floor of the living areas provided additional, natural warmth for their owners.

DOMESTIC ARCHITECTURE

Poorer village sites, such as that excavated at Tell Raddana (near Ai), provided only the most minimal comforts of home and living space. In this small village of six, closely packed houses, the basic design is a simple, windowless rectangle divided into two living areas by a row of four roof supporting pillars. These pillars are usually placed within 5 feet of one long wall thereby creating a "great room" in the remaining 10-foot-wide living area. This "great room," illuminated by the fire pit and sputtering oil lamps, functioned as the place for most of the family's activities: cooking, entertaining, and sleeping.

Wooden beams, set in niches cut into the walls and supported by the pillars, supported the roof. Slats were made from smaller pieces of wood, brush, or thatching, which was sealed with a layer of clay. The ceiling thereby created was about 6 feet from the floor with the beams lowering that height by 5 or 6 inches in places. Based on such a low roof, it can be surmised that the Israelites were not much more than 5 feet tall.

With living space at a minimum, there was no room for luxuries or privacy. Cooking was done

outside the front door on small clay ovens or in a courtyard shared by two or three other households. There was no furniture, only stone ledges built along the wall and a few flat stones spaced around the central fire pit. Bathrooms were a convenience not yet provided for in these dwellings. The bodily needs of each individual were taken care of outdoors. If the villagers continued the pattern prescribed in the wilderness (Dt 23:12–13), they utilized latrines outside the immediate area of the village. Some may have simply gone into the fields where their excrement could serve as fertilizer.

Pillar buildings at Ai. Photo by LaMoine DeVries.   2-4

The only innovation and true convenience designed into these homes was an interconnected cistern system that brought rainwater into the house. Chiseled out of the chalk and limestone, which forms the bedrock under these hill-top settlements, bell-shaped cisterns provided a continuous supply of water. It was unnecessary to put additional lime plaster on the cisterns in the Ai/Raddana area because of the impermeability of the rock strata. Elsewhere, however, this type of "waterproofing cement" was used to hold the moisture.

Rainwater ran off the roofs and into these cisterns. Rocks were placed at the bottom to trap larger impurities and a hole was drilled in the side allowing water to travel into a series of adjoining cisterns and eventually inside the house. This system also filtered the water as it passed from one cistern to the next.

There are few natural springs on the hill tops and so it was the cistern system which made life possible here. The springs and rivers of the plains and coastal areas had attracted the cities and villages of the Canaanites. The Israelites therefore had to make the most of the resources of the area in which they could initially settle. Later, when judges and kings began to conquer the Canaanite strongholds, the Israelites were able to move down into the more hospitable and better watered areas of the land.

Excavated buildings at Megiddo. Photo by LaMoine DeVries. 2-5

Another style of house which was very common in ancient Israel in this period and down into the time of the monarchy was the courtyard house. Houses of this type have been excavated at Tell el Farah (Tirzah), Hazor, Shechem, and Tell beit Mirsim. Its basic design may have evolved from simple structures built around an animal enclosure in earlier periods. The general pattern consists of a long courtyard surrounded by partitioned rooms on three sides. The courtyard, with its hard packed, earthen or plastered floor, was used for domestic activities like cooking and dining. Excavations of these areas reveal clay ovens, hearths, and a small group of pottery types (more than 50% are storage jars and cooking pots). In some cases storage jars have been found arranged around the walls of the courtyard. These might have contained water for cooking or the grain, oil, or olives that would have gone into the next day's meal.

The close-packed rooms which box in the courtyard provided security and privacy for the

Megiddo gate, showing headers and stretchers building technique. Photo by V. Matthews. 2-6

Let us make a small roof chamber with walls, and put there for him a bed, a table, a chair, and a lamp, so that he can stay there whenever he comes to us. — 2 Kgs 4:10

family. Doorways opened from each room into the courtyard so that the central hearth located there could provide heating to the entire house. These chambers were sometimes subdivided into smaller rooms. They served as sleeping quarters, gathering places for the family and their friends, and as storage spaces. There was also a section cordoned off near the entrance to the courtyard to stable animals.

Walls in these simply constructed houses are quite thick, thereby providing good insulation against the cold and some relief in hot weather. In the hill country where uncut rock is plentiful, the foundation and the walls were made of uncut stone. A mud plaster, mixed with small stones, was applied to the walls to smooth it over and to protect against the weather. The areas of the plain and foothills, however, used sun-dried, mud brick for all but the foundation. These bricks, like cut stone in larger buildings, were laid in a pattern known as "headers and stretchers," which strengthened the construction and stability of the walls. Some houses appear to be sturdy enough to have supported a second story, and this may have been the case for the wealthier village families. What has been uncovered by archaeologists may in fact reflect the housing of the well-to-do while the more primitive dwellings of the poor have left no trace.

The roof over these dwellings provided additional living and work space. It was thatched with a mixture of reeds, branches, and palms leaves and then covered with earth or bricks. Extra sleeping accommodations could be provided on the roof (2 Kgs 4:10), and it could serve as an excellent spot for drying mud bricks or flax stalks (Jos 2:6). As a rule, access to the room was provided by a staircase on the outside of the wall, although ladders may also have been used. In warm weather, the roof was a favorite gathering place for family and friends. The breeze provided relief from the heat and domestic tasks could be performed in more comfort.

Another area of the house which held both functional and traditional importance is the threshold and doorway. Doors were at first simply skin coverings, but these were eventually replaced by a more permanent wattle or wooden barrier and barred from within. On the doorpost was placed the *mezuzah,* which contained a fragment of the law and marked the family's adherence to the covenant. The threshold marked the legal entryway of the dwelling, and in some cases may have served as a place where justice was done (Dt 22:21) or demanded (Jdg 19:27). Shoes were removed before crossing the threshold as a sign of respect and the obligations of hospitality began at this point.

Then they shall bring the young woman out to the entrance of her father's house and the men of her town shall stone her to death, because she committed a disgraceful act in Israel by prostituting herself in her father's house. So you shall purge the evil from your midst. —Deut 22:21

II. AGRICULTURAL METHODS AND TOOLS

What agricultural methods were employed by the Israelite settlers?

Constrained to live in the hill country, the Israelites adapted to this environment by building terraces on the hill sides. This required a large part of the villagers' energies to construct and maintain, but it provided them with farmable strips of land that could support the growing agricultural needs of the people. Terracing in this period was not as extensive as it was in the monarchy period, when 50% of the hill sides were terraced. The growth in population of the villages, however, was one of the prime reasons for initiating such a monumental construction project. Since these terraces have been rebuilt and reused by villagers throughout the centuries, the primary means of determining when they might have originally been built is through the examination of pottery remains. This is not always a re-

He built towers in the wilderness and hewed out many cisterns, for he had large herds, both in the Shephelah and in the plain, and he had farmers and vinedressers in the hills and in the fertile lands, for he loved the soil.

— 2 Chr 26:10

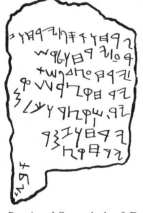

Drawing of Gezer calendar. 2-D

liable test, but indications are that the process that turned the hills of Judea and Ephraim into farm land began in the early settlement period and then was expanded and maintained throughout the monarchy (see Uzziah's emphasis on agriculture in 2 Chr 26:10).

The terraces are not designed to prevent erosion of existing topsoil. The hills have little soil to lose due to previous deforestation (Jos 17:18) and pasturing of animals. Thus much of the soil found in the terraces was brought from elsewhere and was usually a mixture of different soil types. Channels were sometimes dug to direct rainwater down into the terraces. These terraces were constructed all the way down the face of the hill to ensure natural filtration of the water and a better distribution of moisture to all of the farming strips. Since rain only falls during four months of the year, it is essential that none of it be allowed to run off without benefiting the fields through increased soil moisture levels.

A. GRAIN PRODUCTION

Wheat and barley were the most common crops grown in the hill country by the Israelites. While it comes from the 10th century BC, the so-called Gezer Calendar records a pattern of the agricultural year that must go back to earlier times. This schoolboy exercise, written on a broken limestone tablet, describes the seasons as including two months for storage, two months of planting, two months for the summer planting, one month each to hoe flax and harvest barley, and another to harvest all other crops and to feast. Finally, two months were set aside for vine-tending and a month for tending the summer fruit.

The agricultural calendar was thus based on the division between the rainy winter months and the dry spring and summer. Once the rains had loosened the ground, ploughing and plant-

ing of various crops began in November and continued until January. Wheat and barley were the first to be planted while crops like sesame, millet, and lentils, and garden vegetables like cucumbers, garlic, onions, and leeks were planted from January till March. Harvest seasons varied according to the temperature ranges of specific regions with the Jordan valley the first to harvest and the cooler mountain areas the last. This meant that barley, which ripened before the wheat, was harvested from April to May while the latter was harvested from May to June.

To prepare the ground for planting, a wooden plow (sometimes with a metal sheath or boot attached), drawn by a team of oxen (1 Sam 11:5), opened the furrows. The smaller villages probably shared a team of oxen or perhaps even rented one from a nearby village. One text from Mari (*ARMT* 14:80.4–10) mentions a similar arrangement in which a village obtained the use of a team of oxen in exchange for its labor service for the government. The importance of work ani-

Some "modern" farmers use methods not far removed from their ancestors. Photo from Elmendorf, A Camera Crusade through the Holy Land.   2-7

mals to a village also figures into Gideon's sacrifice of his team to Yahweh after using them to tear down his father's Baal altar in Jdg 6:25–28. In another instance, the slaughter of his oxen could have symbolized the seriousness of Saul's plea for the tribes to assemble for war (1 Sam 11:7).

Sowing involved simply casting the grain into the furrows by hand and trampling it into the ground with the foot or the tread of the animals. Harvesting of the ripened grain was done with sickle blades (Joel 3:13). These were made of bronze, although in the poorer villages wooden sickles, with flint embedded as the cutting edge, continued to be used. Once iron technology and tools were introduced into the Israelite villages, these improved farm implements would have been greatly prized over their primitive predecessors.

The harvested grain was taken to a central threshing floor. This was a flattened area, ranging in size from 160 to 320 feet in diameter (depending on the number of villages and fields

Gleaning fields. Photo from Elmendorf, A Camera Crusade through the Holy Land.   2-8

it serviced). It was located in an open place where the prevailing winds would aid in the winnowing process. The circular earthen floor was used to separate the kernels of the grain from the stalks. This was accomplished by driving oxen over the grain, trampling it. The concern the Israelites had for the animals that aided them in

The threshing floor. Photo by V. Matthews. 2-9

this important activity is reflected in Dt 25:4, which states that a man is prohibited from muzzling his ox while it treads out the grain. It was thus free to breathe and to eat a portion for its hire.

In later periods a more efficient method of threshing was developed using a type of threshing sledge with stone and bits of metal attached to its under side. These extra edges allowed the sledge to do a more thorough job of crushing the stalks. A sledge like this is mentioned in 2 Sam 24:25 as a part of David's purchase of the threshing floor of Araunah, which became the site of the temple in Jerusalem.

Because the threshing floor was also used as the site for the distribution of grain to the villagers, it eventually became associated with the well-being of the community and the administration of the law. In the Ugaritic legend of Aqhat (*ANET,* p. 151), Dan-el, the hero's father, is portrayed as sitting in the threshing floor of his village deciding the cases of widows and orphans (cf. Deborah's activity in Jdg 4:5). A similar case is found in the book of Ruth where the widowed heroine went to see Boaz at the threshing floor. He was spending the night at this installation to guard his grain, but it does not seem out of place that Ruth should have come to him here to make a petition regarding her upcoming marriage (Ruth 3:6–13).

The next step in the process of preparing the grain for milling is winnowing. This was done using a long wooden fork which tossed the grain and chaff into the air. Then, as Ps 1:14 says of the wicked, the chaff was driven away by the wind. Jeremiah 15:7 also used this common village activity to describe God's testing of the people "with a winnowing fork in the gates of the land." Two places associated with justice are used here: the threshing floor where the winnowing was done and the gate, which was the

Women were responsible for grinding the harvested grain into usable flour or meal. Photo from Elmendorf, A Camera Crusade through the Holy Land.   2-10

center of business and legal activity when the Israelites inhabited walled cities during the monarchy period.

Sieving of the grain is the final step in separating the grain from the chaff. These small wicker screens trapped tiny stones or bits of pottery and allowed the grain to fall to the floor where it could be collected. Amos, an 8th-century prophet from the farming village of Tekoa, used this activity to describe how God in his wrath will "shake the house of Israel among all the nations as one shakes a sieve, but no pebble shall fall upon the earth" (9:9).

Once the kernels of grain were collected, they were then distributed to the people by the village elders. A portion was ground into flour with a simple millstone on a larger stone quern shaped like a saddle. It was then pulverized in a stone mortar with a rounded pestle. Another portion was "parched" to be eaten as journey provisions or pressed into cakes. The remainder was stored in pottery jars and stacked around the walls of homes or courtyards, or in plastered storage pits. Only the larger villages and towns had communal silos for the storage of large quantities of grain.

B. CULTIVATION OF VINES AND OLIVE TREES

Every village in this and later periods had its vines and trees. Terraces are actually better designed for these crops than for the cultivation of grain. This fact, plus evidence from the sites and the biblical text, suggests that grapes and olives were staples in the diet and the farm production of ancient Israel.

Tub used for crushing olives to extract oil. Photo by William Dever.   2-11

Monarchy-era tower bordering terraced vineyard. Photo by Ralph Harris. 2-12

As Isaiah notes in his "Song of the Vineyard" (5:1–6), the cultivation of vineyards on terraces was a time-consuming and sometimes frustrating activity. It involved the maintenance of the terrace wall, the clearing of the field of stones, and the planting of proven vine cuttings. A watchtower was sometimes constructed to guard the vines, and a wine press and vat were carved out of the rock of the hillside. In addition, a hedge or fence was also built to keep out small animals and grazing herds (Ps 80:12–13).

The vines required constant care, with pruning done from June to August to allow for new growth and the removal of nonproductive or old vines (Lev 25:4). Supports for the vine clusters were constructed to prevent bruising and rot, and the area around the vine was regularly hoed to cut back on weeds that would steal moisture needed by the fruit to ripen (Isa 5:6).

The grapes were harvested with pruning hooks (Isa 2:4) in August and September. Some were dried into raisin clusters (1 Sam 25:18) and the rest taken to the wine press to be trod into wine. The resulting liquid squeezings were poured or channeled into a fermentation vat and then stored in jars or skin bags. With so much communal activity associated with this installation, it is no wonder that its importance is second only to the threshing floor in Israelite tradition (Hos 9:2).

Like many places of business or manufacture the wine vat became associated with scenes of community life. One of the best known from this period involves the Judge Gideon. When the Midianite raiders had ravaged his village's fields, he secretly ground his remaining wheat in a wine press to prevent the invaders from suspecting that he was holding out on them (Jdg 6:11).

The harvesting of the grapes and the production of wine was a time of celebration in the villages comparable to the grain harvest (Jdg 9:27). The people's joy was based on the fact that wine was paired with bread as the chief staples of life (Jdg 19:19). At times the festival may have gotten out of hand, leaving the village open to attack. For instance, in Jdg 21:20–21 the decimated Benjaminite tribe took advantage of the celebration at Shiloh to steal wives from among the dancers.

*So they said, "Look, the yearly festival of the LORD is taking place at Shiloh, which is north of Bethel, on the east of the highway that goes up from Bethel to Shechem, and south of Lebonah." —*Judg 21:19

Olive and fig trees provided the other noncereal agricultural crops. The fruit of these trees added spice and variety to an otherwise monotonous diet. In addition, crushed olives provided oil for lamps, cooking, and personal care products. The olive tree was long-lived and well suited to the hot dry summers and cool damp winters of Israel and the rest of the Mediterranean basin. It was seen, along with the other produce of the land, as one of the blessings provided to the people by God (Dt 7:13).

Ripe olives were gathered in the autumn with the villagers striking the tree branches with sticks and gathering the fallen fruit in baskets. The olives were then crushed under a revolving, flat stone and the stream of oil and juice was caught in a cistern. The remaining pulp was then placed in wicker baskets to be crushed again by a stone-

weighted lever. Squeezings were then channeled into a larger catchbasin. Gradually, the finer grade of oil rose to the top of the cistern and was skimmed off for use in lamps (Ex 27:20). The remainder was further refined and used among other purposes as a base for cosmetics, in cooking, and as medicine.

Basalt oil mill used to crush olives — N.T. innovation.
Photo by Ralph Harris.   2-13

Fig trees, whose fruit was the last to appear in the summer (the summer fruit of the Gezer Calendar and Amos 8:2) were also among the items characteristically exploited in arid farming areas like the hill country (Jer 40:10–12). Because of their high sugar content, figs could be dried and pressed into cakes that were stored for later consumption or given as gifts in the dry, fruitless summer. First Samuel 25:18 lists fig cakes as one of the items Abigail took to David's camp to prevent his attack on her husband's household.

This same passage could also serve as a typical menu of the foods eaten by the people in the settlement period. Abigail took David's men 200 loaves of bread, 2 skins of wine, 5 butchered sheep, 5 measures of parched grain, 100 clusters of raisins, and 200 fig cakes. With this as a guide, it can be seen that the land did yield its agricultural wealth to the Israelites, although not without a struggle and not always in the abundance they desired.

III. WEAPONS AND WARFARE

What were the weapons used by the Israelites and what were the methods of warfare used in the periods of the conquest and settlement?

A discussion of weapons and warfare in this period of Israel's history must take into account the differences between the accounts in Joshua and in Judges. The book of Joshua describes the conquest and highlights Yahweh's role as the "Divine Warrior," who provides one victory after another to the Israelite forces. This pattern is found in the capture of Jericho (Jos 6), the defeat of the five Amorite kings when God caused the "sun to stand still" (Jos 10:6–13), and in the wilderness period in the battle against the Amalekites (Ex 17:8–13). In these battles it is God's intervention that determines the outcome, not the strength of the Israelite tribes.

And the sun stood still, and the moon stopped, until the nation took vengeance on their enemies.
—Josh 10:13a

In contrast to this theme, in Judges the "holy war" or *herem* was admitted to have failed. Many Canaanite cities are listed as being too strong for the Israelites to capture, and the iron chariots (1:19) of these people of the plain kept the Israelites bottled up in the hill country (1:34). A rationalization for this failure is spelled out in Jdg 3:1–4 which states that God spared these Canaanite and Philistine cities so that "the people of Israel might know war, that he might teach war to such at least as had not known it before" and "for the testing of Israel, to know whether Israel would obey the commandments of the Lord."

Thus during much of the settlement period the Israelites were either vassals of the more powerful Canaanite rulers or were engaged in nearly continuous armed conflict with their neighbors and fellow tribesmen. This state of affairs can be illustrated by two passages: Jdg 15:11 and 12:1–6. In the first of these texts, Samson had been pursued into the territory of Judah by an army of Philistines. Eventually, he was captured and turned over to his enemies. However, his captors were men of Judah who told him, "Do you not know that the Philistines are rulers over us?"

Judges 12 relates that Jephthah had just completed a war with the Ammonites in Gilead and was faced with the militant jealousies of the Ephraimites. Claiming they were denied their share of the glory in the now concluded campaign, these tribesmen crossed into Jephthah's territory.

Beni hasan slinger. 2-E

Unlike Gideon, who was faced with the same charge in Jdg 8:1–3, Jephthah denied the Ephraimite claim saying they had failed to come when called. This precipitated a civil war; Jephthah's forces took the fords of the Jordan to prevent the invaders from escaping and slaughtered 42,000 of them.

One other portion of this narrative which demonstrates the obvious differences between the tribes in this period is the so-called *Shibboleth* Affair. As the Ephraimites attempted to sneak across the Jordan, Jephthah's men stopped them and asked them to pronounce the word *shibboleth*, which means an ear of grain. The Ephraimites, however, spoke a different dialect of Hebrew and therefore pronounced the word as *sibboleth*. This gave them away and they were executed on the spot.

A. The Contrast in Weapons

Although the Philistines and Canaanites began to experiment with an iron-based military technology in the 12th and 11th centuries BC, the metal of choice throughout this period remained bronze. Israelites also used bronze weapons, but their lack of metallurgical knowledge and the monopoly over the tin trade exercised by the Philistines probably forced many of their soldiers to use slings and farm implements to defend themselves. Some iron weapons were undoubtedly captured by raiding Israelite forces, but without the knowledge of metallurgy to repair and fabricate new weapons out of scrap metal, they would have eventually become useless. This may explain why the forces under Joshua chose to burn the chariots of the northern coalition of Canaanite kings (Jos 11:9) rather than use them themselves. The Israelites could not repair the chariots and they did not want to leave them behind for the Canaanites to use against them in the future. The chariots would have also been of little use to raiding Israelite bands operating out of the rugged hill country.

And Joshua did to them as the LORD commanded him; he hamstrung their horses, and burned their chariots with fire.
—Josh 11:9

The Israelites' lack of skill in working metals is repeatedly mentioned in the narratives. First Samuel 13:19 explains that the Israelites were deliberately denied this knowledge by the Philistines "lest they make themselves swords or spears." As a result the Hebrew tribesmen were ill equipped for war and were constantly being forced to rely on inferior weapons and the element of surprise. For instance, the Joseph tribe's attack on Bethel (Jdg 1:22–25) was successful because a man of that community was captured, and he showed them "the way into the city."

In an episode involving the Benjaminite judge Ehud, the hero had to resort to assassination (Jdg 3:15–26) to free his people from the tribute demands of Eglon of Moab. Concealing a dagger on his person before his interview with the Moabite king, Ehud then told Eglon that he had a message for him from God. This caused the greedy monarch to send away his guards and gave the left-handed Ehud the opportunity to draw out his dagger, stab him, and escape.

Gideon was another Israelite judge who used trickery rather than force of arms to achieve his goals. When faced with overwhelming odds in a war against the Midianites, he divided the 300 men that God had allowed him to bring into three companies. They surrounded the Midianite camp and then in the dead of night raised such a racket by smashing pitchers, shouting, and blowing horns that the confused enemy soldiers began fighting among themselves (Jdg 7:19–22).

Other weapons mentioned in the text include some very primitive items. For example, Shamgar, in Jdg 3:31, killed 600 Philistines with an ox goad—not an unusual weapon for a hill country farmer. The Kenite woman Jael killed the sleeping general Sisera by driving a wooden tent peg through his skull (Jdg 4:21). Samson, judge of the tribe of Dan, victimized the Philistines using a "fresh" (nonbrittle) jawbone of an ass to slay a thousand men (Jdg 15:15). His exploits also included burning the Philistine fields of standing grain with torches tied to the tails of foxes (Jdg 15:5), and carrying away the doors of the gate of the Philistine city of Gaza (Jdg 16:3).

When Israelite forces were marshalled against walled cities, the siege was never prolonged and generally included scenes of fierce fighting. The ultimate goal of the besieging army, once the gates or walls were breached, was the citadel tower, which was the final defense of the citizenry. According to Jdg 8:17, Gideon tore down the tower of Penuel; his son Abimelech captured the city of Shechem in Judges 9. In this latter narrative, Abimelech still had to decimate the Shechem's fighting forces by ambushing men as

He also broke down the tower of Penuel, and killed the men of the city. —Judg 8:17

they came out to the fields and by rushing a segment of his army through the open gate into the city (vv 44–45).

Those people that survived the initial attack took refuge in the city's citadel tower. Abimelech used fire to weaken the tower's masonry, thereby forcing the people to abandon its defenses or be buried in the collapsing rubble. The remainder were slaughtered by Abimelech's men (vv 48–49). This wily general tried to use the same strategy at Thebez, but he got too close to the wall of the tower and was struck with a millstone flung from above by a woman (vv 50–53). The death of their leader disheartened the Israelites and they gave up the siege.

Even after the monarchy was established and Saul provided the centralized leadership that the people had lacked since the death of Joshua, iron weapons were scarce. First Samuel 13:22 records that only Saul and his son Jonathan had spears and swords (most likely meaning iron spears and swords). The remainder of the troops that were about to face a Philistine army had only what weapons they could acquire — probably bronze sickle swords, slings, bows, and clubs. The battle, as in the Gideon narrative (Jdg 7:19–22), was eventually won as a result of a raid that threw the enemy camp into confusion. Jonathan and his armor bearer secretly entered the camp, causing a large enough disturbance to give his father's army the opening they needed to gain the victory.

The contrast between military technologies is also graphically portrayed in the David and Goliath episode. This reflects the classic confrontation between the heavily armored knight and the more mobile auxiliary fighter. Goliath is described in 1 Sam 17:4–7 as a giant soldier, clothed in a bronze helmet, bronze chain mail, and bronze greaves which protected his legs. He carried a huge spear with an iron head and was accom-

So on the day of the battle neither sword nor spear was to be found in the possession of any of the people with Saul and Jonathan; but Saul and his son Jonathan had them. —1 Sam 13:22

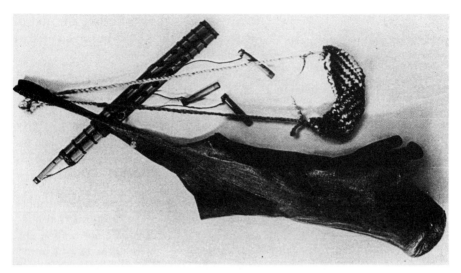

panied by a shield-bearer. David, on the other hand, wore no armor (having turned down the use of Saul's) and relied on a sling and 5 stones as his only weapons.

Perhaps the ancient shepherd's equipment included a sling, a flute, and a goatskin pouch. Photo from Elmendorf, A Camera Crusade through the Holy Land.   2-14

Again, victory for the Israelites seemed impossible, and in the text it is ascribed to God's intervention on the side of his people (v 47). In any case, sling stones could be thrown with incredible force and were a part of every army's arsenal. They have been found in great quantities by archaeologists in the levels of the city of Lachish associated with its capture by the Assyrians about 700 BC. David used his to good effect and opened the way to an Israelite victory.

B. Similarities in the Practice of War

The rules of warfare practiced by the Israelites and their enemies seem to be very similar. Each side was striving to either exterminate or subjugate the other. Goliath's challenge states that the winner of the contest between champions would turn the loser's people into servants (1 Sam 17:9). The principle of winner take all is quite typical of this violent age and is even found in the Babylonian version of creation, the *Enuma*

Elish (*ANET,* p. 67), where Marduk, the god of Babylon, challenges the chaos beast Tiamat to single combat.

The taking of spoils from the bodies and animals of the vanquished foe was an accepted and anticipated practice. In Judges 5:28—30 the mother of Sisera, general of the Canaanite city of Hazor, rationalized that her son was late in returning because of the rich spoils he was collecting from the defeated Israelites:

> Out of the window she peered, the mother of Sisera gazed through the lattice: ''Why is his chariot so long in coming? . . . ''Are they not finding and dividing the spoil?—A maiden or two for every man; spoil of dyed stuffs for Sisera, spoil of dyed stuffs embroidered, two pieces of dyed work embroidered for my neck as spoil?'' (Judges 5:28—30, RSV)

Gideon, after defeating the Midianite kings Zebah and Zalmuna (Jdg 8:21–26), gathered the golden earrings, pendants, and purple garments of the enemies. He also took the pendants from the necks of their camels.

Mutilation of corpses as well as surviving enemy soldiers was also established policy for both the Israelites and the people of Canaan. This can be seen in David's bringing back 200 Philistine foreskins to Saul as bride price for Michal (1 Sam 18:27). In Judges, Adonibezek, king of the Perizzites, said that he had cut off the thumbs and big toes of 70 kings whom he had defeated. The same thing was then done to him when his forces were defeated by the tribes of Judah and Simeon (Jdg 1:6–7). Following this same policy, Nahash, king of the Ammonites, told the people of the Israelite village of Jabesh-Gilead that he would massacre the entire population if they did not surrender. However, submitting to his demand would then cost all the men of the city their right eyes (1 Sam 11:2).

IV. SOCIAL ORGANIZATION AND ADMINISTRATION OF LAW

How were villages organized and how was law administered?

"In those days there was no king in Israel; every man did what was right in his own eyes" (Jdg 17:6). This observation from hindsight, written in the time of the monarchy, is the theme of the book of Judges and a powerful argument for the establishment of the monarchy. The leadership of Moses, Joshua, and the tribal leaders appointed to judge the Israelites in the wilderness (Ex 18:21–22) seems to have disappeared in the settlement period along with the covenant and the Decalogue. Even the ark of the covenant, the visible symbol of God's presence with his people, is almost totally absent from the Judges narrative (found only in 20:27). All this points to a time, not of anarchy, but of local administration of justice. Individual households and village assemblies administered justice and chose to listen or not listen to the rallying calls of the judges.

In those days there was no king in Israel; all the people did what was right in their own eyes.
—Judg 17:6

A. THE HEAD OF HOUSEHOLD

The social organization of the Israelites from the time of the exodus through the settlement period was based on the extended family. A man determined his lineage first by his father, then his clan, his tribe, and finally (if at all) by his people. In nearly every introduction of a character he is described as "_____ son of _____." This is also indicated in the narratives describing the casting of lots: Achan in Jos 7:16–18 and Saul in 1 Sam 10:20–21. The man who was singled out was found by the process of selecting tribe, clan, and family.

In the tents in the wilderness and in the villages of the hill country, the family was the focus of life. Individual dwellings were often too small to house more than the nuclear family. The villages, however, were organized into clusters of multiple-family compounds. Thus the head of the household, in an extended family arrangement, would have been the grandfather or oldest active male member. His home would have formed the physical and social center of a cluster of dwellings which housed his extended family. The death of the grandfather may have caused a temporary readjustment of the power structure of the group, but this would have settled back into the traditional pattern fairly quickly.

An example of the way the family adjusted to new leadership is found in Judges 17–18. In this passage, Micah's father had died and he quickly moved into the position as head of the household. This is demonstrated by his installation of his sons in adjacent dwellings and his hiring of a Levite to officiate in his private shrine. The family is thus portrayed as living within a cluster of houses within the village.

When all the people saw the pillar of cloud standing at the entrance of the tent, all the people would rise and bow down, all of them, at the entrance of their tent. — Exod 33:10

The head of the family represented its members in the assembly of the people, as a village elder, and in worship. One example of his responsibilities appears in Ex 33:10, where each man stood at the door of his tent and worshipped while Moses consulted with Yahweh. This communal role is also highlighted in Num 1:4–16, where a select group of clan heads is chosen to aid in the census of the people.

In matters of law, the head of the household exercised the powers of the *pater familias* in much the same way as in the patriarchal period. It was his right to punish or reward the members of his family without the interference of the other villagers. For instance, in Jdg 6:28–31, when Gideon is accused by the people of his village of destroying the altar of Baal, his father refuses to allow him to be punished saying it is a dispute between Gideon and the god. This power of the father was protected in the law by the commandment to "honor your father and your mother" (Ex 20:12) and by the tradition of respect that was due them (Prov 30:17). Under extreme circumstances, the death penalty could be imposed upon a man who struck his father or his mother (Ex 21:15).

The responsibilities of leadership and the guarantees of respect given to the head of a household, however, also brought with them an element of danger. If a man willfully broke the law, thereby endangering the survival of the community, his crime could bring destruction to the entire family group. This occurred when Achan stole from the spoils of the *herem* at Jericho. The result of his crime was a defeat in the next battle at Ai and the sentencing of his entire household to be stoned as a sacrifice for his sin (Jos 7:24 – 25).

Her husband is known in the city gates, taking his seat among the elders of the land.
— Prov 31:23

B. Village Elders

Beyond the level of the household, authority in the village was vested in the hands of the elders. These men, all heads of households and property owners, represented the collective wisdom of the community (Prov 31:23). It was their responsibility to deal with cases involving the general welfare of the entire village. As individuals within an assembly, they were responsible for formulating legal policy based on the legal traditions and customs of the group. The Decalogue (Ten Commandments), given to the covenant community at Sinai, especially its injunctions against theft, murder, and adultery, would have formed a large part of their traditional legal knowledge.

In the small, unwalled villages of the hill country, the elders probably met in the cleared threshing floor (like Aqhat's father Dan-el in the Ugaritic epic). This circular, open space, associated with the harvest and the survival of the people, was the first "courtroom." Here disputes over the distribution of grain were heard and the cases of widows and orphans dealt with publicly.

During later periods, when the villages acquired walls or grew into towns, the gate area became the place of judgment where cases were brought before the elders. Thus after Ruth confronted Boaz at the threshing floor, he went to the gate and called on the elders to sit with him and decide her case (Ruth 4:1–2). This involved restating the legal situation, hearing testimony, and resolving the problem before the witnessing elders.

C. THE JUDGES

Then the LORD raised up judges, who delivered them out of the power of those who plundered them. —Judg 2:16

The only other authority figures during the settlement period, after the deaths of Moses and Joshua, were the judges. They are portrayed in the book of Judges as charismatic leaders chosen by Yahweh to liberate the people from oppression. For the most part, the judges were military leaders, not judicial or religious leaders. Their role was to carry out a God-directed campaign against a Canaanite, Philistine, or other enemy group. The combined intervention of Yahweh and the judge then relieved the people of the burden of taxes, slavery, or oppression, which they had originally brought upon themselves by their sin (Jdg 2:11–19).

Individual skills as a military leader, however, were not the chief qualification for a judge. Gideon, who was reluctant to serve and considered himself unqualified to lead men (Jdg 6:15), defeated the Midianites with a force of only 300 men and an unorthodox strategy (Jdg 7:19–23). In preparing for a battle against the king of Hazor, Deborah relied upon the generalship of Barak and a promise of victory from Yahweh to inspire the troops (Jdg 5:6). Samson, the most unusual of the judges, took on the entire nation of the Philistines, single-handedly killing thousands of them. Eventually, however, he succumbed to inflated pride and a failure to keep his Nazirite vows to God (Jdg 16:4–22).

None of the judges, other than Samuel, were national figures. They operated in specific, limited areas and dealt with local problems. Occasionally, the judge called on other tribes to aid in a military campaign, but it was apparently up to the tribal leaders to decide whether they would come. Thus when Deborah called on the Israelites to join in the war against Jabin the king of Hazor, five tribes sent their warriors. The "clans of Reuben," Gilead, Dan, and Asher, for their own reasons, chose not to respond (Jdg 5:14–18).

The 12-tribe league, as it is described in Joshua, does not appear to have operated during the settlement period. The narrative does not include a single instance in which all 12 tribes are described as working together during this period. In several instances, in fact, they are described as fighting among themselves (Jos 22:10–12; Jdg 8:1; 12:1–6; 20:12–48).

Some tribes are not even mentioned by name in the text of Judges. It seems likely therefore that several of the smaller tribes, like Simeon (mentioned only in Jdg 1:3), were absorbed into larger ones. Thus when Saul was proclaimed king by the tribes of both the north and the south at Gilgal (1 Sam 11:14–15), all 12 would no longer have existed as identifiable, independent groups.

A description of the role played by the judges in the religious activities of the people will be dealt with in the unit on religious practices. The legal function of the judge is mentioned only with regard to Deborah and Samuel. While their legal activity is not described in detail, it is interesting to note that both operated in the vicinity of the cities of Ramah and Bethel in the "hill country of Ephraim." Deborah is pictured (Jdg 4:5) as sitting in judgment over people who had brought their cases to her. Samuel, in contrast, traveled a circuit from Bethel to Gilgal and Mizpah, going from village to village and administering justice (1 Sam 8:15–17). His territorial

She used to sit under the palm of Deborah between Ramah and Bethel in the hill country of Ephraim; and the Israelites came up to her for judgment.

—Judg 4:5

authority was widened as far south as Beer-sheba when he appointed his sons to be judges over that region (1 Sam 8:1–2).

The types of cases heard by a judge would probably include those that could not be decided by the heads of households or the assembly of elders. Since both Deborah and Samuel also functioned as prophets, it may have been assumed by the people that their judgments would be based on both the legal tradition and divine revelation.

V. FAMILY LIFE

What were the customs that governed everyday life for the Israelites?

A. MARRIAGE CUSTOMS

First-time marriages continued to be arranged by the bride's father in this period. In principle, endogamy, marriage within the group, would have still been the norm in the Israelite villages. However, once the Israelites settled in Canaan mixed marriages were probably more common. For instance, Samson was encouraged by his father to marry a "woman among the daughters of your kinsmen, or among all our people," but he was insistent that a marriage be arranged with a Philistine woman (Jdg 14:3).

In contrast to the arranged marriage for young couples, the customs regarding widows apparently allowed for a more direct contact between the two participants. Ruth went directly to Boaz at the threshing floor to obtain his aid in arranging their marriage. David simply sent a go-between to ask Abigail, the widow of Nabal, to become his wife (1 Sam 25:39–42).

The custom of paying a bride price figures in several episodes during the settlement period. It also very often involved accomplishing some great deed in order to obtain a wife. A good example of this occurs when Saul offered riches and a daughter in marriage to the man who was able to slay Goliath (1 Sam 17:25). Later, though, he demanded 100 Philistine foreskins of David as an additional bride price for his daughter Michal (1 Sam 18:25). Similarly, Caleb offered his daughter Achsah to the conqueror of the city of Kiriath-sepher (Debir). Once Othniel had accomplished this deed, further negotiations then occurred in arranging the marriage. Othniel was encouraged by his future wife to also ask for a field, perhaps as her dowry. Achsah in turn asked for water rights, since the field they had been given was in the arid Negeb region (Jdg 2:12–15).

Polygamy was not uncommon during this era. Gideon is said to have had 70 sons and many wives (Jdg 8:30) and Elkanah, the father of Samuel, had two wives, Hannah and Peninnah (1 Sam 1:2). Such an arrangement must have led to occasional conflict between the wives and disputes over the inheritance. Deuteronomy 21:15–17, a law in the Deuteronomic Code (dated to c. 650 BC), deals with this matter and probably originated in the family customs of the settlement period. In this situation a man with two wives could not shortchange any of his children with regard to the inheritance simply because he favored one wife over the other (cf. also CH 167, 170–171; *ANET,* p. 173).

If a man has two wives, one of them loved and the other disliked, and if both the loved and the disliked have borne him sons, the firstborn being the son of the one who is disliked, then on the day when he wills his possessions to his sons, he is not permitted to treat the son of the loved as the firstborn in preference to the son of the disliked, who is the firstborn. He must acknowledge as firstborn the son of the one who is disliked, giving him a double portion of all that he has; since he is the first issue of his virility, the right of the firstborn is his. —Deut 21:15–17

B. CHILDBIRTH AND CHILD REARING

Where they were available, midwives often helped with the birth of children. The mention of the team of Shiphrah and Puah in Ex 1:15 probably reflects the use of two women, one to aid with the delivery and the other to support the back of the woman on the birthing stool. The primitive and isolated environment of the Israelite villages may have forced many women to give birth alone or only with the help of female family members. This was undoubtedly a contributing

Figure of mother and child. 2-F

factor to the high mortality rate among infants as well as their mothers. For example, Rachel died giving birth to Benjamin as the family traveled between Bethel and Bethlehem (Gen 35:16–19). In another case, Phinehas' wife went into premature labor after hearing the news of her husband's death in the battle against the Philistines at Aphek. The double shock to her system caused her death, although the child did survive (1 Sam 4:19–20).

Children had to grow up fast in the hill country villages. As soon as they were able to take directions (Isa 7:15), they were put to work in the home or the fields. As they grew older some were sent to guard the herds (1 Sam 16:11) or were apprenticed to craftsmen in the village. Occasionally a child was also sent to serve in the religious shrines like that at Shiloh. After he was weaned at the age of three or four, Samuel was taken to Shiloh to begin his training as a priest (1 Sam 1:24).

Honor your father and your mother, so that your days may be long in the land that the LORD your God is giving you.

— Exod 20:12

Israelite children were expected to be respectful and obedient to their parents (Ex 20:12). They were to answer the call and orders of their elders (1 Sam 3:5). A disobedient child was considered a disgrace to the family and the community (e.g., 1 Sam 2:22–25 — Eli's sons). The ultimate expression of obedience by a child is found in the case of Jephthah's daughter (Jdg 11:34–39). She willingly submitted to being sacrificed so that her father's oath could be honored.

C. Burial Practices

The narrative's description of burials during this period generally functions as a means of establishing or solidifying claim to tribal territories. For instance, the bones of Joseph, which had been carried by the people out of Egypt at the time of the exodus, were buried in a plot of ground near Shechem (Jos 24:32). This piece of land had been purchased centuries earlier by his father Jacob from King Hamor (Gen 33:18–20). By this action the Joseph tribes legitimized their claim to that area. Similarly, Joshua was buried "in his own inheritance at Timnath-serah" in the hill country of Ephraim (Jos 24:30).

The burials of Gideon and Samson, in contrast to the proprietary burials mentioned above, were in family tombs. Gideon was buried in the "tomb of Joash his father, at Ophrah of the Abiezrites" (Jdg 8:32) and Samson "between Zorah and Eshtaol in the tomb of Manoah his father" (Jdg 16:31). As in the patriarchal tomb at Hebron, the cave of Machpelah, these burial places imply multigenerational residency in the area.

The burial caves or rock-cut tombs themselves were located outside the village proper. Some personal possessions were buried with the corpse, but they were often simply symbols of who the person was in life. Still some items may have been designed as comforts in the afterlife or as wards to drive away evil spirits. Superstitions about the spirits of the dead may have existed, but they do not figure in any narrative other than the story of Saul and the witch of Endor in 1 Sam 28:8–19.

VI. RELIGIOUS PRACTICES

In what ways did the Israelites in the exodus and settlement period worship God?

The religious practices of the Israelites in the period of the exodus and settlement range from the magnificent spectacle of thousands of people confirming the covenantal obligations at Sinai (Ex 19:17 and 24:3–8) to private family worship at the shrine of Micah with its graven image (Jdg 17:4–5). Coming out of the polytheistic environment of Egypt, the Israelites were not immediately able to adapt themselves to a strict monotheism.

The signs of power displayed by Yahweh and his spokesman Moses would have been enough to convince the people to leave Egypt and return to Canaan. Nevertheless, once they arrived there, many found the lure of other cultures and other gods irresistible (Jdg 3:6).

A. ALTARS

Altars served a variety of purposes. They were sometimes expressions of thanksgiving for a military victory (Ex 17:15–16) or part of a purification ritual preparing the people to ask God what must be done to achieve victory (Jdg 21:4–23). At times an altar was built as a memorial or "witness" of the faithfulness of the people to the covenant (Jos 22:10–34). For the most part, however, altars were used to make sacrifices to God.

According to the Covenant Code in Ex 20:24–25, altars were to be constructed of earth or uncut stone. This injunction reflects the basically nomadic character of the people during the wilderness period. It goes well with the command that

The remains of an altar at Megiddo. Photo by Ralph Harris.   2-15

there should be no steps going up to the altar so as not to expose "your nakedness" (v 25). Both instructions probably reflect an attempt to differentiate Israelite altars and sacrifices from those of the Canaanites.

The further stipulation (v 24) that their altars were to be built "in every place where I cause my name to be remembered" ties them to specific events in the nation's history and perhaps to long-used sacred sites. Thus Gideon built an altar after experiencing a theophany and a command to liberate his people from the Midianites (Jdg 6:23 – 24). In Jdg 21:4 – 23, the tribes gathered at Bethel, a site associated with Israelite worship as far back as Abraham and Jacob, built an altar, sacrificed, and asked God's guidance in preparation for battle.

B. TYPES OF SACRIFICES

There were two major types of sacrifices made on these altars: burnt offerings (holocaust) of animals and peace or thank offerings of animals or cereal. These were done to expiate sin, offer thanks, or give God his due (firstfruits; Ex 22:29 and 23:19). All expressed the people's respect for the power of their God, and all eventually acquired very elaborate rules and rituals (Lev 1– 7). It was their lack of respect in stealing from a portion of the sacrifice that was set aside as God's alone (Lev 7:1– 21) that caused the deaths of Eli's sons in 1 Sam 2:12–16.

You shall not delay to make offerings from the fullness of your harvest and from the outflow of your presses. The firstborn of your sons you shall give to me.
— Exod 22:29

C. RELIGIOUS HOLIDAYS

Some sacrifices are associated with national gatherings (Jdg 2:5) or communal events like the Passover (Ex 12 and Jos 5:10). This latter type is tied to the development of a calendar of religious holidays. These feasts centered on the major events of the agricultural year: planting season, wheat harvest, and the autumn ingathering of fruit, grapes, and olives (Ex 23:14–17). The number of feasts and the rituals associated with them also became more elaborate after the settlement period (Lev 23:1–44 and Dt 16:1–17).

D. SPONTANEOUS SACRIFICES

Spontaneous sacrifices also occur in the narrative although some of these appear to be tied to the laws of hospitality. In Jdg 6:17–21, Gideon is visited by an angel. He did not at first perceive that his visitor was a divine being and offered him a "present" of a "prepared kid," unleavened cakes, and a pot of broth. The angel instructed him to place the food on a rock and pour the broth over it as a libation. After the angel touched it with his staff, flames consumed the offering and he disappeared.

A similar case occurs in Jdg 13:15–19. Samson's parents were visited by a "man of God" who foretold the birth of their son. When he appeared a second time to Manoah and his wife, they offered him a meal as an expression of hospitality and thanks for his good news. The angel refused their food but suggested that they offer the kid as a burnt offering on a rock. When this was done the angel ascended in the flames from the makeshift altar.

The Levites took down the ark of the LORD and the box that was beside it, in which were the gold objects, and set them upon the large stone. Then the people of Beth-shemesh offered burnt offerings and presented sacrifices on that day to the LORD.
—1 Sam 6:15

One final example of spontaneous sacrifice occurs in 1 Sam 6:14–15. Here, the people of Beth-shemesh were surprised by the return of the ark of the covenant from its Philistine captivity. They rejoiced by breaking up the Philistines' cart for fuel and sacrificing the two cows which had drawn it to their fields. Two Levites elevated the ark during the ceremony by placing it on a rock which overlooked the sacrifice.

E. HUMAN SACRIFICE

The only example of human sacrifice by the Israelites in the settlement period is found in Jdg 11:30–39. Jephthah, the Gileadite judge, in preparing to fight a battle against the Ammonites, took a vow that he would sacrifice the first person who came out of his tent to greet him on his return. This turned out to be his virgin daughter. He was probably reluctant to carry out his promise, but she insisted that he fulfill his oath, although she did ask for a two-month period to mourn her untimely death.

Then whoever comes out of the doors of my house to meet me, when I return victorious from the Ammonites, shall be the LORD's, to be offered up by me as a burnt offering. —Judg 11:31

This practice seems uncharacteristic of Israelite society and therefore may be an example of a Canaanite practice which the Transjordanian tribes had adopted. Jephthah's rash oath (prohibited in Lev 5:4) may be another sign of this cultural borrowing. His oath is also similar to the one taken by Saul in 1 Sam 12:38 – 39 — also in a war against the Ammonites.

F. NATIONAL PLACES OF WORSHIP

A few sites in the period of the settlement have national religious significance. Some, like Shechem and Bethel, have a previous history of Israelite religious and social activity. Others, like Shiloh and Keriath-jearim, are tied to the presence of the ark of the covenant and have no pre-settlement background as an Israelite cultic site. In no case, however, is there one site that is preeminent over the others like Jerusalem will be in later periods. This was probably due to the fragmented nature of the tribes during the settlement period. They could not always travel to a central shrine when they did not control all of the country.

National gatherings at particular sites, therefore, represented significant events in the history of the people. According to Jos 18:1, the "whole congregation of the people of Israel assembled at Shiloh, and set up the tent of meeting." The tent of meeting and the ark had traveled with the people during the conquest. Now that the conquest was over, the ark was brought to a centralized location in the hill country where the distribution of the land could be made to the tribes. Since Shiloh had no previous ties to Israelite history, it was an ideal, neutral site for the distribution.

Shiloh was not the site, however, of the overriding religious event of the late conquest period. Instead, Shechem is where Joshua gathered the tribes and performed a covenant renewal ceremony (Jos 24). He recited the epic history of the people from the time of the patriarchs through the conquest and demanded that they put away the old gods and old religious practices and worship Yahweh. To register their assent to the covenant, he wrote down the statutes and ordinances on a stone and placed it as a memorial stele "under the oak in the sanctuary of the Lord" (vv 25 – 26). Shechem's association with the very beginnings of Yahweh worship (Gen 12:6 – 7) provided the proper symbolic background for this ceremony.

Bethel serves as a central shrine in Jdg 20:27, just as it will in the monarchy period (1 Kgs 12:29). With the ark standing in their midst, the tribes gathered here during a war against the rebellious tribe of Benjamin. The tribes were initially defeated by Benjamin and now were "weeping" before the Lord at Bethel. This is reminiscent of Jdg 2:5, where God told them he would no longer drive the Canaanites out of the land for them and they wept (*bochim*). The key may then be that national weeping and repentance were to be done at Bethel.

Now this man used to go up year by year from his town to worship and to sacrifice to the LORD of hosts at Shiloh, where the two sons of Eli, Hophni and Phinehas, were priests of the LORD.   —1 Sam 1:3

During the late settlement period, Shiloh once again is described as the site where the ark of the covenant resided. The people journeyed here once a year to bring their sacrifices (1 Sam 1:3). This narrative presupposes a fairly long residence for the ark and a temple to house it (1 Sam 3:3). The yearly pilgrimage by Elkanah and his wives may reflect the injunction in Ex 23:16 to keep the feast of ingathering and implies that the

Israelites held fairly tight control over the area around Shiloh. Even so, it seems unlikely that all of the villagers throughout the hill country would have made the trip each year.

After the Israelites were defeated by the Philistines at Aphek (1 Sam 4:5–11) and the ark was captured, Shiloh was probably destroyed. Archaeological excavations at the site show a destruction level around 1050 BC, and the transference of the ark to Kiriath-jearim (1 Sam 6:21) implies that Shiloh no longer existed. Immediately after this, Mizpah, in the territory of Benjamin, served as the site of a gathering (1 Sam 7:5). On this occasion Samuel purified the people through fasting and a libation of water. He completed the ritual by sacrificing a whole nursing lamb as a sin offering for the people (v 9) and by setting up a memorial stone (Ebenezer, v 12).

Throughout the remainder of Samuel's career as judge and during Saul's early kingship, Mizpah (another Mizpah in Transjordan was the assembly point for Jephthah's army, Jdg 10:17) was the site for national gatherings. It was the gathering place in Jdg 20:1 for the tribes to hear the complaint of the wronged Levite, and it was one of the places on Samuel's judicial circuit (1 Sam 7:16). He also called the people together at Mizpah to choose a king by lot (1 Sam 10:17).

Then the Ammonites were called to arms, and they encamped in Gilead; and the Israelites came together, and they encamped at Mizpah. —Judg 10:17

G. LOCAL SHRINES

Since the tribes were scattered throughout the hill country and travel was difficult at best, local shrines and local religious customs were the norm for the majority of Israelite villagers. As it says in Jdg 3:5, the Israelites dwelt among the Canaanite people "and they took their daughters to themselves for wives, and their own daughters they gave to their sons; and they served their gods."

Despite the injunction against sacred images (Ex 20:4–5), several of the narratives in Judges mention them as accepted objects of worship. In Gideon's village, his father built an altar to Baal and set up a sacred pole or Asherah (Jdg 6:25 – 26). Gideon tore this altar down but later he had a golden ephod (a garment worn by priests, but also used to adorn idols in Canaanite worship) made from spoil taken in a war against the Midianites (Jdg 8:24 – 28). He set it up in his home town of Ophrah and it eventually became an object of worship.

The most blatant record of the worship of sacred images within a household or local shrine appears in Jdg 17:3 – 5, 7 – 13. Micah, a man of the hill country of Ephraim, received a large quantity of silver from his mother; he used a portion of it to fabricate a graven image, an ephod, and other sacred images known as teraphim. These were placed in a shrine in his housing cluster, and one of his sons was designated as officiating priest. Later, a man from the city of Bethlehem was hired by Micah as his official Levitical priest. Micah was sure he had done the right thing and said, "Now I know that the Lord will prosper me, because I have a Levite as priest" (v 13).

High place at Dan. Photo by V. Matthews. 2-16

Micah's shrine and images strictly cut across Israelite legal boundaries. But this is practically excused with the statement that "In those days there was no king in the land and every man did what was right in his own eyes" (v 6). This same statement (20:1) was also used to justify the theft of the images and the hiring away of the priest by the migrating tribe of Dan in 20:14 – 31.

The question then arises, why did a Levite, a man charged with teaching and maintaining the law, consent to serve a group of sacred images? Why did Micah set them up in the first place and why did the Danites jump at the chance to steal them for themselves? The answer almost certainly is that popular religion, the religion of the local villages, was not the pure monotheism required by the law at Sinai. Recent excavations at the Judges' period settlement of Tell Qiri revealed a similar household shrine with incense burners and a large number of animals bones. A substantial percentage of the bones proved to be the right foreleg of goats. This is reminiscent of the law in Ex 29:22, which calls for the sacrifice of the "right shoulder" of the ram.

Evidence such as this suggests that the Israelites found it hard to give up household gods and were attracted to the agricultural gods and ritual practices of the Canaanites. For example, the original ritual behind the Day of Atonement (Lev 16:7–10) may have a Canaanite or pre-Yahwist background with its use of a sacrificial goat upon whose head the sins of the people were placed. Driving it out into the wilderness as an offering to a demon (Azazel) is also out of character for later Israelite worship.

Thus it can be seen that much of what the later biblical writers (Dt 12:2–3 and 2 Kgs 23:8–9) described as Canaanite worship practices were also common to the Israelites throughout much of

Cult incense stands. Photo by LaMoine DeVries. 2-17

their history. This is especially true of the use of the "high place" or *bamah* for worship. For instance, in 1 Sam 9:12–13 Samuel went to a city to bless a sacrifice being made on the "high place." In later periods, however, many of the kings were condemned for not outlawing the high places (2 Kgs 12:3 and 16:4).

So many examples of idolatry and the borrowing of Canaanite rituals suggest that during this period the people were still polytheistic or at best henotheistic in their beliefs. This latter term implies that they may have accepted the worship of Yahweh as their chief God but still continued to believe in the existence of other gods. This can be seen in Joash's statement to his friends after Gideon destroyed their Baal altar (Jdg 6:31):

> Will you contend for Baal? Or will you defend his cause? . . . If he is a god, let him contend for himself, because his altar has been pulled down.

A similar note of henotheistic beliefs surfaces in Jephthah's reply to the Ammonites' demands for the return of the land "from the Arnon to the Jabbok and to the Jordan" (Jdg 11:13–24). He first recited the history of how Yahweh had given the Israelites victory over Sihon, king of the Amorites (see Num 21:21–32). Then, summing up their right to keep these captured lands he stated:

> Will you not possess what Chemosh your god gives you to possess? And all the Lord our God has dispossessed before us, we will possess. (v 24)

H. CIRCUMCISION

Circumcision, like sacrifice and fasting, functions within the biblical narrative as a means of purifying the people. It continues to function as a distinctive sign of the covenant, differentiating the Israelites from the "uncircumcised" Philistines. However, its reintroduction at crucial points in the narrative implies a ritual purification role for circumcision.

This practice was first introduced in Gen 17:10 in the time of Abraham. It is not mentioned again until Ex 4:24–26, where Moses' wife Zipporah circumcises their son as they begin their journey back to Egypt. The significance of this act is uncertain except in terms of the need to be fully in compliance with the covenant before beginning to serve Yahweh once again. This interpretation can also be used to explain the circumcision of the Israelite men before they left Egypt in the exodus (Jos 5:5) and just before they began the conquest (Jos 5:2–3). It is also tied, in these last two instances, with the Passover ritual, which was performed before they left Egypt (Ex 12) and while they waited to heal after being circumcised in Jos 5:8–10.

I. CULT PROSTITUTION

While it is not described as a widespread problem in the settlement period, cult prostitution does appear to have been practiced by the Israelites. In the neighboring communities of the Canaanites, their worship of fertility gods commonly included the use of both male and female cult prostitutes. Sexual activity at local shrines was designed to promote the fertility of the land and symbolize the primary function of the storm god Baal and his consort Asherah.

First Samuel 2:22 suggests that Eli's sons had subverted the activities of women whose job it was to clean up the debris of the sacrifice "at the entrance to the tent of meeting" at Shiloh. This function originated in the wilderness period (Ex 38:8). What was now happening at Shiloh, however, was that the priests were lying with these women and in effect forcing them to play the role of cult prostitutes like in Canaanite religion. For this action and others, the entire priestly clan of Eli was killed and the shrine at Shiloh ceased to function (1 Sam 2:31–36).

None of the daughters of Israel shall be a temple prostitute; none of the sons of Israel shall be a temple prostitute.
—Deut 23:17

3

MONARCHY PERIOD

HISTORICAL INTRODUCTION

A reconstruction of Solomon's temple. 3-A

The transition from a loosely formed tribal league to an urban-based monarchy was the single-most important political event in Israel's history. This was not accomplished overnight, nor did it begin without dispute or dissent. Once it was instituted, however, a new social and religious phase began for Israel that would see the establishment of Jerusalem as the capital of David's kingdom and the emergence of the temple of Yahweh as the focal point of worship and the symbol of God's presence for the nation. The covenant made at Sinai was expanded to include obedience to the king, and Yahweh's shift to Zion spelled the establishment of a priestly community that would orchestrate the ritual of sacrifice and define for all what obedience to God entailed.

It took a variety of factors to bring the monarchy into being—no one of which could have been the single cause. These factors included the growing population of the Hebrew tribes in the hill country villages, continued hostilities and economic competition with the Philistines' and other Canaanite city-states, a lack of outside interference by the superpowers of Egypt and Mesopotamia, and the emergence of several charismatic military leaders whose exploits built them a reputation and following that served as a springboard for national leadership.

The winds of change that swept the monarchy into existence begin in the late judges/settlement period when it became evident to the tribal leadership that the only way to meet the threat of Philistine and Canaanite domination was to unite the tribes under a centralized administration. Samuel had had some success in uniting the central hill country of Ephraim into a loose confederation. The towns and villages in this area looked to him and the priestly group that was previously housed at Shiloh for leadership. The text (1 Sam 7:15–17) describes his "circuit" within the region and it may be assumed that his powers were employed to settle tribal and clan disputes that might otherwise have torn the area apart.

The first indication that this arrangement would not continue to work after Samuel's time appears in 1 Sam 8:1–5. In this passage Samuel is said to have appointed his sons as judges in the southern region of Beer-sheba. This was probably an attempt on his part to expand his effective area of administration into Judah. However, his sons took bribes and "perverted justice" to such an extent that the elders of the tribes called Samuel to a meeting at his base in Ramah and asked for a king to be named to rule them. From that point on the text contains two strands of tradition: one which favors the idea of a monarchy and the other which strongly opposes it. This dispute which began with the inception of the kingship continued even after the monarchy ceased to exist in the post-exilic period.

Then all the elders of Israel gathered together and came to Samuel at Ramah, and said to him, "You are old and your sons do not follow in your ways; appoint for us, then, a king to govern us, like other nations."

—1 Sam 8:4–5

A. EARLY MONARCHY

Saul's rise to power, like David's a generation later, hinged upon his influence as a war chief. His command of a professional force of fighters and his initial success against the Ammonites and Philistines gave him the credentials the tribal elders needed to name him as their king. The support he received from the priestly community in the person of Samuel gave his leadership position the sanction of Yahweh.

Now I know that you shall surely be king, and that the kingdom of Israel shall be established in your hand. —1 Sam 24:20

The difficulty of maintaining the loyalty of the tribes for his position as king became evident when Saul ceased to win every battle and his relationship with Samuel began to deteriorate. This latter development seems to have been the direct result of his merging of the functions of church and state. On three separate occasions (1 Sam 12–15) the narrative describes how Saul failed to follow tradition regarding sacrifice and the rules of the *ḥerem* (holy war). A case was built against him designed to justify his and his family's replacement on the throne by David. He is even portrayed on more than one occasion admitting to David that his rival was destined to take the throne from him and his sons (1 Sam 24:20; 26:25).

These events were written long after Saul's reign when the Davidic monarchy was well established and court historians as well as priests would be expected to make every effort to legitimize the current ruler's right to the throne. Still, it is quite likely that Saul did in fact overstep the bounds set by the priestly community; thus it chose a successor whom it thought it could control. David is described as the youngest of seven sons from an undistinguished clan of the tribe of Judah. By choosing him, Samuel and the Shiloh priesthood could not be accused of favoring only the Ephraimite region. Plus, David's lack of experience and political connections would make it more likely that he would look to Samuel and the priests for support and advice.

David, however, quickly proved himself to be his own man, perfectly capable of acquiring the leadership and military skills necessary to become a rival chief to Saul. He entered Saul's royal court as a musician, a skill for a younger son without prospects of a large inheritance (1 Sam 16:18–23). As 16:18 notes, David had other useful qualities that would also be attractive to Saul: "a man of valor, a man of war, prudent of speech, and a man of good presence." These qualities aided David in rising to the position of royal armor-bearer and later to a leadership position in Saul's army.

Most important to later events was David's marriage to Saul's daughter Michal. This tie to the royal household gave David a claim, however remote, to the throne. Just how important she was to him becomes clear after Saul's death. David insisted on Michal's return as a prerequisite to his joining Saul's old general Abner in uniting the kingdom (2 Sam 3:13). He realized that for the northern tribal leaders to join him he needed some visible link with Saul's rule. This would make it easier for them to accept David as the legitimate successor of the former king.

The final break between Saul and David was caused by the king's growing awareness of David's increasing popularity (1 Sam 18:7–8). Certainly, the popular chant, "Saul has slain his thousands, and David his ten thousands" (1 Sam 18:7), would have been cause for Saul's royal jealousy. What results is a period of conflict between them that sees David branded as an outlaw and eventually joined with the Philistines as a mercenary chief.

And the women sang to one another as they made merry, "Saul has killed his thousands, and David his ten thousands."
—1 Sam 18:7

Like Jephthah in Jdg 11:3–11, who became an outcast from his tribe and formed an outlaw band, David built a following of his relatives and those discontented with Saul's rule (1 Sam 22:1–2). They played a cat and mouse game with Saul's army while operating on the fringes of society. Several of these men, including Joab and Abiathar, stayed with David throughout his career and formed the nucleus of his advisory circle when he became king.

Even as an outlaw David made a name for himself with the people, protecting the city of Keilah from the Philistines (1 Sam 23:1–5) and helping shepherds guard their flocks while in the hill country (1 Sam 25:7–8). Marriage alliances (e.g., Abigail, 1 Sam 25:39–42 and Ahinoam, 1 Sam

25:43) during this period also solidified David's position as king of Judah after Saul's death.

David's service with Achish, the Philistine king of Gath, seems to be an attempt on his part to remove himself from Saul's area of control. While there he continued to build support with the tribal chiefs by sending them portions of the spoil he took in raids (1 Sam 30:26). During this period David learned Philistine military tactics and strategies as well as the use of iron technology. Such an intimate knowledge of the enemy proved to be invaluable when he led his armies against them as king of Israel.

With the death of Saul and his sons in battle against the Philistines at Gilboa (1 Sam 31), David was free to establish himself as a political force within the tribes. At first, however, this was only with his own tribe of Judah. Loyalties among the Ephraimite tribes still centered on Saul's family with Ishbosheth installed as their king. The defeat at Gilboa meant, however, that his capital had to be set up outside of Israel in the Transjordanian city of Mahanaim (2 Sam 2:8). David, having been proclaimed king by the elders of Judah, chose Hebron, long associated with the patriarchs and the worship of Yahweh, as his capital (2 Sam 2:1–4).

A border war raged between the forces of David and Ishbosheth for seven years until a falling out between Saul's son and his general Abner led to the unification of the two kingdoms. A series of negotiations and political assassinations (2 Sam 3–4) then followed which removed all remaining obstacles to David's assuming the full leadership of the tribes. The tribal elders of Israel were forced to come to David in Hebron to acknowledge him as their king (2 Sam 5:1–3).

Unification of the tribes into a single kingdom was still a tenuous arrangement and required delicate political handling by David and his court. To remove the hint of favoritism to his own

So all the elders of Israel came to the king at Hebron; and King David made a covenant with them at Hebron before the LORD, and they anointed David king over Israel. — 2 Sam 5:3

tribal group of Judah, a new capital was established at the more centralized and politically neutral site of Jerusalem. This Jebusite city, never captured by the Israelites, provided a clearly defensible location with access to trade routes and an informed population from which to draw bureaucrats to help manage the affairs of state (2 Sam 5:6–9; 1 Chr 10:4–9).

Jerusalem also served as virgin ground in which the Yahweh cult could grow and flourish under David's leadership. When he had the ark of the covenant brought to his new capital (2 Sam 6:12–19), David was signalling to the priests of the old cultic centers of Shiloh, Shechem, and Hebron that he intended to use his status as king to drive an independent political and religious course. His desire to do this was curtailed at least in part when he was denied the right to construct a temple to house the ark (2 Sam 7:4–16). In the next generation, however, his son Solomon was able to overcome the opposition of the old priestly group and build the primary Yahwist temple in Jerusalem with the help of Phoenician expertise (1 Kgs 7).

Now therefore thus you shall say to my servant David: Thus says the LORD of hosts: I took you from the pasture, from following the sheep to be prince over my people Israel; . . .

—2 Sam 7:8

Once established in Jerusalem, David and his general Joab consolidated Israel's political control over large areas of Palestine and Transjordan. Nearly continuous wars kept the sense of loyalty directed on the capital and the king and accelerated the decline of old loyalties to tribe and clan. However, the concept of kingship was still new in Israel and disputes arose that threatened to rip the nation apart. The question of succession within David's household was one of the primary causes of dissension. In the last part of David's reign, Absalom precipitated a civil war in an attempt to seize the throne from his father (2 Sam 13–19). This proved to be the severest test of David's leadership, although it did unmask some whose loyalties were questionable (Ahithophel and Mephibosheth). It also gave David the opportunity to reaffirm tribal obligations to the monarchy while demonstrating the potency of his own personal army.

Absalom's revolt may in fact have smoothed the way for Solomon to succeed his father to the throne by eliminating enemies of the monarchy. Solomon began his campaign by obtaining David's blessing (1 Kgs 1:29 – 30), the backing of the prophet Nathan, and the support of Benaiah, the commander of the king's personal bodyguard, and Zadok, a member of the Jerusalem priesthood. He could then argue that his power base was more legitimate and broader than that of his brother Adonijah. The tribal leaders obviously feared another civil war would weaken the nation's ability to protect itself and chose the course of continued stability by proclaiming Solomon king.

Solomon's first actions as king were designed to demonstrate that he was truly in charge of the nation. First, he ousted some of David's old advisers, Joab being the most conspicuous victim. The new monarch's intentions to rule as a true king, not just the war chief of the tribal confederation, were then shown in three extremely important actions. To begin with, by redrawing the boundaries of the 12 administrative districts of the kingdom, Solomon further weakened tribal loyalties and reduced the threat of revolts (1 Kgs 4:1 – 21). Royal bureaucrats were appointed to administer them, to collect taxes, and to provide work gangs for public works and defense projects. Each of these districts was made responsible for supporting the royal household one month in each year (1 Kgs 4:7). Since some districts were larger and richer than others, some provision must have been made to balance the load.

Solomon had twelve officials over all Israel, who provided food for the king and his household; each one had to make provision for one month in the year. —1 Kgs 4:7

The second major action taken by Solomon was to turn Jerusalem into a true administrative and religious center for Israel. He was able to accomplish this with the aid of King Hiram of Tyre, who provided the building materials and architects to construct Solomon's palace and the temple of Yahweh (1 Kgs 5:7-12). The temple, built after the fashion of similar Canaanite temples, housed the ark of the covenant and more importantly "housed" the presence of Yahweh among his people. The God of the desert and of Mt. Sinai had been transformed. His presence had now been transferred to Mt. Zion and his role as the God of a confederation of tribes had been expanded to that of a national God who sanctioned the rule of the king in Jerusalem, his holy city. Israel could now join the other nations with king and God enthroned in a well-established capital city.

As part of the process of installing the official worship of Yahweh in Jerusalem, Solomon initiated a new priesthood to serve in the temple. This new group was headed by his ally Zadok. Abiathar, David's old companion and a priest of the Shiloh cultic group, was exiled from Jerusalem and sent to the nearby city of Anathoth (1 Kgs 2:26). This served the king's purpose by gaining a stronger hold over the activities of the priests. However, it also set up a competition between the Jerusalemite and Levitical priesthoods that would continue until the fall of the temple in Jeremiah's time (587 BC).

Solomon's third major innovation as king was the establishment of close ties with several foreign nations. His ties to Hiram and Phoenicia were primarily economic and were reflected in the aid in constructing the temple and palace complex. Other alliances were made through marriage, the most important of which was with a daughter of the king of Egypt (1 Kgs 3:1). This marriage as much as anything else mentioned in the text testifies to the fact that Israel had indeed become a nation to be reckoned with in Near Eastern affairs. Egypt at that time was weak and divided. This may be why no clear record of its relations with Israel during this period has been found. However, the Amarna Tablets from the

Solomon made a marriage alliance with Pharaoh king of Egypt; he took Pharaoh's daughter and brought her into the city of David, until he had finished building his own house and the house of the LORD and the wall around Jerusalem.
—1 Kgs 3:1

15th–14th century BC (*ANET*, pp. 483–90) confirm that royal marriages were quite common. They gave an influential king the chance to establish political ties and alliances with other nations through marriage.

Whether this was an appropriate action to be taken by an Israelite monarch or not, the text indicates that Solomon's wives were the prime cause of his downfall and the division of the kingdom (1 Kgs 11:1–13). In fact Solomon's marrying foreign women and introducing the worship of foreign gods, coupled with the people's deep dissatisfaction over high taxes and labor service, all contributed to the schism in the next generation.

Solomon had tried to establish a true monarchy on the foundation of the tribal confederation and their loyalty to David. He fortified the nation's borders with monumental defenses at Megiddo, Gezer, and Hazor (1 Kgs 9:15–19), and extracted huge amounts of the nation's produce to feed his army and labor gangs and to pay his debts. His actions fulfilled the worst prophecies of Samuel (1 Sam 8:10–18) about the tyrannies of kings and made it easier for the tribal leaders to dissolve the union when Solomon's son and successor Rehoboam refused to compromise with their demands for shared leadership. The cry went up quite easily:

> What portion have we in David? We have no inheritance in the son of Jesse. To your tents, O Israel! (1 Kgs 12:16),

and a new man, Jeroboam, who would perhaps be more pliable to the demands of the tribal leaders, was named king of the northern confederation (1 Kgs 12:20).

B. DIVIDED MONARCHY

Rehoboam was left with David's original kingdom—the tribe of Judah—plus the city of Jerusalem. Jeroboam had obtained through his

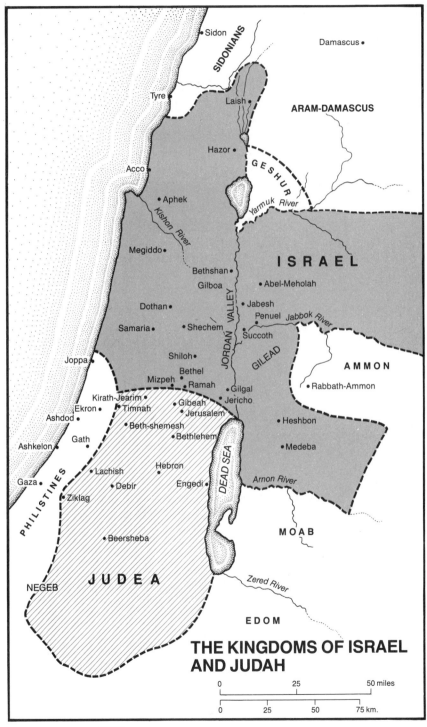

THE KINGDOMS OF ISRAEL AND JUDAH

Sidon

Damascus •

SIDONIANS

Tyre •

Laish •

ARAM-DAMASCUS

Hazor •

Acco •

GESHUR

Aphek •

Yarmuk River

Kishon River

Megiddo •

ISRAEL

Bethshan •

Gilboa

• Abel-Meholah

Dothan •

• Jabesh

JORDAN VALLEY

Penuel Jabbok River

Samaria •   • Shechem

Succoth

GILEAD

Joppa •

Shiloh •

AMMON

Bethel

Mizpeh •   • Ramah

Kirath-Jearim •   • Gibeah   • Gilgal   • Rabbath-Ammon
Ekron •   • Timnah   • Jerusalem   Jericho
Ashdod •   • Beth-shemesh
    • Bethlehem   • Heshbon

Ashkelon •   Gath

DEAD SEA   • Medeba

PHILISTINES

Gaza •   • Lachish   Hebron •
    • Debir   Engedi •   Arnon River

• Ziklag

MOAB

• Beersheba

Zered River

J U D E A

NEGEB

E D O M

0   25   50 miles

0   25   50   75 km.

CMP 1006

So the king took counsel, and made two calves of gold. He said to the people, "You have gone up to Jerusalem long enough. Here are your gods, O Israel, who brought you up out of the land of Egypt." —1 Kgs 12:28

election by the tribal leaders and Ahijah the prophet (1 Kgs 11:30–33) leadership over most of central and northern Palestine as well as portions of Transjordan. However, he lacked a religious center upon which to focus the people's worship of Yahweh and thus he reinaugurated the old cultic centers of Dan and Bethel to serve this function. In these shrines, located at either end of his kingdom, Jeroboam placed golden calves, restructured the religious calendar to bring worshippers there instead of Jerusalem, and established a non-Levitical priesthood to serve in them (1 Kgs 12:25–33).

These actions became in the biblical tradition of the history of the kings the "sin of Jeroboam." The shrines, however, were a shrewd political move by a king who could not afford to allow his people to retain any loyalty to Jerusalem. The non-Levitical priesthood also made it easier for him to control the cult. It cut short interference from priests and prophets, like Ahijah, who had helped him gain the throne. Plus, his promotion of the use of the *bamoth* (high places) in the local villages and towns (1 Kgs 12:31) gained him the support of those tied more closely to popular or local religion than to a national cult.

Despite his attempts to consolidate his power through political and religious reforms, Jeroboam still lacked one thing that his rival Rehoboam possessed. This was the sense of legitimacy of rule that comes with a multigenerational ruling dynasty or family. Rehoboam had made mistakes, but the idea of loyalty to the Davidic line kept him in power at least in Judah and protected his descendants on the throne for the next three centuries. The idea of the "everlasting covenant" with David's house (2 Sam 7:18–29; 1 Kgs 11:34–39) grew in power and tradition over the years and became the central focus of the idea of the Messiah in the later prophets and the postexilic period.

Without a tradition of dynastic rule, Jeroboam was subject to political pressures from the tribal leaders and the army. He also had to face the wrath of the priestly community that was excluded from the central shrines of Dan and Bethel. It is not surprising then that the pattern of succession in the northern kingdom became one of succession by assassination. On occasion this involved simple military coups, as in Omri's rise to power with the backing of army (1 Kgs 16:15–22). In other cases the prophets gave their sanction to a new claimant through the traditional means of anointing him. This was the situation with Jehu, who was anointed king by one of Elisha's associates (a "son of the prophets"), and who was commissioned to seize the throne from Ahab's son Joram (2 Kgs 9).

Zimri came in and struck him down and killed him, in the twenty-seventh year of King Asa of Judah, and succeeded him.
—1 Kgs 16:10

The general lack of stability in a monarchy without roots or tradition of smooth transition of power played into the hands of the emerging superpower nations of Egypt and Assyria. While Israel and Judah exhausted themselves in wars with Syria (1 Kgs 20, 22 and 2 Kgs 6–7) and the nations of Transjordan (2 Kgs 3), the superpowers consolidated their control at home and prepared to expand into Syro-Palestine. The last period of relative independence for Israel and Judah came in the reigns of Jeroboam II (786–746) and Uzziah (782–742).

The shortsightedness of their policies with regard to other nations emerges in the prophecies of Amos and Hosea and comes to full bloom after 740 BC in the face of the military might of the Assyrian king, Tiglath-Pileser III (biblical Pul, 2 Kgs 15:19). The Assyrian war machine had first entered the area in 853 BC when their king, Shalmaneser III, was defeated at the battle of Qarqar by a coalition of Phoenician and Palestinian kings, including Ahab. After defeating the Syrians in 841, however, Jehu, king of Israel, was forced to pay tribute to the Assyrians (as recorded

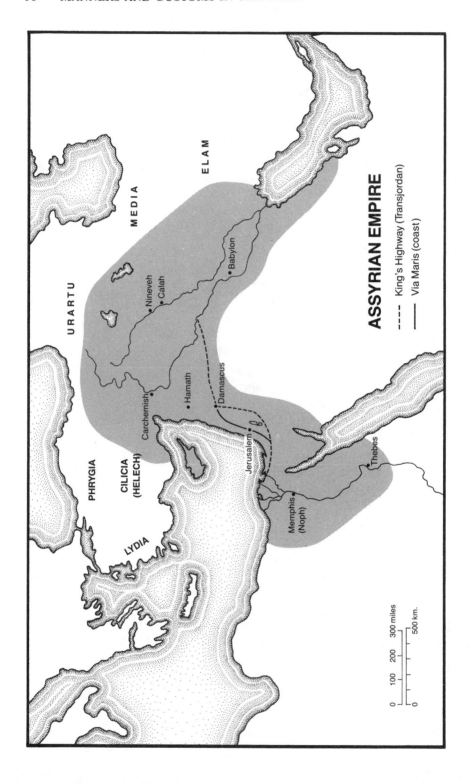

ASSYRIAN EMPIRE

- - - - King's Highway (Transjordan)
——— Via Maris (coast)

in the "Black Obelisk" inscription of Shalmaneser; *ANET*, p. 281). From that time on the Assyrians, devastating large areas and massacring entire city populations, repeatedly forced their way into Syro-Palestine. Situated on the major trade route of the Via Maris, Syria, Israel, and the Philistine city-states were eventually absorbed into the growing Assyrian empire.

These new vassal states of Assyria were restive under foreign rule and repeatedly revolted. In 736 BC, Israel and Syria declared war on King Ahaz of Judah in order to get him to join their revolt against the Assyrians. Ahaz subsequently allied himself with the Assyrians (against the advice of the prophet Isaiah, Isa 7:1–9), and this led to the defeat of the rebels. However, the price Ahaz paid for Assyrian help was full submission to the stronger nation, including the introduction of Assyrian worship practices in the temple in Jerusalem (2 Kgs 16:1–18).

A subsequent revolt by Israel's King Hoshea in 722 BC caused the Assyrians to take the drastic measure of destroying Israel's capital at Samaria and deporting a large proportion of the population to some other part of the Assyrian empire,

Assyrian warrior leads prisoner away. 3-D

never to return (2 Kgs 17:1–6). The kingdom of Judah also felt the effect of Assyrian displeasure with repeated invasions and the destruction of many cities. King Sennacherib recorded in his royal annals (*ANET*, p. 287) that on one occasion he held King Hezekiah of Judah prisoner in Jerusalem "like a bird in a cage" while he captured and enslaved the populations of 46 cities. The biblical account of the siege of Jerusalem credits divine intervention for the miraculous survival of the city (2 Kgs 19:32–37). Internal politics within the Assyrian empire may have also contributed to the lifting of the siege. Second Kings 19:37 states that Sennacherib was murdered by his sons on his return to Nineveh.

The traumatic effect of the destruction of the

In the eighteenth year of King Josiah, the king sent Shaphan son of Azaliah, son of Meshullam, the secretary, to the house of the LORD, saying, . . .
— 2 Kgs 22:3

Assyrian scribe. From Assyrian wall painting, ca. eighth century B.C. 3-E

northern kingdom and the Assyrian invasions lead Judah in the period after Hezekiah's death into a state of quiet vassalage to the Assyrians. No prophetic voice was heard during the reign of King Manasseh. Only after the Assyrian empire began to crumble under assaults from the Babylonians and Medes was Judah able to once again assert a measure of independence. This came in the reign of Josiah (640 – 609 BC) who inaugurated a religious and political reform designed to purge the people of foreign gods and Canaanite worship practices. A concerted attempt was made to centralize all power and authority in the city of Jerusalem (2 Kgs 23).

Josiah's reform was instigated and carried out by a group of priests from the city of Anathoth, including Hilkiah, Shaphan, and Ahikam. Their intent and that of the king was to restore the powers of the monarchy and of the Jerusalem priesthood with themselves as its leaders. To do this they instituted the legal code found in Deuteronomy 12 – 26, a code which set Jerusalem aside as the only true place of sacrifice and worship for the people. First, however, all vestiges of Canaanite and Assyrian worship were to be eliminated throughout the land. To ensure that this became a national effort, the high places and local altars were to be destroyed, the seasonal religious festivals were to be centered on the capital, and the Levitical priesthood was to officiate only within the precincts of the temple in Jerusalem.

Such a radical reform could not be put into effect overnight. Enforcement must have been difficult in the face of long years of polytheistic religious activity by the people. Archaeological findings from this period point to some successes such as the incorporation of abandoned altars into the walls of buildings and the lack of deposits of sacrificial remains at cultic sites during this time. The fact is, however, that Josiah's reform was only enforced for 13 years until his death

in battle at Megiddo against Pharaoh Necho II
(2 Kgs 23:29 – 30).

Josiah's death spelled the end for most of his reforms and a new era of submission to the superpowers. First, Egypt claimed Palestine after the
defeat of the Assyrians at the battle of Carchemish in 605 BC. This meant a new master for Judah
and a puppet king. Josiah's son and immediate successor, Jehoahaz, was taken hostage back to Egypt
and his brother Eliakim was put on the throne.
His status as a servant of the Egyptians was
graphically portrayed when his name was changed
to Jehoiakim by the pharaoh (2 Kgs 23:34).

*Pharaoh Neco made Eliakim son
of Josiah king in place of his
father Josiah, and changed his
name to Jehoiakim. But he took
Jehoahaz away; he came to
Egypt, and died there.*
— 2 Kgs 23:34

What followed were the last days of Judah's
monarchy. A series of political mistakes and revolts eventually led the superpowers to crush the
nation. The sequence of events began with a
shift of masters. In 603 BC the Babylonian King
Nebuchadnezzar wrested Palestine from the
Egyptians, and suddenly Jehoiakim found himself a Babylonian vassal (2 Kgs 24:1). Perhaps because of Egyptian promises of aid, Jehoiakim
revolted three years later bringing the might of
the Babylonian army on his people.

During this period the prophet Jeremiah condemned Jehoiakim's policies (Jer 36) and denounced the reliance the people of Jerusalem had
on the temple of Yahweh to save them from any
threat (Jer 7 and 26). Nebuchadnezzar besieged
the city and captured it, taking the son of Jehoiakim back to Babylon as a hostage along with a
group of Judah's leaders and priests (2 Kgs 24:10 –
17). The Babylonian king then installed as his
puppet-king the last of Josiah's sons, Mattaniah,
and changed his name to Zedekiah (2 Kgs 24:17).

Again there was a period of relative quiet as Jerusalem licked its wounds. However, in the ninth
year of his reign, Zedekiah revolted (probably
again under the urging of Egypt, Jer 37:7); this
time Nebuchadnezzar chose to totally destroy this
source of continual irritation and rebellion. While

Jeremiah urged the people to surrender to the Babylonians (Jer 38:17–18), Zedekiah continued to hold out until the city fell to Nebuchadnezzar's army. The last reigning king of Judah was forced to watch the execution of his sons and then had his eyes gouged out (Jer 39:6–7). The only remaining member of the royal house, Jehoiachin, eventually died in Babylonian exile without an heir, never having returned to Jerusalem.

The fall of Jerusalem and the Babylonian exile spelled the end of the Davidic monarchy and the beginning of a community that was ruled by foreign officials and an increasingly rigid priesthood. The monarchy period itself witnessed the heights of power in the time of David and Solomon, and the slow decline to near oblivion after the division of the kingdoms. The life of the people included the growth of an urban-based culture in Jerusalem and other administrative sites, while an emphasis on agricultural village life was retained. Both aspects of this society will now be examined.

I. THE ISRAELITE CITY

Megiddo seal belonging "to Shema" (8th cent. B.C.). 3-F

What were Israelite cities like during the monarchy?

The transition during the monarchy period from a village culture to an urban culture brought enormous changes to the lives and religion of the people of Israel. A large proportion of the population continued to live in villages, but these settlements became associated with the life and economy of the cities in their region. They supplied produce for the cities' markets and men for the king's armies and labor battalions. Their focus was now centered in large part on the urban center. Despite some feelings of hostility, such as those expressed by the prophet Micah (6:9–16), the villagers' fate—for good or bad—was hereafter intimately tied to that of the city.

Many of the Israelite cities occupied during the monarchy period were built over the ruins of older Canaanite cities (Megiddo, Gezer, Hazor). Jerusalem, David's capital, was originally a Jebusite city. When he made it his capital of the united kingdom, he built his first palace within the old citadel and extended the walls of its enclosure to accommodate his growing bureaucracy and to house his closest followers (2 Sam 5:9–11).

Where a new city was established, such as Samaria (1 Kgs 16:24), certain considerations went into the choice of the site. These included whether the prospective city site was easily defensible and whether it had an adequate water supply for a growing population. In addition, its access to major commercial routes and its distance from supporting agricultural areas also had to be considered.

This is the account of the forced labor that King Solomon conscripted to build the house of the LORD and his own house, the Millo and the wall of Jerusalem, Hazor, Megiddo, Gezer
—1 Kgs 9:15

A. CITY WALLS

Cities in the ancient world contained several major features. Most important among these was the wall. Ancient cities unearthed in Palestine had walls as much as 30 feet thick, rising to a height of 50 feet or more. They were constructed of a mixture of stone and mud brick, with larger quantities of stone being used in the hill country sites where it was more easily quarried. Stone from earlier cities on the site were also recycled, thereby mixing the stratigraphy of the site and adding to the chronological puzzle for the archaeologist. Particular types of stone dressing and the engraving of mason marks on the stones do help in unraveling this problem, however.

Iron I four-room house. Photo by V. Matthews. 3-1

The walls were the major defense of the city and thus were constantly maintained and refortified with towers and in some cases with the addition of a glacis. This latter feature consisted of a clay and stone slope built up against the face of the wall. Some were also plastered over to present a smooth surface that would be more diffi-

Iron II period glacis at Tell Halif. Photo by Patricia O'Connor-Seger, Lahav Research Project.   3-2

cult for attackers to scale. The glacis was also designed to prevent the effective use of battering rams against the wall or city gate (see Joab's attack on Beth-maacah in 2 Sam 20:15–16).

Generally, wall construction followed the slope of the hill or promontory on which the city was built. As a result, they were seldom straight for any great distance. Eventually, this feature was incorporated into the defensive design with the introduction of an "offset-inset" or redans wall construction. Walls of this type, with sections indented along their line of construction, presented less direct frontage to the attackers and gave the defenders a broader field of fire from the battlements.

Where defense was not as much of a concern and more commercial space was needed, cheaper to construct, casemate walls were used. This became the standard pattern in the more peaceful reign of Solomon. Archaeologists have discovered that each of his fortress cities at Megiddo, Hazor, and Gezer (1 Kgs 9:15–19) were built with casemate or hollow walls. While not affording the protection of solid walls, they did have the advantage of a lower cost, quicker construction, and the creation of premium space within the walls for warehouses and shops.

B. STREETS AND PUBLIC SQUARES

Since the inhabitants were in effect recycling these old sites, city planning was practically impossible without razing large portions of the tell (artificial mound). Many of these cities had been captured and rebuilt in the past without much attempt at establishing thoroughfares or market squares. Being built on the crown of the hill or tell there was only a small amount of space within the citadel area and this was reduced each time the city was rebuilt.

The average size of city sites in the biblical period was 5–10 acres. This meant that planning considerations often were set aside when the need arose to build an extension on to the administrative complex. As a result, the city often expanded beyond its walls and down the slope of the tell. Often this new area was then walled in with fortifications. Such a process led to the expansion of the sites of Hazor to 200 acres and of Dan to 50 acres in size.

With space at such a premium, it is no wonder then that there is no word in biblical Hebrew for street. Ḥuṣ, which is to be translated "outside," may refer to bazaars in the city streets of Samaria in 1 Kgs 20:34; however, these "streets" would have only been narrow paths between buildings, ending many times in a blind alley. They were also often choked with traffic, carts and booths, and accumulated garbage.

What little open space did exist for public assembly and market activity was in front of important buildings like the palace and temple and in the vicinity of the city gate. These relatively open areas are called a reḥob. This term is to be translated simply as "broad area." In Dt 13:16 and 2 Sam 21:12 it can be loosely translated as "public square." In the first of these texts the

Ben-hadad said to him, "I will restore the towns that my father took from your father; and you may establish bazaars for yourself in Damascus, as my father did in Samaria." The king of Israel responded, "I will let you go on those terms." So he made a treaty with him and let him go.
—1 Kgs 20:34

"square" served as the site for the burning of captured loot following the capture of a Canaanite city. In the second instance the *rehob* was a place of execution and assembly. It functioned as the marshalling area for Hezekiah's troops in yet another text (2 Chr 32:6).

Considering the space limitations in most ancient walled cities, however, the most likely place for the *rehob* would have been immediately outside the city gate area. Evidence for this occurs in 1 Kgs 22. An impressive event was staged, according to this passage, involving King Ahab of Israel and King Jehoshaphat of Judah. They sat enthroned before the city gate of Samaria in the *rehob* surrounded by court officials and 400 prophets. Such a spectacle would have been too cramped within the confines of the city walls.

C. CITY GATE

Among the busiest and most vulnerable features of the walled city was the city gate. The gate provided access for the inhabitants, it served as an assembly area for important governmental and religious announcements, and it functioned as the commercial and legal center of the city. However, because it was an entry way through the walls it was invariably the focal point of any attack upon the city (Jdg 9:44 and 2 Sam 18:4). The multi-use character of the gate area required ingenious construction that would provide a fairly broad entrance and activity space for the population and visiting merchants. At the same time, it had to present a significant obstacle to potential attackers.

Abimelech and the company that was with him rushed forward and stood at the entrance of the gate of the city, while the two companies rushed on all who were in the fields and killed them. —Judg 9:44

During the monarchy period the diagonally positioned, six-chambered gate became the norm. It has been found by archaeologists at Beth Shemesh, Hazor, Shechem, Gezer, Megiddo, and Tirzah. This multistoried entrance way provided meeting areas for business and legal matters,

Six-chambered gate; chambers were used for defense as well as for legal and business activity. Photo by LaMoine DeVries.
3-3

as well as garrison space for watchmen and defenders. It may be that the gate in which David awaited word of the battle with Absalom's army in 2 Samuel 18 was one of this type. He is described as sitting between the two gates while the watchman went up on the roof of the gateway (v 24). This would have been the first line of defense within the gateway. Each segment of the gate complex would have contained a set of metal-hinged, wooden doors. These were flanked by indented chambers where defenders would be stationed.

David's sitting between the gates signalled to the people his personal command of the city and his desire to be kept informed about the battle and the defense of the city. After David learned of the death of Absalom, he then went "up to the chamber over the gate" to mourn the loss of his son (2 Sam 18:33). This may have been in one of the towers flanking the gate or in one of a set of rooms in the upper story of the gateway itself. Again, architecture varied based on the topography of the site and its wealth and importance.

During peace times the gate served as a gathering place for merchants (Gen 19:1 and 2 Kgs 7:1). Here would be found the stalls and booths of craftsmen and hawkers as well as the produce market for the surrounding villages. Fresh produce was bartered for bread, pottery, leather goods, and clothing. Egyptian jewelry, Phoenician furnishings, perfumes from Arabia, and ingots of metal from Cyprus and Anatolia all were available in these open air bazaars (see Isa 3:18–24 for a list of some of these imported products).

Like the threshing floor in the unwalled villages (cf., Ruth 3:10–14 and Aqhat v:5–8), the city gate functioned as a gathering place for legal activity. Each of these places was intimately tied to the economic and social well-being of the community and each was large enough for a crowd to gather and a trial to be held. Deuteronomy 21:18–21 provides a good example of how the gate area served as a legal forum. In this text the parents of a "stubborn and rebellious" son were required to bring him to the gate where they had to testify against him to the elders. Following

The city gate was of central importance to the social life of a city. Photo by Ralph Harris.
3-4

their testimony, the son was stoned to death by "all the men of the city." This type of communal execution was designed to bring home to the entire community that crime was not just an individual matter — it was a physical and religious threat to the entire population of the city.

The gate thus became the place of judgment for the city. Here the elders habitually sat (Prov 31:23) awaiting the summons to hear testimony and make pronouncements based on the law. On a higher level of authority, the king was also supposed to listen to the cases of his people. Thus when David failed to provide a hearing for the complaints of tribal officials, this gave Absalom an opening for his rebellion. He stood "in the way of the gate" and commiserated with these men, assuring them that he would have given them a fair judgment if he were king (2 Sam 15:1–6). The legal role played by the gate area is also found in the period just before the fall of the northern kingdom of Israel (c. 750 BC). Amos listed as one of the gravest crimes of the people that justice had been perverted "in the gate" (Amos 5:10–15).

You shall bring both of them to the gate of that town and stone them to death, the young woman because she did not cry for help in the town and the man because he violated his neighbor's wife. So you shall purge the evil from your midst. — Deut 22:24

D. PALACE AND TEMPLE

The two monumental structures which represented the power and prestige of the Israelite monarchy and the worship of Yahweh were the king's palace and the temple in Jerusalem. These buildings mark the transition from tribal to national status and from village to urban culture. Unfortunately, little physically remains of these monuments to the power of David's and Solomon's kingdom. Despite the fact that Jerusalem is one of the most excavated ancient cities in the world, most of the remains of the palace and temple have disappeared as a result of repeated destructions and the reuse of materials in later structures.

What has been revealed in the most recent

excavations is evidence of the establishment of an Israelite city on the site in the 11th–10th century BC and a succession of expansion projects that extended the original "city of David" (2 Sam 5:7–9) over a much larger area. Further excavations, made difficult by current occupation of the site and political and religious pressures, should reveal an even more complete history of the life of the city.

The descriptions of Solomon's temple in 1 Kgs 6, 7:13–51 and his palace in 1 Kgs 7:1–12 point to a drastic change of fortunes. In just two generations the Israelites had risen from a people subject to Philistine and Canaanite warlords to a major power with control over all of Palestine and much of Transjordan. Solomon had made a marriage alliance with the Egyptian pharaoh (1 Kgs 3:1) and had a working arrangement with Hiram the king of Tyre to provide craftsmen and building materials for his construction projects.

One result of this reliance on foreign expertise was the use of a basically Canaanite and Egyptian decorative and architectural style. Although no archaeological remains of Solomon's temple have been found, its description in 1 Kings 6–7, 2 Chronicles 3–4, and in Ezekiel 40–48 provides a good picture of its basic structure. Standing on a platform (Ezk 41:8), the temple was an oblong with two courtyards leading up to a porch area and the inner "Holy of Holies" where the ark was housed (1 Kgs 6:23–28). At the entrance of the temple stood two carved pillars, Jachin and Boaz (1 Kgs 7:21). Since they did not support the roof, their purpose is unknown. Bases for similar free-standing pillars have been found at the entrance to Canaanite temple sites at Hazor and Arad. These pillars are also represented on carved ivories from Phoenicia. They may have symbolized the presence of God, like the pillar of cloud before the tabernacle (Ex 33:9), or marked the passage from secular to sacred precincts.

He set up the pillars at the vestibule of the temple; he set up the pillar on the south and called it Jachin; and he set up the pillar on the north and called it Boaz.
—1 Kgs 7:21

Palace and temple also represented a new form of government in which the people were subject to the single rule of the king. Social stratification became more pronounced as the king created a new elite group comprised of his advisers (2 Chr 22:11, *ben hammelek*, "son of the king") and family (2 Chr 11:23). This process began in Saul's reign with his granting of "fields and vineyards" to his loyal followers (1 Sam 22:7). Such a distinction marked them specifically as "his men" as opposed to the "people of the land" (2 Kgs 21:24), who accepted the king's authority but were neither granted special privileges nor placed under special obligation.

He dealt wisely, and distributed some of his sons through all the districts of Judah and Benjamin, in all the fortified cities; he gave them abundant provisions, and found many wives for them.
— 2 Chr 11:23

A growing royal bureaucracy (1 Kgs 4:1–19) managed affairs in the former tribal districts, collected taxes, and recruited manpower for the army and labor battalions. The resources of the nation were expended in monumental construction projects and the enhancement of the powers of the court. The citadel of the city became a nerve center of administrative activity with its offices and warehouses squeezing out previous inhabitants. This now signalled the boundaries between the zones of the powerful and the powerless within the city. In Samaria for instance, there was actually a wall built to divide the two areas of the town and the architecture was markedly different in each.

New forms of worship and an expanded priesthood also came into being at this time. The ark was housed within the temple of Solomon and a group of priests was charged with its care and the maintenance of the sacrificial routine (1 Kgs 8:5–8). The religious calendar was expanded or revised. Festivals and sacrifices were now to be held in Jerusalem, and the "high places" (1 Kgs 3:2) were officially discouraged in favor of the national religious shrine.

Such a transition from regional administration and popular religious practices was not accomplished overnight. Opposition to Jerusalem and the monarchy surfaced in the next generation and led to the division of the kingdom. However, the kingdom of Israel in the north immediately adopted a similar form of government with a monarchy and national shrines at Dan and Bethel to serve as a focus of the people's worship and as rivals to the Jerusalem temple (1 Kgs 12:25–33). Clearly, once the temple/palace process had begun, it could not be reversed.

As the kingdoms of Judah and Israel gradually fell prey to the expanding superpowers of Egypt and Mesopotamia, the temple and palace became symbols of both the sins of the people as well as of future hope and restored glory. Isaiah centered much of his prophetic message around the "everlasting covenant" which God had established with the "house of David" (2 Sam 7:19–29; Isa 11:1–3). His assurance was that Jerusalem, while punished for the sins of the people, would never be destroyed (Isa 10:24 and 29:7–8). Living at this same time (late 8th century BC), Micah put the blame for the destruction of the people by invading Assyrian armies squarely on the cities of Samaria and Jerusalem (Mic 1:5).

All this is for the transgression of Jacob and for the sins of the house of Israel. What is the transgression of Jacob? Is it not Samaria? And what is the high place of Judah? Is it not Jerusalem? —Mic 1:5

After the northern kingdom had been destroyed, Jerusalem and its temple became the last bastion of hope for Yahweh's chosen people. Josiah's religious and political reforms (2 Kgs 22:3–24) came at a point (622–609 BC) when Assyrian control of Judah was weakening. They were designed (using the laws in Dt 12–26) to redirect the people's political and religious focus on Jerusalem and the Davidic monarchy. Such central events as Passover (2 Kgs 23:21) were restored to prominence and provisions were made to increase the power of the Jerusalem priesthood by eliminating all of the local shrines and recalling all the Levites to Jerusalem (23:8).

Josiah's untimely death in battle against the Egyptians (2 Kgs 23:29) spelled the end for many of his reform measures. However, the idea of the temple as the supreme expression of Yahweh's power and presence survived. It became the symbol of hope for the people of Jerusalem. Thus, when Jeremiah prophesied just before the fall of the city to the Babylonians (600–587), he offered the inhabitants hope of a restored city and people after their punishment was complete. However, he also called for the destruction of the temple, which had become since Josiah's time an idol and symbol of false hope for an unfaithful people (Jer 7:8–15 and 26:4–6).

Do not trust in these deceptive words: "This is the temple of the LORD, the temple of the LORD, the temple of the LORD."
—Jer 7:4

E. Private Dwellings in the City

The style and size of private dwellings in Israelite walled cities varied based on available space, construction materials, and the relative importance of the inhabitants. Excavations of Iron Age (8th century BC) levels at Megiddo and Hazor reveal houses of the standard four-room style with central courtyard. The fact that these are old sites with many previous occupation levels may explain why small, poorly constructed houses are found next to much larger and more complex dwellings. These newer homes probably represent the houses of the new Israelite elite who now ruled these cities. Space limitations thus had squeezed the social classes closer together, while squeezing most of the nonadministrative inhabitants out of the walled cities into surrounding towns and villages.

In newer cities like Samaria and Tirzah, however, there was a clearly defined distinction between the poorer areas and those of the elite. This latter area was usually on the western edge of the mound where the prevailing west wind would cool the houses and carry away cooking and human odors. The houses in this area were much larger and better built, generally showing additions and repairs made over the long periods of time they were occupied. Like those in the villages they were pillared structures with stone foundations and few window openings (Hos 13:3). There was more use of tooled stone, however, in the walls, including square-stoned corners. The central courtyard contained the oven and cooking storage jars and served as a gathering area for the family and its friends.

The entrance to these dwellings usually led into an alleyway, and there were stairs on the outside of the house leading up to the second story. If the house was built next to the city wall, these stairs were built against the wall. An economy of materials can be seen in the construction of the doorways at the end of the wall so that only one doorjamb was required. The ceiling consisted of log beams thatched over with several layers of a clay and straw mixture.

Therefore they shall be like the morning mist or like the dew that goes away early, like chaff that swirls from the threshing floor or like smoke from a window.
— Hos 13:3

Sanitary conditions within these homes continued to be unhealthy. Poor ventilation, the odor and gases arising from decaying food and waste matter, and the heat both contributed to the growth of bacteria and the spread of disease. Frankincense and other sweet-smelling aromatics were burned in small incense stands in these homes. While these stands, which have been excavated in large numbers at Megiddo, Gezer, Beth-Shan, and Shechem, may have also had a cultic purpose, their smoke helped to cover the household odors and drive away insects.

Excavations at Jericho, Bethel, and other sites have revealed stone-lined drainage systems for sewage and excess rain water. However, these are only associated with the houses of the wealthier families. References to muck and mire in the streets (2 Sam 22:43) suggest that they were still the principal area for the disposal of waste. Waste was also deposited in near by fields and in communal dung heaps.

Archaeological evidence shows that at least some houses within the city served as both dwelling places and industrial and commercial establishments. This again is probably a reflection of the lack of space within these walled cities. At the site of Shechem a house was uncovered which contained dye vats and loom weights, suggesting a clothing manufacturing enterprise. Elsewhere booths were discovered attached to the outside of a house. They contained rows of clay storage jars containing the carbonized remains of grain. This may have been a shop selling grain to city dwellers. A similar shop unearthed at Hazor with a large number of small pottery bowls may have been a primitive cafe or food market.

II. SOCIAL LIFE

In what ways did the lives of the Israelites change during the monarchy period?

Even with the establishment of an urban centered culture during the monarchy period, the vast majority of the Israelite population continued to live in small, unwalled villages and towns. Life there would have remained much the same as it was in the settlement period except for the demands and opportunities afforded by the regional urban centers. Cities like Beer-sheba, Jerusalem, Lachish, Samaria, Megiddo, and Hazor became focal points of royal power and major defense posts for the rest of the land (1 Kgs 9:15–20). They served as regional markets for farm produce and provided a clearing house for manufactured and imported goods. Farm families made the trek from their villages once or twice a year to sell their surplus grain and to buy new farm implements, pottery, and luxury goods (jewelry, perfumes, cosmetics). They also came to Jerusalem and other religious centers to make sacrifices and to celebrate major religious holidays.

Those Israelites who did live within the walled cities (until the Assyrian occupation of the 8th century BC) were primarily government workers

He bought the hill of Samaria from Shemer for two talents of silver; he fortified the hill, and called the city that he built, Samaria, after the name of Shemer, the owner of the hill.
—1 Kgs 16:24

and prominent merchant families. Their "service area" jobs made it necessary for them to live close to the administrative hub. However, having to devote full-time to managing the affairs of the government and the economy also meant that the cities and their inhabitants were not self-supporting. They depended on the rural farm belt to supply them with food and the raw materials for manufacturing. The local villages also provided surplus manpower for construction projects and military campaigns.

A. SOCIAL MOBILITY

A symbiotic arrangement between the rural and urban areas is quite common in the ancient Near East. In such a culture the basic traditions and loyalties of extended family relationships can remain intact in the villages, but the opportunities of joining the royal elite or the military may dissolve old ties among the city dwellers. The drive to advance in a period when social mobility is possible can lead to the abandonment of old values and the establishment of new loyalties to the state and to oneself.

The man Jeroboam was very able, and when Solomon saw that the young man was industrious he gave him charge over all the forced labor of the house of Joseph. —1 Kgs 11:28

One possible example of this may be Jeroboam, son of Nebat. This son of a widow from the tribe of Ephraim rose to a position of high authority, having "charge over all the forced labor of the house of Joseph" (1 Kgs 11:28). Solomon gave him this position because he had proven himself to be "industrious." He was later singled out by the prophet Ahijah to rule the northern ten tribes because of Solomon's worship of the gods of his foreign wives (1 Kgs 11:29–40). Subsequently, he led the revolt against Rehoboam after Solomon's death (1 Kgs 12:12–20). His loyalty to his former benefactor ended when the opportunity arose for him to become king himself.

The later history of the monarchy yields other examples of individuals taking advantage of a situation to advance themselves. In the 9th century, the succession to the throne of Israel was in dispute; factions among the army and assassination were the primary means to power. King Elah was murdered by Zimri, "commander of half his chariots" (1 Kgs 16:9–10) and then Zimri was overthrown after only seven days by Omri, another army commander (1 Kgs 16:15–23). A brief civil war then occurred with Omri overcoming a rival claimant named Tibni (vv 21–22). Neither Zimri nor Omri have a genealogy, which may indicate that they came from unimportant families and rose to power on the strength of their skills as soldiers.

B. CLOTHING AND PERSONAL ADORNMENT

Although the general style of dress for the people of Israel did not change markedly during the monarchy period, there were some shifts in costume, jewelry, and other personal items — especially among the well-to-do. Some of these changes were the result of increased wealth and the desire to differentiate between the social classes. Others were borrowed by or imposed upon the people by foreign rulers along with other customs and regulations.

Items of clothing were prized possessions, handed down to children and given in pledge (Amos 2:8 and Prov 20:16). Designed to be draped loosely around the body, garments regulated body heat and allowed for ease of movement. They were most commonly made of wool, although linen was also used. Woolen garments, however, were difficult to launder. They were nearly always moist with perspiration and soiled with food and dirt on the sleeves. This led to skin infections and the transmission of bacterially based diseases.

Take the garment of one who has given surety for a stranger; seize the pledge given as surety for foreigners. — Prov 20:16

The basic dress for both men and women was the *kethoneth*, a shirtlike garment which is depicted in ancient art in a variety of styles. Usually made of wool, it could reach as far as the ankles or just to the knees; it might have either long or short

"Jehu son of Omri" bows in submission in panel 2 of the Black Obelisk. Photo courtesy of the British Museum.

The "Black Obelisk" of Shalmaneser III affords invaluable glimpses into the ancient past. Photo courtesy of the British Museum.   3-5

sleeves. This garment is mentioned in the "Black Obelisk" inscription of the Assyrian king Shalmaneser III (842 BC). In a series of sculpted, captioned registers, Jehu, king of Israel, is depicted bowing before the king; his servants are shown carrying gifts as tribute payments.

Jehu is wearing a fringed *kethoneth* tied with a girdle which also has tassels hanging from it. His head is covered by a pointed cap, and his beard, like those of the Israelite porters carved on this monument, is trimmed to a point. The porters have a slightly different costume. They also are wearing a *kethoneth*, but it is covered by a fringed *simlah*, or mantle, which is draped over their left shoulders. Their beards are trimmed to a point like the king's and they are wearing pointed caps and sandals with upturned toes.

An Assyrian relief and inscription from 701 BC shows Judean captives from the city of Lachish. This monument to the conquests of Sennacherib comes from the period of his invasion of Judah and siege of Jerusalem (2 Kgs 18:13–16). The barefooted prisoners on the relief are wearing a shortsleeved, full-length *kethoneth*. They are bareheaded and have closely trimmed beards. This may reflect different styles between Israel and Judah or simply the changes in style from one period of time to the next.

The rather elaborate hems with suspended tassels found on most garments in the ancient Near East symbolized the rank of kings and their advisers as well as the military. This can be seen in David's remorse over cutting off the hem of Saul's garment in 1 Sam 24:6–7. He realized that by doing this he had symbolically weakened the king's authority. Hem and tassels, parts of which were dyed blue with an extract taken from the hypobranchial gland of the murex snail, were also worn as a sign of wealth among the nobility and merchant class (Ezk 23:6). Even the poor, however, were expected to have at least four blue threads in their tassels as a sign of devotion (Num 15:37–41).

The girdle, which was used to tie the *kethoneth* and *simlah*, also functioned as a weapons belt and

> He said to his men, "The LORD forbid that I should do this thing to my lord, the LORD's anointed, to raise my hand against him; for he is the LORD's anointed." So David scolded his men severely and did not permit them to attack Saul. Then Saul got up and left the cave, and went on his way.   —1 Sam 24:6–7

a sign of rank. In 2 Sam 20:8 Joab is described as wearing a "soldier's garment" tied with a girdle, *hagor*, through which he had sheathed his sword. David uses the same term in describing Joab's crimes to Solomon in 1 Kgs 2:5. In this case, however, the *hagor* of David had been soiled with the blood of Joab's murder victims. The girdle therefore also represented the power of David as king.

The garments specifically worn by aristocratic men and women are mentioned in Isa 3:18–24. The list contained here is primarily that of the wealthy, but it does point out the large variety of items that could be found in a their wardrobe. Headcoverings in this list include scarfs, headdresses, turbans, and veils—all but the last worn by both sexes and worn by priests as symbols of authority. Sashes, mantles, and girdles would have been used to tie the undergarments, some of which are said to be made of linen, gauze, or silk (Ezk 16:10). Special robes and festal garments, with embroidered cloth (Ezk 16:13), were used for festive occasions, weddings, and entertaining.

You were adorned with gold and silver, while your clothing was of fine linen, rich fabric, and embroidered cloth. You had choice flour and honey and oil for food. You grew exceedingly beautiful, fit to be a queen.

—Ezek 16:13

C. JEWELRY AND PERSONAL ITEMS

The list in Isa 3:18–24 also includes items of jewelry and personal care products. While some of these pieces of jewelry were also worn by men, the list in Isaiah seems to be a catalogue of what the well-dressed (extravagant) woman wore. Various adornments covered their owner from head to foot. These included delicately carved, garlanded frontlets and moon-shaped crescents, drop pendants on twisted golden necklace cords, armlets (note Saul's armlet of office in 2 Sam 1:10), nose and signet rings, and tinkling anklets (3:16). Each of these items would have been fabricated of gold or silver. In some instances, especially in the case of signet rings (used to stamp documents or as symbols of office), precious and semiprecious stones were mounted and engraved (Ezk 28:12–

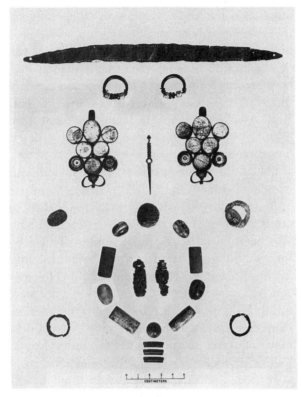

Jewelry found in a ca. 1400 BC burial at Megiddo. Photo courtesy of the Oriental Institute of the University of Chicago.
3-6

13). Larger pieces, like the breastplate of the high priest (Ex 28:17 – 21), also contained mounted precious stones.

A similar passage, Ezk 16:10 – 13, describes the clothing and jewelry of Yahweh's royal bride. She has bracelets on her arms and a gold and silver chain around her neck. Her head is adorned with a crown, earrings and a nose ring. Items made of gold or silver, such as these, were also used as money in this time before the introduction of minted coins (Job 28:15 – 18).

D. COSMETICS

Jezebel's preparations before meeting the triumphant Jehu and her own inevitable death have served as the classic example of the use of cosmetics by Israelite women (2 Kgs 9:30). She, of course, was a Phoenician princess who had

They even sent for men to come from far away, to whom a messenger was sent, and they came. For them you bathed yourself, painted your eyes, and decked yourself with ornaments; . . .
— Ezek 23:40

married King Ahab. Her use of eye paint, *puk*, may have just been the Phoenician style. That both Jeremiah (4:30) and Ezekiel (23:40) speak of women who enlarged their eyes with eye paint, however, suggests that it was a common practice in Israel as well as the rest of the ancient Near East. Analysis of deposits of this eye paint from Egyptian tombs and from cosmetic palettes found by archaeologists has shown that it consisted primarily of crushed galena mixed with gum and water.

Red dyes made from iron oxide (red ochre) or crushed leaves of the henna plant (SS 1:14) have also been found in Egyptian tombs. This mixture would have been applied to cheeks, lips, finger and toe nails, and hair to add color to a woman's appearance. Other shades of color were produced with a mixture of clays or crushed plant matter. The "perfume boxes" of Isa 3:20 may well refer to receptacles for these dyes as well as powdered or liquid fragrances.

Perfumes of various types were used by the Israelites to mask household odors and as incense offerings in shrines and temples. Several personal fragrances and soaps (Jer 2:22) were used by women as part of their attempts to cleanse and purify the body. These scents were applied to the body along with oils and other ointments (Prov 27:9) as well as being sprinkled on clothes (Ps 45:8) and on room furnishings (Prov 7:17).

A number of these scents are mentioned in the Song of Songs. Among them are spikenard (4:13–14), taken from the root of the gingergrass imported from Arabia, myrrh (5:5), and saffron (4:14), extracted from crocus and turmeric. The spices mentioned among the gifts of the queen of Sheba to King Solomon in 1 Kgs 10:2 probably included those used for cooking as well as those which were burned as incense and used as personal fragrances.

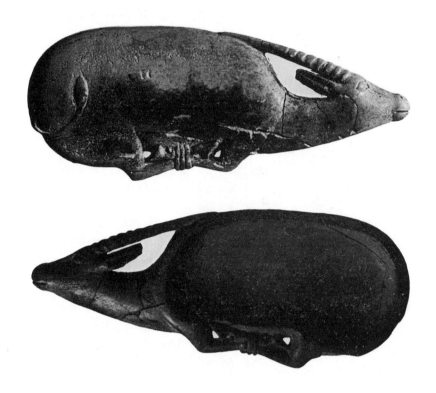

E. FORMS OF ENTERTAINMENT

The variety of entertainment in the Israelite cities would have increased during the time of the monarchy. A larger and more varied population in the cities, the significantly greater personal wealth of some individuals, and the increase in leisure time would have ensured that this was the case. As in earlier periods, occasions for celebration such as marriages and births, religious festivals (2 Sam 6:14–15), and military victories (1 Sam 18:6) all could spark individual and mass entertainments. These could include feasts (2 Sam 20:5), singing and dancing to a variety of musical instruments, board games (many examples of which have been excavated in Palestine), games of skill and strength (2 Sam 2:13–16), and riddle contests (Jdg 14:12). During the monarchy, how-

Cosmetic dish in the form of an ibex. Photo courtesy of the Ashmolean Museum.   3-7

ever, these events would have been more common and more elaborate as the king, the nobility, and the priesthood drew the people's attention to themselves and the Yahweh festivals.

Music was at the center of many of these celebrations and entertainments. For instance, when Jehoshaphat returned with his army to Jerusalem after a victory over Moab and Ammon, his victory processional marched to the temple playing harps and lyres and trumpets (2 Chr 20:28). Similarly, the wine and merriment of the feast described in Isa 5:12 was accompanied with the music of lyre, harp, timbrel, and flute. The text also indicates that the royal court was entertained by professional musicians and singers (2 Sam 19:35 and Ecc 2:8). Dancing would have been a natural accompaniment to these songs (1 Sam 29:5 and Ps 30:11).

Temple ritual included music and the singing of psalms in procession by pilgrims and priests. Psalm 24 and the "songs of ascent" (Pss 120–

This bas relief from Carchemish shows four military musicians. The musician on the left is blowing a shophar. Photo courtesy of the British Museum.
3-8

134) are good examples of hymns that might have been used in public processions to the temple. An indication of how organized temple music became during the monarchy appears in David's appointment of men who were "in charge of the service of song in the house of the Lord" (1 Chr 6:31–48). Choirs sang psalms on particular occasions (Ps 92, a song for the Sabbath) and as continuous praise to Yahweh (Ps 66).

Choirmasters were given specific instructions on how to orchestrate performances of these songs — contained in the superscriptions to each psalm. For example, the superscription to Psalm 22 instructs the choirmaster to perform this song according to a popular tune of the time, "The Hind of the Dawn." These instructions also include specific instrumentation to be used and some technical terms, such as *Selah* (Ps 32:4), whose meanings are still unknown to modern scholars.

F. TREATMENT OF DISEASE

The text describes quite a number of different diseases that afflicted the people of Israel. Among these are a disease of the bowel (amoebic dysentery — 2 Chr 21:15, 18–19), boils or tumors (perhaps bubonic plague in 1 Sam 5:6–12), and various types of plagues (2 Sam 24:15 and 1 Kgs 8:38). The common denominator for most of these diseases was that they were considered the result of sin or the sign of God's displeasure. As a result, treatment of disease was in many cases a matter of discovering why God was displeased (2 Sam 24:10–25) or submitting to the instructions of God's prophet (2 Kgs 5:10–14).

So the LORD sent a pestilence on Israel from that morning until the appointed time; and seventy thousand of the people died, from Dan to Beer-sheba.

— 2 Sam 24:15

In the case of leprosy (a general term for what were probably several different skin conditions), Lev 13 prescribed ʾ complicated set of procedures in which the afflicted person went to the priest to be examined. Certain primary appearances of eruption or discoloration of the skin were listed as well as several secondary features. A waiting period in increments of 7 days was set for the disappearance of these outward symptoms. If they were still present after that time the priest declared the individual unclean and outcast from the community and the temple. The contagion was also considered transmissible to clothing and these were burned if washing did not remove the stain of contamination (vv 47–59).

Physicians are mentioned only in a few scattered instances in the biblical text. Even then, they seem to have been associated with magicians and pagan priest-healers. This was apparently the case when King Asa was condemned for consulting physicians instead of Yahweh (2 Chr 16:12). Jeremiah 8:22, in speaking of spiritual healing of the people, mentioned the "balm of Gilead" and physicians to administer it. The implication here is that herbal medicines were known and used (Jer 51:8). Isaiah, for example, prescribed a "cake of figs" poultice be applied to a boil which was troubling King Hezekiah (Isa 38:21).

Is there no balm in Gilead? Is there no physician there? Why then has the health of my poor people not been restored?

—Jer 8:22

For the most part, however, medicine and the treatment of disease remained a primitive business with some health problems being described by the biblical writer as incurable (Dt 28:27). When this happened the afflicted person or a relative sometimes sought a holy man whose intercession with a god might effect a cure. For instance, in 1 Kgs 17:17–24, a woman asked Elijah to restore her comatose son to life. The prophet laid on the boy three times and called on God to "let this child's soul come into him again" (v 21). Once the boy was revived by this procedure, his mother testified that "now I know that you are a man of God" (v 24). Similarly, Na'aman, the Syrian general "cleansed" of his leprosy by Elisha's intercession, stated "I know that there is no God in all the earth but in Israel" (2 Kgs 5:15).

G. Conceptions of Death

Isaiah, taunting the king of Babylon (14:4–11), provides the common Israelite belief that the dead go down to *Sheol* where they, king and pauper alike, are all the same. Following the painful loss of his son, David summed up this general belief concerning the dead (2 Sam 12:21–23). As the child lay ill, the king fasted and wept, lying on the ground. But after his death, David simply stated: "Can I bring him back again? I shall go to him, but he will not return to me" (cf., Job 7:9–10).

As the cloud fades and vanishes, so those who go down to Sheol do not come up; they return no more to their houses, nor do their places know them any more.
—Job 7:9–10

Conceptions regarding *Sheol*, a poorly defined region from which there was no resurrection, and in which there was no reward or punishment, remained the same throughout the monarchy period. It was a place so cut off from the world of the living that "the dead praise not the Lord, neither any that go down into silence" (Ps 115:17–18). In the only instance in which the dead are described as communicating with the living, Saul has the witch of Endor bring up Samuel's shade from the netherworld (1 Sam 28:8–19). Samuel complained that his rest had been disturbed and prophesied the end of Saul's reign.

H. Mourning

Conventional mourning rituals were quite elaborate and expressive. For example, the messenger who brought the news of Saul's death had torn his clothing and placed earth on his head. David's and his men's reaction to the news was to also tear their robes, weep, and fast until evening (2 Sam 1:2–12). In addition, David composed a eulogy (2 Sam 1:19–27) for Saul and again for his son Absalom (2 Sam 18:33). Other expressions of mourning included a procession (2 Sam 3:31–32), the wearing of sackcloth, putting dust on the head, and shaving the hair from one's head (Mic 1:2 and Ezk 27:30–31). Jeremiah also mentions the custom of bringing food and drink to the mourning family and cutting oneself as a sign of mourning (16:6–8), a practice prohibited in Dt 14:1.

I. BURIAL CUSTOMS

Failure to be buried was the greatest disgrace for the Israelite dead. The prophets often spoke of a day of vengeance when Yahweh would destroy the family of a king who had broken the law (1 Kgs 14:11; 21:24). Similarly, God's unfaithful people would be defeated by the armies of Egypt, Assyria, or Babylon, and their bodies would be left for birds and animals to consume (Jer 16:4) or cast on to dung heaps (Amos 4:3).

His corpse must not remain all night upon the tree; you shall bury him that same day, for anyone hung on a tree is under God's curse. You must not defile the land that the LORD your God is giving you for possession.
— Deut 21:23

The law required that even executed criminals must be buried as soon as possible (Dt 21:23) and that bodies found beside the roadway be buried by the people of the nearest village (Dt 21:1–9 and 1 Kgs 13:29). On one occasion, however, seven of Saul's sons were hung to pay "blood guilt" to the Gibeonites. These non-Israelites left them hanging for a full season. David was eventually shamed into burying them, along with the bones of Saul and Jonathan, by the faithfulness of Rizpah, one of the mothers of the hanged men, who stayed with the bodies to prevent them from being eaten by animals (2 Sam 21:10–14).

The bodies of the dead were buried in tombs that reflected the social station of the individual. Cremation was almost unknown, although the bodies of Saul and his sons were burned after being retrieved from the walls of Beth-shan by the men of Jabesh-gilead (1 Sam 31:12). This may be because of the dismemberment and advanced state of decay of the bodies. After the cremation, the bones were buried under a tamarisk tree and a seven-day fast was observed as a mourning period (v 13).

Burial for kings and the wealthy was in family tombs (2 Sam 21:12–14) in caves or carved into

the rock of nearby hillsides. The often repeated phrase at the end of a king's reign, "he slept with his fathers, and they buried him in the city of David" (1 Kgs 15:8) was used of most of the kings of Judah (cf., 2 Kgs 14:16 for Israel's kings). Excavations in Jerusalem have uncovered several tombs which would have been within the walls during the monarchy period. It seems unlikely that these could be anything but royal tombs because of the skill of carving and the lack of space for tombs within the city.

A group of rock-cut tombs have been found on the northern end of Ophel Hill on Zion and these may also be royal sepulchers. This may be the spot where Absalom prepared an elaborate monument tomb for himself "in the King's Valley" with a pillar to mark the spot (2 Sam 18:17–18). The mention of Manasseh's tomb (7th century BC) in the Garden of Uzzah (2 Kgs 21:18) may be a new site after the original area for royal burials was filled.

Rock-cut tombs like that identified by archaeologists as the tomb of the "Steward of the House" generally had a single large chamber, although there are some with more. This elaborate tomb, located in the Silwan Valley across from the City

Ophel Photo by LaMoine DeVries.   3-9

What right do you have here?
Who are your relatives here, that
you have cut out a tomb here for
yourself, cutting a tomb on the
height, and carving a habitation
for yourself in the rock?
— Isa 22:16

of David, contains an inscription giving the name of the owner and cursing anyone who would disturb it. It may be the tomb of Shebna, the steward of King Hezekiah who was rebuked by Isaiah (22:16) for carving a tomb higher up on the hill than his social status would allow.

An additional feature of the rock-cut tomb was a charnel pit in which the bones of older burials were placed. They no longer had the principal place within the tomb, but at least were still interred with the rest of the family. Bench shelves are carved into the walls for the most recent burials. They have rounded pillows carved at one end and often have clay lamps placed at the head, perhaps to light the way to the underworld for the dead. Jars of wine, water jugs, and open-mouthed food jars are also found in these tombs, designed to aid the dead in their journey. Personal items like arrowheads and seals are also common grave goods.

The burial of the poor or lower classes would have been much less elaborate, perhaps simply involving the scooping of holes out of the earth. Their bodies may have even been placed into abandoned or pillaged tombs which once belonged to a prominent person or family (2 Kgs 13:20). Infants were often interred within the house itself. The large number of these burials gives further evidence of a high infant mortality rate in the cities.

III. LAW

How did legal custom and the administration of justice change during the monarchy period?
The introduction of the monarchy and the movement of a large number of people into urban centers contributed to significant changes in legal custom and the administration of justice in ancient Israel. The king naturally wished to ex-

ercise as much control over the law and its enforcement as possible in order to increase his
own authority. This meant he had to be identified with the dispensing of justice to all segments
of society, especially the weak. The ideal was to
create a perception of him among the people that
he was a "just king." With this accomplished, it
would be more likely that they would look to him
first for justice under the law.

The other major factor at work in transforming the law as it was first formulated at Sinai was
the legal problems of city dwellers. They simply
overtaxed a system that was originally designed
to meet the needs of a nomadic and rural-based
people. New situations arose that had not been a
part of their society before, such as regulations
concerning commerce or making loans (Dt 23:19–
20) or the accuracy of weights and measures
(Dt 25:13–16). As a result new laws or new interpretations of the law had to be made. This necessity may be at the heart of Solomon's request for
wisdom "to discern between good and evil" in
order to rule his people (1 Kgs 3:9).

You shall not charge interest on loans to another Israelite, interest on money, interest on provisions, interest on anything that is lent.
—Deut 23:19

During the early monarchy royal judicial authority was held as a prerogative of the king and
little delegation of authority to local judges was allowed. However, by the reign of King Jehoshaphat (c. 873–849 BC) the complexity of running
the nation of Judah and the sheer number of
cases led to a major reform of the judicial system
(2 Chr 19:4–11). The king, who had expanded his
area of control and fortified the border regions,
now used these new fortress cities as judicial centers where district courts were held and judges
heard cases (vv 5–7). Differentiation between secular and religious matters was also made by Jehoshaphat. He appointed Levites and priests in
Jerusalem to hear appealed cases dealing with
religious crimes, defined by the categories of
"bloodshed, law or commandment, statutes or ordinances" (v 10). To supervise this new judicial

When Abner returned to Hebron, Joab took him aside in the gateway to speak with him privately, and there he stabbed him in the stomach. So he died for shedding the blood of Asahel, Joab's brother. — 2 Sam 3:27

A. FAMILY LEGAL CUSTOMS

bureaucracy, Jehoshaphat set the chief priest, Amariah, over the Levitical judges, and Zebadiah, one of the king's chief officers, was made the head of the secular judges.

The introduction of royal authority forced some changes in legal custom but was unable to supersede others. Early in David's career as king at Hebron, he faced a legal problem that had the potential to tear his political hopes of a united kingdom apart. His general Joab had murdered Abner, the commander of Ishbosheth's army (2 Sam 3:26–27). This was done in the name of blood revenge, since Abner had killed Joab's brother Asahel in battle (2 Sam 2:18–23).

The blood feud was an extension of familial responsibility to protect its own and was also tied to clan affairs since it involved a dispute between two extended families. However, it directly threatened the authority of a king trying to establish a system of royal justice. The solution (2 Sam 3:29–39) was for David to disclaim any responsibility for Joab's act and to disgrace Joab by forcing him to mourn publicly at Abner's funeral (cf., Jehu's disclaimer over the death of Ahab's 70 sons in 2 Kgs 10:9–10). In the fictitious case of the woman of Tekoa, David went a step further by invoking royal authority to protect the accused murderer from clan vengeance (1 Kgs 14:4–11).

The ultimate solution to this problem came with the establishment of the six Levitical "cities of refuge" as described in Jos 21:13–40. Here a man who had accidentally caused the death of another could flee from the vengeance of family and clan to a city of refuge. There he would be tried by the elders of the city and either granted asylum or punished for his crime (Num 35:9–34). In the time of Josiah's reform (late 7th century BC), when all worship and royal authority were centralized in Jerusalem, the number of cities of refuge was cut to three and there was no Levitical involvement (Dt 19:1–13).

B. MARRIAGE AND BETROTHAL

The more cosmopolitan atmosphere of Solomon's court and the increased contacts with other nations led to a greater acceptance of intermarriage between Israelite and non-Israelite. Solomon solidified foreign alliances through his marriages to foreign royal princesses such as the pharaoh's daughter (1 Kgs 3:1), and Ahab strengthened already strong ties with the Phoenicians when he married Jezebel, the daughter of the king of Sidon (1 Kgs 16:31). These diplomatic marriages do have a dark side in the text, serving as prime causes for the adoption of idol worship (vv 31–33) and the suppression of the Yahweh prophets (1 Kgs 18:13). However, with the precedent set by the king it is not surprising to find mixed marriages among the rest of the people (Bathsheba's marriage to Uriah the Hittite in 2 Sam 11:3 may be a precursor of this policy).

And as if it had been a light thing for him to walk in the sins of Jeroboam son of Nebat, he took as his wife Jezebel daughter of King Ethbaal of the Sidonians, and went and served Baal, and worshiped him.
—1 Kgs 16:31

The parallels between Israelite marriage laws and those found in other ancient Near Eastern law codes suggest further evidence of an acceptance of cultural borrowing during the monarchy period. For instance, the sanctity of the betrothal vows is found in both Dt 22:23–27 and the 18th century BC Code of Hammurabi #130 (*ANET*, p. 171). The presumption in both cases is that the father contracts the marriage and once a girl has been betrothed she is technically the wife of another man. Any crime against her is also, however, one against both her father and her betrothed husband.

The Babylonian law states that a betrothed virgin, who has been raped, will be freed while her attacker is executed. The Deuteronomic law is more specific, making provision for the location of the crime and using this as the basis for the

*In the case of a seignior's
daughter, a virgin who was
living in her father's house,
whose [father] had not been asked
(for her in marriage), whose
hymen had not been opened since
she was not married, and no one
had a claim against her father's
house, if a seignior took the
virgin by force and ravished her,
either in the midst of the city or
in the open country or at night in
the street or in a granary or at a
city festival, the father of the
virgin shall take the wife of the
virgin's ravisher and give her to
be ravished; he shall not return
her to her husband (but) take her;
the father may give his daughter
who was ravished to her ravisher
in marriage. If he has no wife,
the ravisher shall give the (extra)
third in silver to her father as the
value of a virgin (and) her
ravisher shall marry her (and)
not cast her off. If the father does
not (so) wish, he shall receive the
(extra) third for the virgin in
silver (and) give his daughter to
whom he wishes.   —MAL 55*

punishment of the couple. If the crime took place within the city, both were to be executed, since the woman could have cried out for help. However, if the rape was committed in the "open country" where no one could hear her cries, she went free and only the man was to be executed.

The 12th century BC Middle Assyrian Law Code also contains evidence of a place-oriented criminal system. MAL 55 (*ANET*, p. 185) is concerned with the rape of an unbetrothed virgin, who is still living in her father's house. The code states that it does not matter whether this crime has taken place in the city or the country, after dark or during a religious festival. The rapist must pay a fine in silver to the father for the loss of his daughter's virginity and the father has the option of forcing this man to marry his daughter, with no possibility of divorcing her later. Deuteronomy 22:28–29 is almost an identical version of this law. The rapist must also pay a fine of 50 shekels of silver and marry the girl without later recourse to divorce.

Divorce was an option for an Israelite man whose wife had committed some "indecency" (Dt 24:1–2). This was probably adultery, although other ancient Near Eastern law codes also list childlessness (CH 138) and taking a job outside the home (CH 141) as grounds for divorce (*ANET*, p. 172). There is no law in the biblical text allowing a woman the right to divorce her husband. However, he may not make unsubstantiated accusations of adultery or shameful conduct against her, on pain of paying a fine and being publicly whipped (Dt 22:13–19).

C. INHERITANCE LAWS

Samuel's earliest arguments against the establishment of the monarchy included the statement that the king "will take the best of your fields and vineyards and olive orchards and give them to his servants" (1 Sam 8:14). Saul did attach

"any strong man, or any valiant man . . . to himself" (1 Sam 14:52), and presumably he was able
to do this by granting them privileges at court
and tracts of land. The kings would have been
able to do this by transferring land to these advisers which was no longer being used or whose
owners were dead. There is ample evidence for
this in both Hammurabi's Code (CH 30; *ANET*,
p. 167) and the royal correspondence from Mari
(*ARM* IV 1:5 – 28).

These five men abandoned their territory (and) came to me because their brothers had been entrusted with wheat and a field here (and) were satisfied. Now on this matter I have sent their sugāgum *to you. These men should be taken and entrusted to his hand (so that) they may be brought to me. They should be given satisfaction and go with their brothers. — ARM*

The sale of land outside the family or clan was
unusual in ancient Israel. Even during the des-
perate time of the siege of Jerusalem by Nebuchadnezzar in 587 BC, Jeremiah was offered the
option to purchase a field in Anathoth from his
cousin. Before the land could be offered to a
stranger, Jeremiah had "the right of possession
and redemption" (Jer 32:7 – 9). This transaction
was made and signed before witnesses. Its stipulations were recorded on a legal contract which
was then placed in a sealed earthenware vessel
for safe storage (vv 10 – 14).

On occasion kings tried to exercise their powers so as to infringe upon inheritance traditions.
Thus, in 1 Kgs 21 King Ahab attempted to purchase the vineyard of a Jezreelite named Naboth.
As was his right, Naboth refused to sell his land
to the king citing the fact that he could not give
him "the inheritance of my fathers" (v 4). Ahab
had no legal recourse after being refused and
went home to sulk. His Phoenician wife Jezebel,
however, had no qualms about taking what she
wanted. She was not bound by tradition or the
law and promptly trumped up charges of blasphemy against Naboth. Two witnesses, per Dt
19:15, were brought forward to testify against
him and he was subsequently stoned to death
(vv 8 – 14). Naboth's sons were apparently also
executed along with their father for this crime
(2 Kgs 9:26).

When Ahab, as the ultimate heir of property

within the kingdom, went to take possession of Naboth's field, he was met there by the prophet Elijah (1 Kgs 21:15–19). The king and his entire family were cursed for having "sold themselves" in order to take possession of land that was not theirs. The theme here is that the king is not above the law. This same theme recurs in the narrative of David's adultery with Bathsheba (2 Sam 12) and Solomon's idolatry (1 Kgs 11).

D. SLAVERY

Slavery was a part of Israelite tribal society from the beginning (Gen 16:1). According to the law, both Israelite families and their slaves were included as part of the covenantal community's Sabbath obligations (Ex 20:8–11). Once they settled in Canaan, the memory of Israel's enslavement in Egypt became the basis for a generally humane treatment of slaves in the law. For instance, the Deuteronomic Code (and Ex 21:2) required that slaves be freed after six years service (CH 117 requires three years; *ANET,* pp. 170–71) and that they should not be sent away empty-handed (Dt 15:12–15). Another law protecting the rights of slaves is recorded in Ex 21:26–27. This statute required that male and female slaves be freed if they had been brutalized by their masters.

When you buy a male Hebrew slave, he shall serve six years, but in the seventh he shall go out a free person, without debt.
— Exod 21:2

Throughout these early periods, however, the number of slaves was quite small. Their numbers did not increase significantly until the time of David when his almost continuous wars provided a steady flow of prisoners. These men and women became household servants, wives (Dt 21:10–14) or concubines, and construction workers (2 Sam 12:31). Not all prisoners, however, were spared to become slaves in war. David, in one instance (2 Sam 8:2), chose to execute two-thirds of his Moabite prisoners, perhaps as a lesson to that nation or because he simply did not need that many slave laborers.

Solomon's public works projects were built by forced labor battalions, drafted from among the Israelite villages (1 Kgs 5:13–18). The text states that Israelites were not used as slaves (1 Kgs 9:22). By whatever title, however, Israelite "workers" would have been required to carry out Solomon's grandiose building program in addition to the levies of captured Amorite, Perizzite, and Hittite slaves (1 Kgs 9:21).

But of the Israelites Solomon made no slaves; they were the soldiers, they were his officials, his commanders, his captains, and the commanders of his chariotry and cavalry.
—1 Kgs 9:22

Poor Israelites occasionally became slaves by selling themselves or members of their family into slavery to satisfy a debt. By law, this servitude for males was to only last six years; in the seventh they were to be freed and their debt cancelled (Ex 21:2). This early code (Ex 21:7–11) also stated that daughters, sold by their father into slavery, did not obtain their freedom in the same way as males. Many of these women became concubines or wives and thus their position as slave or free women was determined by their marital status.

The later Deuteronomic Code simplified the law by including both men and women in this six-year, limited period of servitude (Dt 15:12). The fact that these laws were not always obeyed, however, is attested to in Jer 34:8–16. Here the prophet complained that Hebrew slaves had been freed during the Babylonian siege of the city of Jerusalem and then had once again been enslaved after the immediate danger had passed.

Provision for perpetual slavery for male Israelites only occurs in the law when a slave made the decision to remain a slave himself. He may have done this to prevent falling back into the pattern of poverty that had forced him into slavery originally or because freedom would have separated him from his family. The latter is explained in Ex 21:2–6. A man was given a wife by his master and they had children while he was still a slave. When his period of servitude ended he could go free but not his wife and children. At that point he could renounce his freedom by swearing an oath to God and having an awl driven through his earlobe into the post of his master's door (also found in Dt 15:17). The mark of the awl branded him as a slave for life (see CH 226–227 for laws on fraudulently removing the slave-mark; *ANET*, p. 176).

IV. RELIGIOUS PRACTICES

In what ways did the religious practices of the Israelites change during the monarchy period?

The establishment of the monarchy did not initially have a dramatic effect on local and family religious practices. Popular religion remained separate and often quite different from the official religion of Jerusalem and the temple. A single pattern of worship existed only when the monarchy exercised strong control over the entire land—as in Josiah's time. Political developments further complicated the Israelite religious scene. The Yahweh cult and its Levitical priesthood were established in Jerusalem during David's and Solomon's reigns. Shortly after the division of the kingdom, however, rival shrines and high places were set up by the kings of Israel. And, when the Assyrians and Babylonians conquered Palestine, they imposed the worship of their gods on the Israelites.

A. POPULAR RELIGION

In the individual homes and villages of the Israelites at the beginning of the monarchy period, popular expressions of religion centered around seasonal festivals (1 Sam 20:18, 29). Sacrifices were designed to ensure the fertility of the land and their herds. These sacrifices were made on altars in private chapels or collectively on the "high place" (*bamah*, 1 Sam 9:19). Sacred images (*teraphim*) were worshipped, and were even found

Samuel answered Saul, "I am the seer; go up before me to the shrine, for today you shall eat with me, and in the morning I will let you go and will tell you all that is on your mind."
—1 Sam 9:19

in the royal household of Saul (1 Sam 19:13).

Some of these religious practices were copied from those of neighboring peoples. Like clothing styles, jewelry, manners of speech, and architecture, religious practices were also borrowed from the Canaanites, Philistines, and Phoenicians. It was the adoption of Canaanite religious practices that prompted the formulation of much of the law (see esp. Dt 13–14) and the pronouncements of the prophets.

Despite his construction of the Yahweh temple in Jerusalem, Solomon's building of temples for the gods of his foreign wives (1 Kgs 11:4–8) set a precedent for the people that promoted the worship of these other gods. The priesthood in the capital could not police these illicit practices and they apparently continued throughout the history of Judah (1 Kgs 14:22–24). Recent finds at Kuntillet Ajrud, in the northern Sinai desert, add fuel to the argument that Yahweh worship was blended with that of the Canaanite fertility god Baal and his consort Asherah.

Worship of Yahweh in the local areas was further weakened by the division of the kingdom. Popular religion was given nearly free rein by the kings, who only demanded the people's political loyalties. In Ahab's time (c. 874–852 BC), this included the near elimination of open Yahweh worship and the establishment of Baal as the national deity (1 Kgs 16:31–33; 18:4).

Local "high places" were promoted, with the king building shrines on them and appointing non-Levitical priests to officiate there (1 Kgs 12:31). The prophets often pointed to these sacred spots as the justification for the destruction of the nation (Amos 7:9 and Hos 10:8). Standing stones (*massebot*) were erected on the high places as well as in the temple of Baal in Samaria (2 Kgs 3:2). These slabs of stone marked the entrance to sacred precincts or represented the presence of the deity. They were so closely

He also made houses on high places, and appointed priests from among all the people, who were not Levites.

—1 Kgs 12:31

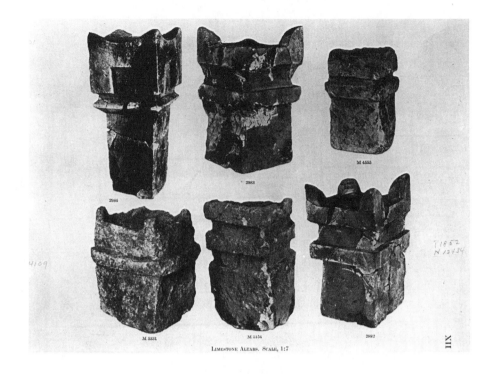

M 4555

2983

2984

4109

M 5331   M 5154   2082

LIMESTONE ALTARS. SCALE, 1:7

XII

Horned household altars made of limestone found at Megiddo. Photo courtesy of the Oriental Institute of the University of Chicago.   3-10

associated with Canaanite worship that Josiah singled them out for destruction, along with the sacred posts (*asherim*), in his 7th-century reform movement (2 Kgs 23:14).

Josiah's reform (2 Kgs 23:4–24) actually provides a long list of Canaanite religious practices engaged in by the people of Judah. Idols and their priests were removed from the temple along with all sacred vessels and incense burners used in their worship. The Asherah, a sacred wooden pillar set up in the temple, was taken out and burned with its ashes scattered over a "potter's field" graveyard (v 6). Cult prostitutes were banished and the "high places" were defiled and abolished from one end of the land to the other (vv 7–8). Archaeologists have found a horned altar from the shrine at Beer-sheba which dates to Hezekiah's time (c. 701 BC). It was re-used as fill in constructing a wall, evidencing an earlier royal

attempt to eliminate the high places (2 Kgs 18:22).
In addition to these efforts to purify religion in
Judah, Josiah also eliminated a shrine in the valley of Hinnom which was being used for the sacrifice of children to the god Molech (2 Kgs 23:10)
and removed horses and chariots that were associated with sun worship from the temple precincts
(v 11). Altars that had been built to foreign gods
by previous kings were pulled down and destroyed (vv 12 – 15), and the graves (vv 16 – 20) of
the Baal priests at Bethel (one of the sites in
which Jeroboam had placed a golden calf, 1 Kgs
12:28 – 29) were defiled. The final expression of
his clean sweep of the land comes in v 24 with
the outlawing of mediums, wizards, teraphim,
idols, "and all the abominations that were seen
in the land of Judah and in Jerusalem."

B. TEMPLE WORSHIP AND THE YAHWEH CULT

There were several temples and shrines scattered throughout Canaan during the pre-
monarchic period. These included the ones at
Shechem (Jos 24:25 – 26), Shiloh (1 Sam 1:3), and
Dan (Jdg 18:28 – 31), and the three corners of
Samuel's circuit as a judge: Bethel (1 Sam 10:3),
Gilgal, and Mizpah (1 Sam 7:16). Archaeological
investigations have shown that after the capture of
the ark of the covenant by the Philistines (1 Sam
4:10 – 11) Shiloh and the temple which had housed
it were destroyed. Shiloh's prominence was ended
at that point and the ark went into obscurity in
the village of Kiriath-jearim (1 Sam 7:1 – 2). The
priestly group which had served at Shiloh transferred their operations to the city of Nob (1 Sam
21:1 – 10). This was not, however, the only priestly
community operating in Canaan at that time.
David and his family were also associated with
temples in Hebron (2 Sam 2:4 and 15:7) and
Bethlehem (1 Sam 20:6).

*Now this man used to go up year
by year from his town to worship
and to sacrifice to the LORD of
hosts at Shiloh, where the two
sons of Eli, Hophni and Phinehas, were priests of the LORD.*
                                    —1 Sam 1:3

C. JERUSALEM TEMPLE

The temple most associated with the monarchy was the one built by Solomon in Jerusalem. Its site, like Jerusalem itself, was on politically neutral ground — the threshing floor of Araunah the Jebusite (2 Sam 24:18 – 25 and 2 Chr 3:1). Suggestion of previous cultic usage was thus eliminated and the priestly community of Yahweh was given exclusive rights to the site. The purchase of the threshing floor (a place associated with justice in the older village culture) by King David and the building of the temple here by King Solomon placed royal sanction on the Yahweh cult.

They brought in the ark of the LORD, and set it in its place, inside the tent that David had pitched for it; and David offered burnt offerings and offerings of well-being before the LORD.
— 2 Sam 6:17

The key to the association of the site of the temple with Yahweh was the ark of the covenant. David had it brought to his new capital with great fanfare and ceremony after he became the king of all the tribes (2 Sam 6:1 – 19). The ark was housed in a tent, a parallel to the wilderness tabernacle (Ex 40:1 – 8), and the sacrificial routine was initiated with David making burnt offerings and peace offerings before the tent (v 17).

The next logical step for David would have been to construct a formal temple for Yahweh worship. However, the text offers a variety of reasons for why David did not then build a temple to house the ark. According to 2 Samuel 7, the need for a temple was replaced by the need to create a ruling house. First Kings 5:3 excused David from this task because of the press of military campaigns to protect the nation and 1 Chronicles 28, despite giving David credit for establishing the priestly bureaucracy that would supervise temple worship, said he was denied the right to build the temple because he was "a warrior and had shed blood" (v 3).

As a result, it was David's successor Solomon who had the leisure time and resources to build the temple to Yahweh in Jerusalem (1 Kgs 5:4 – 6). In his dedication of the completed temple, he followed David's example, initiating sacrifices of various kinds (peace offerings, burnt offerings, cereal offerings), followed by a seven-day feast for all the people (1 Kgs 8:62 – 66). From the beginning, then, there was a precedent set of the king officiating at sacrifices and initiating national worship festivals. Some of David's sons were even described as being priests (2 Sam 8:18).

D. ROLE OF THE PRIESTLY COMMUNITY

David and Solomon were also said to have established the temple priesthood (1 Chr 15:1–24; 1 Kgs 2:35). The idea of the king as both political and religious leader, however, was later disputed by the Levitical priesthood. They eventually gained more complete control of the sacrificial rituals; and the king, while still an advocate for the people with God, had a secondary role (cf., Solomon's actions in 1 Kgs 8 to those of Hezekiah's in 2 Chr 30:13 – 27). This was due in part to the political struggle between the priests and the king. But perhaps even more important was the practice of kings, starting with Solomon (1 Kgs 11:6 – 8) and Jeroboam (1 Kgs 12:28 – 33), of building altars to foreign gods and promoting non-Levitical priests to lead their worship (1 Kgs 13:33).

The people of Israel who were present at Jerusalem kept the festival of unleavened bread seven days with great gladness; and the Levites and the priests praised the LORD day by day, accompanied by loud instruments for the LORD. — 2 Chr 30:21

The result in the biblical text was the portrayal of the kings as either evil idolaters, like Manasseh (2 Kgs 21:2 – 9), or as reformers who looked to the prophets and priests to help them renovate the temple and cleanse the worship of the people (Joash, 2 Chr 24:2 –14; Josiah, 2 Kgs 22:3 – 23:25). This account did not take into consideration the political pressures that were being placed on the kings to conform to the customs of their Assyrian and Babylonian masters. Manasseh ruled for 40 years as a vassal of the Assyrians and his long reign might well be attributed to his success in conforming to their rules.

With the kings fighting for their own survival, the priests became the protectors and interpreters of the law. Josiah's reform, by centralizing worship in the Jerusalem temple, reinforced the priests' position and strengthened their control of popular religion. The Deuteronomic law code of Deuteronomy 12 – 26 provided a blueprint for the religious activities of the people in the villages and towns of Judah. Everything from dietary laws (14:3 – 8) to the proper place and means of slaughtering animals (12:15 – 27) are found here as well as the religious calendar (16:1 – 17) and the referral of difficult legal cases to the Levitical priests (17:8 – 13).

In Jerusalem itself, the actual routine of sacrifice and temple worship was left in priestly hands. Extremely elaborate ritual and sacrificial instructions are described in Leviticus. These included which animals were to be used for particular sacrifices (Lev 1:3 – 17), what portion of the animal was reserved for God (3:16), the use of the sacrificial blood (4:6 – 7), and the offerings that were acceptable from a man who could not afford the normal sacrificial animal (5:11).

Matters such as ritual purity (Lev 10:10), interpretation of the law, and the treatment of disease (Lev 13 – 14) are also found here as the exclusive province of the Levitical priests. This code was most likely an ideal one. It may not have been strictly enforced until the post-exilic period when the monarchy had ended and the priests were the principal leaders of the people.

If the offering is a sacrifice of well-being, if you offer an animal of the herd, whether male or female, you shall offer one without blemish before the LORD.

—Lev 3:1

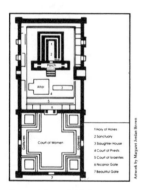

Layout of temple. Mercer Dictionary of the Bible. 3-G

V. WEAPONS AND WARFARE

In what ways did warfare, tactics, and weapons change during the monarchy period?

At the beginning of the monarchy period, the most important element in warfare was the establishment of parity between the Israelites and their enemy neighbors. The time David spent as a mercenary with the Philistines gave him an intimate knowledge of their battle tactics and their skill in the manufacture of weapons. While it is unlikely that iron weapons immediately became the predominant weapon in the Israelite arsenal after this, certainly their use became more common and set the stage for the eventual Israelite victory over the Philistines and other neighboring peoples.

The establishment of the monarchy itself was another important factor in the war against the Philistines. With the tribal groups united under a single leader, they were a much more effective and powerful force. From his capital at Jerusalem, David led his armies (2 Sam 8) or entrusted them to Joab's leadership to protect the villages and towns of his kingdom from invaders (2 Sam 10). As the area of his effective control grew, an advance staging area was established in the valley of Succoth to guard the fords leading into Transjordan from invading armies from Ammon or Syria. Under Solomon, this strategic area of Mahanaim was incorporated as one of the 12 administrative provinces of the kingdom (1 Kgs 4:7–19).

Archer stringing bow. 3-H

A. ORGANIZATION OF THE ARMY

One innovation of the united kingdom was the organization of the army into two different units, the regular army and local militia. Naturally, most strategy was based around the professional soldiers of the regular army. Many of these men, like Uriah the Hittite, were foreign mercenaries whose loyalty was to the crown and who could be expected to have the military experience needed in the wars against the Ammonites and Syrian princes. Others, at least at the beginning of David's reign, were from his family or the group of outlaws he had led before the death of Saul (2 Sam 23). They served as an elite shock force which could be reinforced as needed by the less experienced militia forces drafted from the villages of the kingdom (2 Sam 12:26–29). First Chronicles 27 lists the command structure and

This is the list of the people of Israel, the heads of families, the commanders of the thousands and the hundreds, and their officers who served the king in all matters concerning the divisions that came and went, month after month throughout the year, each division numbering twenty-four thousand: . . . —1 Chr 27:1

size of the militia, with each formation consisting of 24,000 warriors. It is likely that a portion of this force was kept on alert in case the king needed to call them into service quickly.

B. WEAPONRY

One sign that the Israelite monarchs were achieving parity with their neighbors was the incorporation of chariotry into their armed forces. In the settlement and judges period, chariots had been a weapon of the Philistines and Canaanites, not the people of Israel (Jos 11:4 – 9 and Jdg 1:19). David's and Solomon's military success can be gauged, however, by their acquisition of chariots (2 Sam 8:3 – 4) and their building of stables to house the horses (1 Kgs 4:26). Their successors in both Israel and Judah used chariots as a matter of course in every military campaign (2 Kgs 3:7), and the commander of chariot forces became one of the major military officers (1 Kgs 16:9). The chariot had added another dimension to Israelite armies which in earlier periods had been made up primarily of infantry contingents.

David took from him one thousand seven hundred horsemen, and twenty thousand foot soldiers. David hamstrung all the chariot horses, but left enough for a hundred chariots.

— 2 Sam 8:4

In the armies of Israel and Judah and their enemies, infantry was separated into different units and equipped with three basic weapons — spear, bow, and sling. Assyrian reliefs from the period of the divided monarchy (c. 900 – 721 BC) depict spearmen in mailed coats carrying a shield in one hand and equipped with a sword either strapped to their back or thrust into their belt. With weapons designed for close infighting, the spearmen formed the first wave of attackers. Depending on the terrain, chariots and cavalry were used both on the flanks and in formation. Chariots were also used to conduct commanders (1 Kgs 22:31 – 34) and messengers around the field while the entire force was supported by the missiles of the bowmen and slingers.

C. SIEGE STRATEGIES

Open field tactics, terrain considerations, and

strategies based on numbers of chariots and soldiers that can be brought to play are found in a
number of biblical passages (1 Kgs 20:23–30;
22:29–36; 2 Kgs 23:28–30). However, a major
challenge to military strategists in the monarchy
period was the capture of a walled city. The strong
points of the city (walls, glacis, moat, and gate complex) had to be overcome. Again, it was the Assyrians who perfected strategies to offset each of
these challenges. Their reliefs show assault ramps,
wheeled tanks attached with battering rams, sap-
pers tunneling under walls, infantrymen with inflated goat skins crossing rivers and moats, and
mobile towers bristling with archers thrust up
against the city wall. Tactics involving these methods and structures were probably used in the Assyrian capture of Samaria (2 Kgs 17:5–6) and the
Babylonian capture of Jerusalem (2 Kgs 25:1–4).

Then the king of Assyria invaded all the land and came to Samaria; for three years he besieged it. —2 Kgs 17:5

While the people of the city rained down
stones and arrows on their attackers (2 Sam
11:24), the strategy of the besieging army was to
spread the defenders as thinly as possible along
the walls. During lulls in the fighting psychological ploys were sometimes employed. In 2 Kgs
18:19–35, Rabshakeh, the Assyrian spokesman,
called to the people of Jerusalem to surrender
and to overthrow King Hezekiah. His pleas were
not answered but Hezekiah's negotiators were
clearly worried since they asked him to speak in
Aramaic so that the people would not understand him (v 26).

Famine also worked in favor of the besieging
army. They could continue to obtain supplies
from the surrounding countryside and from supply columns. However, if the siege lasted for too
long the defenders found the price of goods rising precipitously (2 Kgs 6:25) and they sometimes resorted to cannibalism (2 Kgs 6:26–29).
Water supplies were a constant matter of concern. Cisterns were dug around the city (Jer
38:6) and built into the roofs of many homes to

A relief of the siege of Lachish by Sennacherib. Photo courtesy of the British Museum. 3-11

catch rain water. In times of war the entrance to springs outside the city walls were concealed (2 Chr 32:4) and a water tunnel was cut from inside the city to the spring. The Siloam Tunnel may have been constructed by Hezekiah to divert the waters of the Spring of Gihon prior to the Assyrian siege of Jerusalem (2 Kgs 20:20). It was driven through solid rock for over 1700 feet by two teams of workmen cutting from opposite directions (Sir 48:17–19). In some places this tunnel is over 155 feet below the ground. Water was stored in the tunnel and was channeled into a pool inside the city. These tunnels could also sometimes be a weak point for the city, as David's men demonstrated when they traversed the tunnel into Jerusalem to surprise and capture the city (2 Sam 5:8).

During the fighting, forces of slingers (2 Kgs 3:25) and archers harried the defenders with flights of missiles, masking the approach of towers or reserve forces. Eventually, an attack was made at a particular spot to breach the wall and enter the city (2 Kgs 25:4). The text indicates that breaching the wall was usually followed by a general pillaging and burning of the city (2 Kgs 14:12–14 and 25:9–11 are two examples of this).

D. POLICY OF DEPORTATION

The ultimate punishment for peoples who continued to revolt against the Assyrians and Babylonians during this period was deportation. Although some cities were used as examples with their entire population slaughtered, this was not something that could be done to every city that revolted. The answer, then, was to deport the trouble-makers to some other portion of the empire where they would have less reason to revolt. Into the empty space created by this deportation, the kings of Assyria transported other subjects from elsewhere in their realm.

In 721 BC the Assyrian king Sargon II captured the Israelite capital city of Samaria after a three-year siege. According to his records, he deported 27,290 people. Second Kings 17:6 states that they were "placed in Halah, and on the Habor, the river of Gozan, and in the cities of the Medes." This ended the monarchy in the northern kingdom and led to the creation of a new people in that area, the Samaritans — a people of mixed origins who inter-married with the Jews who were not deported by the Assyrians.

The other major example of deportation is Nebuchadnezzar's taking of large groups of people from Judah and Jerusalem to the area of Babylon. This was done twice, in 597 and again in 587 BC, following revolts by Jehoiakim (2 Kgs 24:1–16) and Zedekiah (2 Kgs 25:1–11) respectively. Unlike the Assyrian deportation of the people of Israel, however, the descendants of some of Judah's exiles did return to Jerusalem

In the ninth year of Hoshea the king of Assyria captured Samaria; he carried the Israelites away to Assyria. He placed them in Halah, on the Habor, the river of Gozan, and in the cities of the Medes. —2 Kgs 17:6

after 538 BC. This was made possible by the capture of Babylon by Cyrus the Persian king. He
issued a decree (known as the Cyrus Cylinder)
that allowed captive peoples to return to their
countries (Isa 45:1).

The Lion of Babylon. Photo from M. Jastrow,
The Civilization of Babylonia and Assyria. 3-12

4

EXILE AND RETURN

HISTORICAL INTRODUCTION

The period from the Babylonian exile in 597/587 BC until the conquest of the Persian empire by Alexander the Great of Macedon in 332 BC brought drastic changes to the Jewish community in Palestine and in exile. During this period of their history the people of Judah had only minimal control over their own affairs. The power vacuum left by the elimination of the monarchy gave the priestly order new power as the arbitrators for the nation. In order to survive as a people, the Jews in Palestine and in the exilic communities accepted some things which they could not control, while clinging to those aspects of their culture which set them apart as unique: their story of the exodus, the covenant at Sinai, Sabbath observance, and the developing canon of law and history. Even more drastic changes took place in the Hellenistic (331–67 BC) and Roman periods (67 BC–AD 135), but these will be dealt with more fully in the next chapter.

Written sources for this period of Israel's history are incomplete and sometimes difficult to fit together. Aside from the biblical narratives in Ezra and Nehemiah, some information can also be drawn from Haggai, Zechariah, and Malachi. The material in Daniel, while perhaps useful in getting impressions of court life in the Babylonian and Persian periods, has some problems chronologically and may have been written much later than the events it records (note that chs 2–7

Archway of colored and glazed tiles. Photo from M. Jastrow, The Civilization of Babylonia and Assyria. 4-1

*The Cyrus Cylinder. Photo
courtesy of the British Museum.*
4-2

are written in Aramaic, the principal spoken language of the post-exilic era). The apocryphal book of 1 Esdras provides a Greek version of the narrative from 2 Chr 35, through Ezra, to Neh 7:38–8:12. There are some omissions from the biblical narrative in 1 Esdras, which probably reflect the changed concerns of the Maccabean community when the book was compiled.

Extrabiblical sources include the Babylonian court records, the official decrees of the Persian government (including the "Cyrus Cylinder," *ANET,* pp. 315–316), and a variety of legal and business documents from Mesopotamia. There are also letters from the Jewish military colony at Elephantine in Egypt which tell us of life during the Persian regime of the 6th and 5th centuries BC. Josephus, the Jewish historian of the 1st century AD, records some of the events of the return from exile in the eleventh book of his *Antiquities*. His chronicle generally is based on tradition as well as written sources, and thus must be treated carefully by historians.

A. EXILE PERIOD

The traumatic effects of the deportations and the end of the monarchy, plus the destruction of Jerusalem and the temple, forced some drastic shifts in the cultural practices of the peoples of Palestine and the various areas of the exile. One of the most fundamental changes which came to Palestine in the wake of the Assyrian and Babylonian conquests of that region was an end to political independence. The northern kingdom of Israel ceased to exist after 721 BC. A large percentage of the upper and middle class population was deported and was replaced by a mixed population of Jews and non-Jews called the Samaritans. They were ruled as an Assyrian province by a succession of foreign masters and had a strictly limited autonomy in deciding local issues. Provincial boundaries apparently remained the same from the Assyrian through the Persian period. The position of governor, however, appears to have become hereditary in the 5th century with five generations of rulers coming from the Sanballat family.

Judah remained an Assyrian vassal state for another century. For it, the fall of the northern kingdom was coupled with an influx of refugees from the north and the deportation of thousands of its own citizens in 701 after Sennacherib ravaged the Judean countryside. Gradually, however, Assyria's power in Syro-Palestine began to decline. The result was a loosening of controls which set the stage for the Deuteronomic reform movement in Josiah's time (640–609 BC) with its emphasis on religious and political centralization (2 Kgs 23). In particular, Jerusalem and Solomon's temple, more than ever, were identified as the site of Yahweh's presence. The royal theology of the "everlasting covenant" with the Davidic house of kings seemed to have once again been vindicated.

During the wave of enthusiasm associated with the reform movement, Josiah even attempted to expand his control and religious reform to the north at Bethel (2 Kgs 23:4, 8, 15, 19). Eventually, however, Josiah's kingdom also succumbed to the superpower struggles for control of the area. He was killed in an aborted attempt to prevent the Egyptian pharaoh Necho II from reaching the battle of Carchemish (605 BC) in time to help the Assyrians (2 Kgs 23:29–30). Subsequently, Judah became a province first of the Egyptians and then of Babylon.

This period ended with ill-advised revolts by kings Jehoiakim and Zedekiah. In reprisal, Jerusalem was sacked twice and the temple destroyed in 587 BC. A fairly large proportion of the ruling class, including King Jehoiachin, was taken into exile in 597, and two additional deportations took place in 587 and 582 (Jer 52:30). They were settled throughout the Babylonian empire, some perhaps set to the task of rebuilding ruined city sites as the name Tel-Abib suggests (Tel or Tell being the name for an abandoned city mound). Other groups were established near administrative centers such as Calah, Nineveh, Babylon, and Nippur.

Some refugees who fled during the Babylonian conquest went to Egypt, while others scattered into the Transjordanian kingdoms and the Judean wilderness (Ezk 33:24–27). Those that remained behind in Judah were ruled by Babylonian-appointed

In the twenty-third year of Nebuchadrezzar, Nebuzaradan the captain of the guard took into exile of the Judeans seven hundred forty-five persons; all the persons were four thousand six hundred.   —Jer 52:30

governors and were expected to pay tribute from their harvests (Lam 5). For Judah to be able to pay this tribute, however, attempts must have been made to return to normal. For example, an attempt was made to redistribute farm lands to the poor (Jer 39:10). Additional efforts can be seen in the rebuilding of a few city sites (Gibeah, Gibeon, Mizpah, Bethzur, Arad), and the possible resumption of sacrifices in the shrine at Mizpah, or perhaps in the remains of the temple (Jer 41:4 – 5). Still, the realities of foreign domination made life in Jerusalem and the rest of Palestine harsh and dispiriting.

Ishmael son of Nethaniah and the ten men with him got up and struck down Gedaliah son of Ahikam son of Shaphan with the sword and killed him, because the king of Babylon had appointed him governor in the land.
—Jer 41:2

One sign of the indignation the people of Judah felt for their foreign masters was the assassination of the Babylonian-appointed governor, Gedaliah. Although he was a member of a prominent family (Shaphan) previously involved in government affairs (2 Kgs 22:3, 12; Jer 36:10 – 12), the people were apparently angered by his appointment because he was not a member of the Davidic royal house. Their antagonism may have also been increased by his movement of the political capital from ruined Jerusalem to Mizpah. As a result, a faction including members of the royal family took out their frustrations by killing Gedaliah (2 Kgs 25:22 – 26; Jer 41:1 – 3). This act became the justification for the third deportation, although most of the rebels apparently escaped to Egypt (2 Kgs 25:26; Jer 52:30).

The biblical text passes over the historical events of most of the remainder of the exilic period. Babylon went into a swift decline after the death of Nebuchadnezzar in 562. His immediate successor, Evil Merodach, is mentioned in 2 Kgs 25:27 – 30 where he frees King Jehoiachin from house arrest. Jehoiachin, as a ruler in exile, sat at court in a place of honor. He ate from the king's table, and was granted a pension from the royal treasury for life.

However, this Babylonian king was assassi-

Persian emperor. From Biblical Archaeologist. 4-A

I returned the images of their gods to their sanctuaries which had been in ruins for a long period of time. I now established for them permanent sanctuaries. I also gathered all the former inhabitants of these places and returned them to their homes.

Furthermore, upon the command of Marduk, I resettled all The Gods of Sumer and Akkad, which Nabonidus had moved to Babylon, unharmed in their former places to make them happy . . . and I endeavored to repair their dwelling places.

— Cyrus Cylinder

nated two years later and his two successors ruled only five years between them. A palace revolt then placed Nabonidus, a son of a priestess of the moon god Sin, on the throne. His royal chronicle dating from 555 – 539 is filled with references to neglect of his duties as the chief officiant at national religious festivals. This may have been due to his allegiance to his family gods, especially the moon god Sin. Failure to support the chief gods of the pantheon, however, would have angered the powerful Marduk priesthood in Babylon.

Nabonidus made the situation even worse by his long absences from the capital. He spent 10 years fighting the Arab tribes for a portion of the spice trade, and engaged in archaeological projects from his base at Tema in northern Arabia. During this time his son Belshazzar ruled as his co-regent. As a result, opposition grew among the priesthood as well as the general population (Isa 45:1–3). If Cyrus' claims in his victory inscription (Cyrus Cylinder) are to be believed, the priesthood and people of Babylon actually welcomed the Persian king in 539, turning the city and the empire over to his rule with only a minimal amount of fighting.

B. POST-EXILIC PERIOD

Technically the Babylonian exile ended in 538 BC when Cyrus issued a decree allowing all captive peoples to return to their homelands. However, there does not appear to have been a mass exodus of people from Mesopotamia. Initially (Ezr 2:63) only a small group returned to Jerusalem with Sheshbazzar, the new Persian governor of Yehuda (Judea). One tradition is that he was one of Jehoiachin's sons. However, it is just as possible that he was a non-Judean Persian appointee. He is credited with laying the foundations for the new temple and returning the sacred vessels taken by Nebuchadnezzar when he sacked the temple in 587 (Ezr 5:14–15).

A few years later a second and larger group of exiles returned to Jerusalem under the leadership of Jehoiachin's grandson Zerubbabel and the priest Joshua (Hag 1:1). They also experienced some trouble in rebuilding the temple and the ruined portions of the city. The Samaritan governor was suspicious of the returnees, feeling that they might be a threat to his authority. The Samaritans were further angered when Zerubbabel rebuffed their request to help with the rebuilding (Ezr 4:3). Tattenai, governor of the province "Beyond the River," and his associates sent letters to the Persian king trying to delay or end further construction in Jerusalem (Ezr 5:6–8). These tactics worked during the confusing period after the death of Cyrus (530) and his son Cambyses (522), but eventually the Jews received official sanction from the new Persian king Darius and completed construction of the temple in 515.

Once the temple was completed Zerubbabel disappears from the text despite the royal titles given him by the prophets Haggai (2:20–23: "signet ring") and Zechariah (6:12: "the branch"). He may in fact have died or been recalled as governor by the Persian government. However, it is also possible that the biblical writers considered his mission had been fulfilled by the rebuilding of the temple. As a result, his narrative ends and the next stage in the restoration process, rebuilding the walls of Jerusalem, is then addressed.

Speak to Zerubbabel, governor of Judah, saying, I am about to shake the heavens and the earth, . . . —Hag 2:21

One conclusion that can be drawn from this is that political events are of less concern to the biblical authors than religious matters. Thus the revival of the Davidic monarchy takes second place in the narrative to the rebuilding of the temple and the priestly community. A further sign of this shift in priorities is found in the book of Malachi, which is perhaps to be dated to the period immediately after the rebuilding of the

The Mozah jar handle. Photo by Nahman Avigad. 4-3

temple. Attention is given by the prophet to improper sacrifices (1:6–14) and unlawful mixed marriages among the people (2:10–16). However, no real picture of political events can be reconstructed from this book.

Even more frustrating to historians is the fact that the biblical narrative tells us very little about the period from 515 to 445 BC. Reference is made to a succession of governors (Neh 5:15), but no details of the administration of this long period of time are found until the appointment of Nehemiah as Persian governor of Judea by Artaxerxes I (c. 445 BC). The archaeological record is also scanty, providing only a few ring seals, clay bullae (hardened seal impressions), and stamped jar handles that contain the names of provincial governors. No chronological scheme can be determined using this evidence, although it is interesting to note that some of these governors do have Jewish names (Elnathan, Yehoezer, Ahzai).

During the intervening years of the 6th and 5th centuries, the Persian government concentrated its efforts on an attempted conquest of Greece. The energies of the empire were also required to suppress revolts in Egypt (488–484) and in Babylonia (482). Darius and Xerxes, his successor, spent huge sums of money raising and equipping armies for these enterprises. This left little time to consider minor political matters in outlying provinces. Jerusalem's problems were virtually ignored until the war with the Greeks was over. Only then did it became possible to obtain the king's attention for local concerns.

Perhaps taking advantage of this emerging concern for matters within the empire, Nehemiah sought the support of the king to investigate the situation in Jerusalem personally (Neh 1:11–2:8). He had received word of its ruined walls and used his rank within Artaxerxes I's court to obtain permission to rebuild them. Nehemiah is described as the "cup-bearer" of the king. This was a title given to a trusted and generally high-ranking official responsible for tasting the king's food and drink to guard him against assassination by poisoning.

The fact that Nehemiah, a Jew, was in such a high position demonstrates the degree of social mobility within the empire. Apparently, those who chose to remain in exile could find opportunities to advance to even the highest levels of

King Darius I; Xerxes his son stands behind. Photo courtesy of the Oriental Institute of the University of Chicago. 4-4

government. The Persian king also showed good sense by sending a representative to Jerusalem whose cultural and ethnic background were the same as the people he was to investigate.

Upon arrival Nehemiah made a personal inspection of Jerusalem's walls before meeting with the political representatives of the provinces of Judah and Samaria (Neh 2:11–16). Despite the threats of Sanballat the Samaritan governor, Tobiah the leader of the Ammonites, and Geshem the Arab tribal leader, the decision was made to rebuild the walls. Nehemiah brushed aside their opposition saying, "you have no portion or right or memorial in Jerusalem" (Neh 2:20). This may be an assertion of the full independence of the province and the governor of Judah as well as an attempt to separate the religiously suspect Samaritans and other "foreigners" from connection with Jerusalem and the temple.

Sanballat and his allies continued to plot against Nehemiah and the construction in Jerusalem (Neh 4:7). Their plans to attack the city and the workers were not idle threats. Excavations at several sites in central Palestine have revealed destruction levels dating to the period around 480. This evidence may reflect the clashes between Persia and Egypt during this period, but they may also be a sign of intercity warfare. In any case, Nehemiah was able to complete the project and prevent an attack by the Samaritans by arming his workers and posting guards on the walls at night (Neh 4:10–23).

So the wall was finished on the twenty-fifth day of the month Elul, in fifty-two days.
— Neh 6:15

After 52 days the citadel's walls were completed, and the inner city of Jerusalem (the old City of David) was thus secured against attack (Neh 6:15). Sanballat and Tobiah attempted on several occasions to lure Nehemiah into a trap or to discredit him (Neh 6:2–13), but he was able to survive them all (see his statement of honest administration in Neh 5:14–19). Nehemiah then secured his position by appointing Hanani, his brother, and Hananiah, the governor of the citadel, as administrators in Jerusalem (Neh 7:2). Because of the need to resettle the city and provide enough men to defend it (Neh 7:4), a census was taken and lots were cast to determine the one in ten who would live within the newly constructed walls (Neh 11:1).

The remainder of Nehemiah's administration, divided over two terms as Persian governor under Artaxerxes I (Neh 13:6–7), concentrated on civil and religious reforms. A general remission of debts and mortgages was granted to alleviate pressures on the people who had been working on the walls (Neh 5:1–13). Levites were appointed to oversee temple worship, officials were designated to gather taxes and tithes (Neh 12:44–46), and the Sabbath was enforced by closing the gates of the city so business could not be transacted during the holiday (Neh 13:15–21). A further sign of Judah establishing itself as a separate and unique province within the empire was a purge of foreign influence in Jerusalem. For example, Tobiah the Ammonite was expelled from his furnished room within the temple (Neh 13:7–9), and one of the grandsons of Eliashib the high priest was exiled for marrying the daughter of Sanballat (Neh 13:28). In addition, Nehemiah forbade all marriages between Jews and non-Jews (Neh 13:23–27).

And I contended with them and cursed them and beat some of them and pulled out their hair; and I made them take an oath in the name of God, saying, "You shall not give your daughters to their sons, or take their daughters for your sons or for yourselves."
—Neh 13:25

The final stage in post-exilic history chronicled in the biblical text is the career of Ezra the scribe. Although he is traditionally thought to have preceded Nehemiah, there are clear indications in the text that Ezra should be dated to the reign of King Artaxerxes II (404–358 BC). For instance, on his arrival in Jerusalem he found the walls already rebuilt (Neh 9:9). Whatever the time of Ezra, his career also emphasized the religious and social reforms set forth by Nehemiah and brought about the impetus needed to formulate the canon of Scripture.

Ezra's purpose in coming to Jerusalem may have been tied to Persia's desire to control Palestine in the face of growing unrest in Egypt. By establishing a consistent legal system and a strong internal power structure based around the Persian governor and the priests of Yahweh, Artaxerxes may have hoped to ensure the loyalty of the Jews. The Persian government had previously ordered the codification of law in Egypt to prevent disputes over land. Ezra's role in codifying Jewish law could have fit into this administrative practice.

Whatever the reason for his coming, Ezra was given extraordinary powers to administer the province. His letter (Ezr 7:12–26) from the king instructed him: (1) to take with him any Jews who wished to return to Jerusalem, (2) "make inquiries about Judah and Jerusalem according to the law of your God, which is in your hand," and (3) carry with him a great sum of gold and silver with which to purchase animals for sacrifice and for the general fund of the temple. Additional funds, up to a specified limit, could also be obtained from the provincial treasurers for the maintenance of the temple and the cult; and Levites and priests were now to be exempted from the payment of tolls, customs, and other duties (Ezr 7:21–24).

Each of these royal commands was designed to give Ezra a free hand when he arrived in Jerusalem. The large numbers of returnees (over 5,000) would make an impressive entourage, and the wealth Ezra brought to the temple demonstrated the backing of the Persian government and the regard that government had for the religions of its subject peoples. One last stipulation in the letter gave Ezra the power to:

> appoint magistrates and judges who may judge all the people in the province Beyond the River, all such as know the laws of your God; and those who do not know them, you shall teach. (Ezr 7:25; RSV)

Those that chose not to obey Ezra and his judges were subject to punishments ranging from the death penalty to imprisonment or exile and the confiscation of goods (7:26).

Having received his orders, Ezra gathered the group of exiles who would return with him to Jerusalem. After taking a census of these people, it was discovered that there were no Levites among them (Ezr 8:15). A special effort was then made to recruit priests and temple servants "for the house of our God" (8:17). Once these men had been gathered, they were given charge of the gold and silver donated by the king to the temple treasury. The narrative states that they arrived without incident, having escaped ambushes and enemies along the way (8:31). After taking three days to recover from the trip, Ezra publicly placed the contributions in the temple treasury and delivered the king's commission to the provincial officials. Sacrifices of thanksgiving and sin offerings were then made by the newly arrived exiles (8:33–36).

Once these initial steps were taken, Ezra set about investigating the situation in Judah. He heard testimony from officials that mixed marriages between Jews and non-Jews were still occurring (Ezr 9:1–2). Citing the prohibition of these types of marriages as a corruption of the people (Dt 7:3), Ezra demanded that the priests and Levites take an oath to put away wives and children of improper marriages (Ezr 9:12–10:5). He followed this up with a proclamation demanding that all of the exiles assemble for a meeting within three days to deal with this situation (10:7–8).

For they have taken some of their daughters as wives for themselves and for their sons. Thus the holy seed has mixed itself with the peoples of the lands, and in this faithlessness the officials and leaders have led the way.
— Ezra 9:2

This meeting was held in the ninth month (November-December) in an open space in front of the temple. Ezra demanded of the entire assemblage that they separate themselves from the people of the land by putting away (i.e., divorcing) their foreign wives (Ezr 10:9–12). The sheer magnitude of what Ezra was asking them to do caused them to ask for a representative group to be appointed to deal with this issue. These representatives were to investigate the situation in each of the cities and judge individual cases in the local districts (10:13–14). After two months of interviews the names of all of the men who had taken foreign wives were compiled and each man was required to divorce his wife and put away the children of that marriage. In addition, each was forced to make a sin offering of a ram from the flock (10:16–44).

The continuation of Ezra's actions in reforming the religious and social character of the people is found in Nehemiah 8. Using the tradition set at Sinai for a "new beginning" in the life of the people, Ezra staged a covenant renewal ceremony. This involved a public reading of the law and an oath taken by all of the people that they would henceforth adhere to that law (Neh 8:1–6). In conjunction with the reading, however, interpreters of the law helped the people to give "the sense, so that the people understood the reading" (v 8). This was probably due to the fact that Aramaic had become the spoken tongue of that day and the law read by Ezra was in Hebrew.

Following the initial reading of the law, the Feast of Tabernacles was celebrated for seven days. There was a reading of the law on each day of the feast (Neh 8:14–18). Their joyful celebration was then followed by another assembly in which a collective act of penitence was made. Prayers were made confessing past sins while the people stood fasting and in the sackcloth of mourning (Neh 9). The scroll of the law was then signed by the priests and Levites (9:38–10:27), while the remainder of the people took an oath to obey its injunctions (10:28–39). Included in this oath was a set of special regulations involving sacrifice and the payment of tithes in support of the Levites and the temple (10:33–39). These stipulations, as much as anything else, point up

And Ezra opened the book in the sight of all the people, for he was standing above all the people; and when he opened it, all the people stood up. —Neh 8:5

JEWISH HISTORY FROM EXILE TO BAR KOCHBA		
DATE	EVENT	RULERS
587 BC	Jerusalem destroyed by Babylonians. Exile in Babylon begins.	BABYLONIANS
539 BC	Persians invade Babylon. Persian domination begins.	PERSIANS
538 BC	Cyrus' decree permits exiles to return to Jerusalem.	
520 BC	Temple in Jerusalem rebuilt.	
445/444 BC	Walls of Jerusalem rebuilt.	
333 BC	Alexander the Great defeats the Persians. Macedonian rule begins.	MACEDONIANS
323 BC	Alexander dies. His kingdom is divided among his generals.	PTOLEMIES
198 BC	Palestine captured from Egypt by Antiochus III.	SELUCIDS
167-165 BC	Maccabean Rebellion following Antiochus IV's persecution of Jews. Jews recapture temple in Jerusalem.	HASMONEANS
AD 63	Roman general Pompey conquers Jerusalem.	ROMANS
AD 66-70	First Jewish Revolt. Jerusalem destroyed.	
AD 132-135	Second Jewish Revolt (Bar Kochba).	

the enhanced role that the priestly community now had in the shaping of post-exilic Judaism.

No further mention of Ezra or his activities is found in the biblical text. Whether he returned to Persia and the service of the king or remained to enforce the covenant is unknown. However, the strict legalism set forth in his reform galvanized the priests of the second temple into compiling an authoritative version of the law and the history of the people. By the 2nd century, as seen in the writings of Jesus ben Sirach (Sirach or Ecclesiasticus), this had become by tradition the official canon of Hebrew scriptures.

Starting with the Assyrian conquest and deportation of the people of Israel (721 BC), and continuing with the Babylonian destruction of Jerusalem (587 BC), a great Diaspora or scattering of the Jews began. Initially they were spread throughout the Near East, and in later periods under Greek and Roman rule they were scattered throughout the Mediterranean and European countries. What resulted from this and the influences of the Persian culture during the postexilic period was the creation of two basic types of Judaism: Palestinian and Diaspora. While each retained a basic respect for the traditions and the laws as well as the sanctity of Jerusalem, language differences and variances in social climate gradually widened the gulf between them. Even more basic differences arose as a result of Hellenistic (Greek) influences and the politics of the Roman emperors and their administrators. They will be discussed in the next chapter.

I. LIFE IN THE EXILE

What was life like for the people in the various areas of the exile?

With the rule of the monarchy ended and the temple in ruins, many people chose or were forced to leave Palestine. Some were political refugees who fled into temporary exile in the Transjordanian kingdoms. Others founded communities in Egypt (Jer 43:1–7; 44:26). Many of these people chose to remain in Egypt after the exile ended. These and other exiles who came in later periods eventually formed the nucleus of Jewish communities like Alexandria in Egypt. Some of them even served as mercenaries in the armies of that country and Persia. Letters confirming the existence of these communities (dating to the Persian period, c. 420–400 BC) have been found at the Jewish military colony of Elephantine. These documents describe business dealings, contracts, wills, and other aspects of everyday life that suggest the people had settled into their foreign existence.

A similar picture emerges from texts describing life among the exiled Jews in Mesopotamia. They had been forced into exile, carrying a few possessions in their baggage (Ezk 12:1–7), and taken to new settlements where they were required to begin a new life. For some this was a difficult task (Ps 137), but the realities of prolonged captivity must have sobered their hope of a quick return (Ezk 24:15–24) and sparked the energies necessary to get on with their lives.

Despite the loss of their former status and the symbols of past glories, the people were given some hope that the exile would eventually end. For instance, the book of Kings (see also Jer 52:31–34) ends its chronicle with the positive note that Jehoiachin (and presumably his family) was released from house arrest in his 37th year of exile. He was also given a place of honor at King Evil Merodach's table and a pension (2 Kgs 25:27–30). Confirming this are Babylonian ration lists, uncovered by archaeologists, which state that Jehoiachin and his family received yearly allotments from the king.

So Jehoiachin put aside his prison clothes. Every day of his life he dined regularly in the king's presence.
—2 Kgs 25:29

Jehoiachin, while only a king in exile, did apparently function as a sort of mediator for the semi-autonomous Jewish settlements. He was aided in his decisions by the "elders of the exiles" (Jer 29:1), "the elders of Judah" (Ezk 8:1), and "the elders of Israel" (Ezk 14:1; 20:1). Signs that these communities did have some power to manage their own affairs is seen in Ezk 33:30, which describes the freedom of the prophet to speak to the exiles, and in Ezr 8:17–20, which indicates that the temple servants had retained their former status as cultic officials.

As the years went by, many of the exiles became more a part of the land and culture of Mesopotamia. By the second generation they spoke the Mesopotamian dialect of Aramaic and used Aramaic script in writing. They took Babylonian names (Zerubbabel, Mordecai) and functioned as a normal part of the local economy. In calculating their transactions, they went so far as to adopt the use of the Babylonian month names.

Evidence of the cultural adaptation made by the exiled Jews is found in the Murashu documents, found at the southern Mesopotamian city of Nippur and dating to the 5th–4th centuries BC. These legal texts provide documentation that life in the exile was not too restrictive for the Jews. There is no evidence of discrimination against them in matters of business. They paid the same interest rate on loans as everyone else; participated in a wide variety of occupations including date-grower, fisherman, and goat-herder; and negotiated contracts for the use of land as tenant-farmers.

The apparent fullness of life evidenced in these texts may be one explanation of why many of the Jews chose to remain in exile after the Persian decree allowed them the opportunity to return to Palestine. The 1st century AD Jewish historian Josephus suggests that their reluctance to return was based on their "being unwilling to leave their possessions" (*Ant.* 11.59–63).

To be sure, new groups continued to return throughout the Persian period. However, in recruiting these groups of returnees, leaders sometimes found it difficult to obtain a full range of skills and occupations. For instance, when Ezra was gathering the people to return with him to Jerusalem, he found that no Levites had gathered for the trip (Ezr 8:15). As a result, he had to send out messengers to various towns to recruit these temple servants. Ezra may have placed such importance on obtaining Levites for his host of returnees because of his desire to recreate the role of the Levites in the march from Sinai (Num 10:13–28).

I gathered them by the river that runs to Ahava, and there we camped three days. As I reviewed the people and the priests, I found there none of the descendants of Levi. —Ezra 8:15

II. LIFE AFTER THE RETURN FROM EXILE

What was life like for those who chose to return from exile to Palestine?

Perhaps the first place to start in describing life after the exile is with the census lists of those who chose to follow their leaders back to Jerusalem. The list of those who returned with Zerubbabel, the Persian governor (*peha,* Hag 1:1), and Jeshua, the chief priest, is found in Ezr 2:1–70 and Neh 7:6–73. This list contains the names of leaders, clan or family members, temple officials, men of mixed or suspect family origin, servants, and animals. A short appendix to the list is found in Neh 12:1–26, which provides additional information on the priests and Levites who "came up with Zerubbabel." The total number mentioned in the text (45,502) exceeds the numbers of the groups (42,360) listed. However, the total probably includes unnamed or undistinguished members of the group of returnees.

Another census list is found in Ezr 8:1–14. It contains the priestly and secular clans (numbering about 1500) who returned with Ezra. Again the number is probably misleading since only the priestly leaders are listed by name. This emphasis on the priestly members of the company indicates their importance to the writer as well as the post-exilic community. Persian governors, like Zerubbabel and Nehemiah, came and went, but the real character and structure of the post-exilic society was shaped by priests and scribes like Joshua and Ezra.

We can only speculate on exactly who returned to Jerusalem after 538 BC. Certainly, the priests had a vested interest in resuming the cult, and the bureaucrats who accompanied each new governor had a specific job to perform. However, the average individual may have come either out of piety inspired by Isaiah's vision of a glorious procession through the wilderness (40:2–5), or out of a desire to make a new life in a place where land would be easier to obtain and new businesses could flourish.

Now these were the people of the province who came from those captive exiles whom King Nebuchadnezzar of Babylon had carried captive to Babylonia; they returned to Jerusalem and Judah, all to their own towns.

— Ezra 2:1

A. POLITICAL CONDITIONS

Whatever their reason for coming, the former exiles found on their arrival a ruined capital city and a neglected countryside. They also quickly discovered that Judah was only one small province (*medinah*) within the larger administrative unit (*satrapy*) of "Beyond the River" (Ezr 4:11). As such, they could not expect the Persian government to pay any more interest to them than their neighboring states. They could do nothing about the resettlement of some of Judah's former territory by Edomites and Ammonites or the control held by the Arab tribes over Gaza and the routes south to Egypt. It also quickly became evident that their every move was being watched by the neighboring governors. The returned exiles represented a potential political threat to their influence in the region. This was especially true for the governor of Samaria. Thus it is not surprising that Samaritan governors and their allies for over 100 years attempted to obstruct the rebuilding of Jerusalem as an administrative center (Ezr 4:4 – 6; Neh 4:1 – 9).

B. CITY PLANNING

Since the biblical narrative concentrates on the rebuilding of Jerusalem's temple and wall (Ezr 3:8 – 6:15; Neh 2 – 4), little is known about the dwellings of its inhabitants. Some small amount of construction on the ruined site was probably allowed by Babylonian governors as long as it served no military purpose. There are some indications that Jerusalem may have still served as a place where religious pilgrims could come to worship. The passage in Jer 41:4 – 6, which describes pilgrims coming to Gedaliah's court in Mizpah, at least suggests that worship was planned, whether in Mizpah or Jerusalem.

At the end of the exile it seems reasonable, although there is no archaeological evidence to support it, that the returning Jews restored some of the buildings in the ruined portions of Jerusalem to provide themselves with housing and business space (Hag 1:4). After a delay of over 20 years, the temple was rebuilt under the direction of Zerubbabel in 515 BC (Ezr 6:15). At this point, however, the city walls had not been rebuilt and the majority of the people would have lived in nearby villages and farms. The prophets Haggai (1:10–11) and Joel (1:4, 9–12) describe the hardships faced by these farmers, who lost crops to flights of locust and to drought. Still, no substantial number of people would have been attracted to settling in Jerusalem until its fortifications were repaired and it stood once again as a symbol of Israelite nationalism.

And this house was finished on the third day of the month of Adar, in the sixth year of the reign of King Darius.
—Ezra 6:15

This important step in rebuilding the pride of the Jewish people was accomplished by the Persian governor Nehemiah. Because of the limited resources and manpower in Palestine, Nehemiah confined his construction to the eastern hill of the city, the site of the City of David, and the temple mount. Support for this conclusion is provided by modern excavations in Jerusalem. Material from the Persian period has only been uncovered on the eastern side of the site.

Utilizing a mixed workforce, and assigning each group to work on a particular portion of the wall, the new inhabitants completed fortifications and gates of this small area of the total city site in 52 days (Neh 3:1–6:15). Again, it seems likely that further construction took place after this, but archaeological evidence is still lacking.

Housing for the *nethinim* (temple servants) and priests, within the newly walled area, was constructed on the ridge of the Ophel, near the sanctuary. Shops for the tradesmen guilds and artisans, including jewelers, were located to the east and southeast of the walls of the temple mount. Other commercial and industrial districts which supplied the city's needs were

When it began to be dark at the gates of Jerusalem before the sabbath, I commanded that the doors should be shut and gave orders that they should not be opened until after the sabbath. And I set some of my servants over the gates, to prevent any burden from being brought in on the sabbath day. — Neh 13:19

probably located outside the city walls (Neh 3:8, 11). Evidence for this is found in Nehemiah's order that the gates of the city be closed on the Sabbath. His action prevented the entrance of Tyrian fishmongers and other merchants on this holy day (Neh 13:15–21).

Most of what is known about city construction and planning outside of Jerusalem in the Persian period comes from excavations in the more heavily settled areas of the Galilee and the coastal plain. This information is limited, however, since some of the most important cities (Megiddo and Jericho) were abandoned during this period and badly eroded as a result. Others that did survive destruction after the fall of Babylon, like Samaria and Ashdod, had their Persian era strata badly damaged by construction during the Hellenistic and Roman occupation.

Relatively intact evidence of the Persian occupation has been found at the coastal cities of Tell Megadim and Shiqmona, and at Elephantine in Egypt. At these sites a standard gridiron pattern was used in some quarters of the city. This was an obvious innovation over the narrow, twisting street patterns common to earlier periods. Here large tracts of houses were built on either side of a road which was crossed by avenues running perpendicular to it. Similar homogeneous housing patterns have been found in the Persian cities in Greece (Olynthus) and at Sardis in Anatolia, indicating a standard in construction throughout the empire.

Those sites in Judah that were rebuilt and fortified by the Persians and the returned exiles were not strengthened to the extent that they had been in the past. Lachish's wall, for instance, was constructed of fill from previous walls and buildings, and field stones laid over a two-meter layer of collapsed debris. Its gateway was also rebuilt, with both sides enlarged and guarded by towers. The entranceway was plastered with clay and soft chalk over a gravel base to accommodate the flow of traffic to and from the city (also found at Megiddo and Tell Dan in Iron Age strata). This suggests a role for the city more commercial than defensive.

The excavated portion of Jerusalem's wall dating to the Persian era (summit of eastern hill) also shows signs of being built with less care than in the past. For instance, cracks in the spaces between standing stones were simply filled with smaller stones. Perhaps the haste with which Nehemiah rebuilt the walls (52 days) is one explanation for this style of construction (Neh 4:21–23). It may also reflect a lack of materials and a decision on the part of the Persian government to prevent true refortification of these cities at the edge of the empire.

C. DOMESTIC ARCHITECTURE

The one innovation to domestic architecture in the post-exilic period was the introduction of the "open court house." Originally brought to Palestine by the Assyrians, this structure remained practically unchanged in style throughout the Babylonian and Persian occupations. It consisted of a central open court with rooms on three or four sides. This lack of uniformity may have reflected the construction site or the relative affluence of the owner. It also may have been based on a pattern found in Mesopotamian cities in which buildings are linked into units sharing a common partition wall.

The governor's residence at Lachish also contains some Persian architectural innovations. Among these was the use of drum-shaped columns on cut stone bases, which supported the porch and lined the stairways—both of which are found in Persian and Greek palaces and temples elsewhere. The building also had a vaulted stone roof and arched doorways. Rooms containing storage areas and residential apartments were arranged around a central courtyard. The entire structure, except for the columns, was constructed of stone salvaged from the ruins of earlier buildings.

For those Jews who lived in the farming villages in Judah, housing remained much as it had in earlier periods. Depending on the relative wealth of the occupants, the courtyard house, of one or two stories, continued to be the principal style of construction. Excavated levels within these villages from the Persian period contain some new pottery types (some imported from Greece and Cyprus), a few Persian and Greek coins, and the usual array of domestic items common to every Israelite home.

D. MARRIAGE CUSTOMS

One of the chief desires of the returning exiles was to settle quickly and profitably into community life in Palestine. To achieve this, many of them married into the prominent Moabite, Ammonite, and Samaritan families of Judah and Samaria (Ezr 9:1–2). This often required the divorce of Jewish wives in order to make this new, more advantageous family alliance possible (Mal 2:13–16). This practice was apparently quite common from the beginning of the return from exile until Ezra's time at the end of the 5th century BC. It brought with it social acceptability for the exiles, as well as assured title to land.

On at least two separate occasions, however, a concerted attempt was made by governors of Judah to outlaw these mixed marriages. Nehemiah's ordering of strict endogamy (marriage within the group) had a variety of causes. For one thing, these marriage alliances, especially with the noble families of Samaria, threatened the political independence of the province of Judah. If enough of the ruling class from both areas became allied by marriage, a case could be made to the Persian government to unite them under a single ruler.

Thus, when he learned that the grandson of Eliashib the high priest had become the son-in-law of the Samaritan governor Sanballat, he expelled the young man as a defiler of the priesthood (Neh 13:28–29).

Another reason given for banning these mixed marriages is offered in both Nehemiah's and Ezra's reform decrees. They bemoaned the fact that children of these marriages no longer spoke the language of Judah. Instead they were taught the language of their Moabite, Ammonite, and Ashdodite mothers (Neh 13:22–24; Ezr 9:1–2). Their social and religious heritage was quickly being lost in the Persian imperial melting pot. Recognizing this, Nehemiah cited the precedent set by King Solomon, who had married many foreign wives and thus brought idolatry to Israel (Neh 13:26–27). This final argument was his justification for demanding that the people cleanse themselves "from everything foreign" (Neh 13:30).

Ezra took the religious arguments against these marriages a step farther by orchestrating a dramatic series of events. After performing acts which were usually associated with mourning (rent his garments, pulled out his hair, and fasted), and quoting the law (Dt 7:3) which prohibited marriages with the people of Canaan, Ezra further shamed them by praying and weeping in public (Ezr 9:3–10:1). The leaders then proposed making a covenant prohibiting such marriages. Ezra appeared to take this under advisement and then decreed that all of the returned exiles assemble within three days to deal with this issue (10:2–8).

Do not intermarry with them, giving your daughters to their sons or taking their daughters for your sons, . . . —Deut 7:3

The assembly of the people in Jerusalem took place in a rainstorm, further dampening their spirits, but also making it harder for Ezra to achieve a quick solution. As a compromise, a panel of elders was created to investigate mixed marriages throughout the province, including those of priests and other temple officials. Within two months they had completed their job of compiling a list of those men with foreign wives and the children (Ezr 10:17). These men then pledged to put aside their wives and children and make a guilt offering (Ezr 10:16–44; Neh 10:28). Such a radical solution was deemed necessary in order to purify the people, and especially the priesthood. Only then was a covenant renewal ceremony conducted and the nation once again proclaimed as the people of Yahweh (Neh 8–10).

E. ECONOMIC LIFE

As might be expected, the economy of the province of Judah continued to be based on agricultural production. The initial problems of repairing hillside terraces and reclaiming abandoned fields were dealt with by the first groups of returnees. It was the duty of the governor to aid them in this task, since it was his responsibility to see to it that the province became productive enough to pay its taxes (Neh 5:15). The smaller population of Judah after the return from exile meant a larger concentration of land in the hands of a few families and a general labor shortage. Those who attempted to work small farms ran into the double problem of paying taxes and farm debts. When a bad harvest occurred, they were forced to either forfeit on their mortgages or sell themselves and their families into slavery to pay off their debts (Neh 5:3–5).

Nehemiah attempted to deal with this problem, bringing charges against the nobles and officials who had been demanding interest on loans, and thus driving their fellow Israelites further into debt (Neh 5:6–9). He loaned the destitute farmers money and distributed grain to their families. Furthermore, their creditors were required to return all confiscated lands and interest payments (5:10–13).

The former governors who were before me laid heavy burdens on the people, and took food and wine from them, besides forty shekels of silver. Even their servants lorded it over the people. But I did not do so, because of the fear of God. — Neh 5:15

Aside from farming, the other economic activities practiced in the cities and towns of Judah benefited from membership in the Persian empire. Most obvious among these economic benefits came with the granting of the right to strike its own coinage. This helped standardize commercial transactions and also contributed to a return of national pride. From the 6th century on, coins bearing "Yehuda" were circulated within the country and the empire. A sign that they were a product of the Persian period, however, was the inclusion of the Athenian owl on one side of these coins.

Yāw, *coin of Gaza, ca. fourth century B.C.* 4-C

The road system, so important to communication and commerce, was maintained and expanded by the government, and caravans were protected by groups of soldiers and horsemen (Ezr 8:22). Luxury goods and manufactured items were transported by sea and land throughout the empire, coming to the markets of Judah on a regular basis. The traders from Tyre on the Phoenician coast brought all sorts of wares to Jerusalem (Neh 13:16), including dried fish, perfumes and ointments from Arabia, fine pottery and jewelry from Greece and the Persian provinces on Cyprus and in Anatolia, and metal utensils and weapons from Mesopotamia or Egypt.

Tyrians also, who lived in the city, brought in fish and all kinds of merchandise and sold them on the sabbath to the people of Judah, and in Jerusalem.
— Neh 13:16

Craftsmen of various types (Neh 3:31) served the needs of the local population and produced goods which could be exported. A business district outside the walls of Jerusalem was apparently established where the stalls of these craftsmen and traders were constructed (Neh 13:20). Just as Ahab placed Israelite merchants in the bazaars of Damascus in the 9th century (1 Kgs 20:34), this area near Jerusalem most likely included both Israelites as well as foreign merchants from throughout the empire. Having access to such a variety of goods would have raised the standard of living of the city and added to the temptations to adopt foreign customs. This was probably in

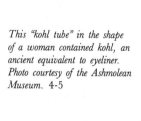

This "kohl tube" in the shape of a woman contained kohl, an ancient equivalent to eyeliner. Photo courtesy of the Ashmolean Museum. 4-5

Nehemiah's mind when he ordered the closing of the gates of Jerusalem on the Sabbath to prevent commercial activity on that day sacred to the Jews (Neh 13:19).

F. BURIAL CUSTOMS

Looking at the 6th century it is difficult to discern any changes in burial customs other than in the grave goods left with the body. Rock-cut tombs with benches along the walls and a straight entrance continue to be used. The chief means of identifying a transition into the Persian period is the increased number of metal burial offerings. These include bowls, mirrors, strainers, and bracelets. Imported Egyptian cosmetic jars made of alabaster and black kohl (eye makeup) sticks are also found in these tombs.

In the 5th and 4th centuries there are two main types of tombs in Palestine: the shaft tomb and the pit grave. The shaft tomb, with either a vertical shaft or sloping steps down to the burial chamber, is found primarily along the coastal plain. These tombs were constructed by wealthy

Phoenicians for themselves or for the Persian officials of the area. Tombs of this type have been excavated at Gezer, Lachish, Dor, Gesher ha-Ziv, as well as several other sites.

Pit graves, in which the body is buried in a shallow depression, were common among the less well-to-do inhabitants of Palestine. Among the sites so far excavated which contain this grave type are Hazor and Tell el-Hesi. Grave goods in these tombs include examples of Greek pottery, alabaster jars, Phoenician coins, and gold jewelry.

III. RELIGIOUS LIFE

In what ways did religious life change during the exilic and post-exilic periods?

In what had been the northern kingdom of Israel, ties to the Yahwist faith were mixed with the ideas of the new settlers brought in by the Assyrians after 721. These peoples included representatives from the Transjordanian kingdoms as well as Mesopotamia. Eventually, their religious practices began to center on the early history of Israel and its link to Shechem and Mt. Gerizim. Their major shrine was built there (*Ant.* 11.346–347) in the time of Alexander the Great (c. 330 BC).

For the exiles and the people who remained behind in Palestine after the destruction of Jerusalem and the deportation of many of its people to Mesopotamia, one direct sign of change came in the message of the prophets. They now began to place a greater emphasis on apocalyptic themes featuring the restoration of the nation and the "reign of Yahweh." Ezekiel's visions of the "valley of dry bones" (37:1–14) and the "restored temple" (chaps 40–48) are good examples of this theme. In addition there emerged in the exilic communities a greater reliance on the law and the priests who interpreted it. This development came at the expense of the monarchy, an institution which had been made defunct by historical events.

Initially the exiles found it difficult to worship away from the Jerusalem temple (Ps 137). Some would have fallen into the worship of the Mesopotamian gods or a mixed religion including both Yahweh and the gods of their captors. Others, who wished to remain strict Yahwists, were reassured by Jeremiah's claim that they could worship God in Babylon (29:5–9). When they came to the realization that the return would not come as soon as they had hoped, they placed greater emphasis on prayer and certain aspects of the law which set them apart from their captors. These included various laws prescribing ritual purity (including dietary habits), Sabbath observance, and circumcision. The prohibition against marriage outside the group was also enforced by leaders of the post-exilic community (Ezr 9; 10:10–15) and may have had its origins among the stricter customs of the exiles in Mesopotamia.

It may be that the synagogue or some similar place of nonsacrificial worship also developed in the period of the Babylonian exile as a response to the loss of the temple in Jerusalem (Ezk 11:16). This is based on the fact that synagogues are prominently mentioned as functioning in the New Testament period (Mt 4:23; Mk 1:21; Lk 4:16). Although no physical evidence has been found for a synagogue prior to the 1st century AD, some time would have been necessary for the synagogue to develop as a part of the community's religious life. It is therefore generally considered that they existed in Mesopotamia, Egypt, and Palestine at least two centuries prior to the Christian era, if not before.

Another factor which suggests the possibility of some sort of worship place being established in the exilic communities is the large numbers of

But seek the welfare of the city where I have sent you into exile, and pray to the LORD on its behalf, for in its welfare you will find your welfare. —Jer 29:7

priests and Levites (including Ezekiel) who were taken into the exile. They undoubtedly continued to provide for the religious needs of the people, even though they no longer had a temple to serve as the focal point of their worship activity. A non-sacrificial cult, which emphasized prayer and the study of the law, would have presented little political threat. Some accommodation with the Babylonian and Persian governments must have been made allowing this to take place. That priests and Levites still existed as something more than ceremonial titles when the exile ended suggests they continued to have an active role in worship.

Why do you provoke me to anger with the works of your hands, making offerings to other gods in the land of Egypt where you have come to settle? Will you be cut off and become an object of cursing and ridicule among all the nations of the earth?

—Jer 44:8

In Egypt, the refugees from Palestine established communities which maintained some contact with Jerusalem. Jeremiah wrote to them condemning their improper rituals, such as burning incense to foreign gods (44:2–10). During the 5th century, the Jewish colony at Elephantine built a temple to serve the cultic needs of its community. This was a clear violation of the Deuteronomic reform that required all cultic activity to take place in Jerusalem (Dt 12 and 1 Kgs 23). In this instance, however, the religious needs of the people in the Diaspora may have outweighed this prohibition (see Isa 19:19–22 for the prophecy of an altar in Egypt).

The influence of the polytheistic society in which they were living may have also softened the restrictions against the worship of other gods. The letters from Elephantine mention worship of Yahu (= Yahweh) by these Jewish mercenaries. However, they also describe sacrifices being made and oaths being taken in the name of the Canaanite goddess Anat as well as several other gods.

A. POST-EXILIC RELIGIOUS PRACTICES

Following the return from exile, several forces were at work which molded post-exilic Judaism. Some voices, perhaps encouraged by the aid given them by the Persian empire, advocated a

he says, "It is too light a thing that you should be my servant to raise up the tribes of Jacob and to restore the survivors of Israel; I will give you as a light to the nations, that my salvation may reach to the end of the earth."

—Isa 49:6

return of all of the people of Israel to Jerusalem where a rejuvenated Judaism would provide a framework of worship for all nations (Isa 49:5–6). Universalism, however, was not the theological path chosen by most of the leaders of the returned exiles or those who remained in Mesopotamia. They had worked to protect the cultural identity of the people while they were in exile by emphasizing the covenant they had made at Sinai. Obedience to the law and maintenance of proper worship practices thus came to represent the unique character of the people of Yahweh. The Torah (Pentateuch) and these ceremonial practices provided them with a sense of continuity with their past and kept hope alive that it could be revived.

B. The Role of the Priesthood

The priests and Levites were considered the protectors of the law and the officiants at all religious ceremonies. As a result, it is not surprising that when the first groups of exiles returned, four families of priests, numbering 4,289, joined the caravan (Neh 7:39–42). What is unusual is that only 74 Levites were in the company (Neh 7:43); fewer even than the number (392) of temple servants and singers who had chosen to make the journey (Neh 7:44–60). One explanation for this is that more priests were taken into exile than Levites, and these numbers simply represented the ratio of their descendants.

Another argument, however, is based on the competition between priestly groups which dated back to David's bringing the ark of the covenant to Jerusalem and his division of cultic responsibilities between Abiathar and Zadok (2 Sam 20:25). In the transition between the reigns of David and Solomon, Zadok and his descendants won the chief place in the priestly community and Abiathar was exiled to Anathoth, 2 1/4 miles north of Jerusalem (1 Kgs 2:26, 35). The Levites were thereafter given a secondary role in the

temple hierarchy behind the Zadokite priesthood. They became "temple servants," but had
no claim to the chief priesthood or to the sacrificial functions of the priests. The only change in
this posture came after the fall of Jerusalem
when most of the priests were killed (2 Kgs 25:18 –
21) or taken into exile. With no one else to officiate at sacrifices, Levites were probably pressed
into service to keep the cultic practices going in
Judah (Jer 41:5).

When it became possible for the exiled Levites
to return to Jerusalem, they may have decided
that exile was better than a return to an inferior
status in Palestine. The Zadokite priests could be
expected to resume their position as the chief religious officials. The descendants of Levites who
had led the worship of the people during the exile
may have had other ideas on this subject. However, when the priests arrived in Judah some compromise must have been made with these Levites
since the text makes no mention of a conflict between them. Feelings between the two groups
may have softened during the exile when they
had to work together to preserve the law. One
sign of this may be the importance Ezra placed
on including Levites within his company of returning exiles (Ezr 8:15 – 20).

A higher regard for the Levites is also found
in the account of the Chronicler (probably written around 300 BC). This suggests that the Levites took on a much more important role in
the worship during the post-exilic period. While
still subordinate to the "sons of Aaron" (perhaps a less offensive title for the priests), the
Levites had charge of the administration of the
temple (2 Chr 24:6, 11). They also had duties
that at least touched on worship: cleansing of
holy objects and chambers, the preparation of
the showbread and cereal offerings, and service
as a choir of thanksgiving during burnt offerings
(1 Chr 23:27 – 32).

But their duty shall be to assist the descendants of Aaron for the service of the house of the LORD, having the care of the courts and the chambers, the cleansing of all that is holy, and any work for the service of the house of God; . . . —1 Chr 23:28

The enhanced role portrayed for the priests and Levites in Chronicles does not fully explain the initial difficulties the clergy had in establishing themselves in Palestine. Like the other returnees, they craved acceptance from the authorities already in the land. For instance, Tobiah the Ammonite was given a specially furnished chamber within the temple precincts by Eliashib the high priest (Neh 13:4–5). The idea may have been to gain the support (political and financial) of this important official and his people for the Jerusalem priesthood. Whatever the case, Nehemiah, representing the strict Yahwism of the exile, refused to allow a foreigner access to the temple and had Tobiah the Ammonite expelled (Neh 13:7–9).

Apparently, a great deal of the energies of the returned exiles was taken up with reopening the land to farming and rebuilding the temple and the city fortifications. The payment of tithes to support the work of the priesthood became secondary to these tasks, and was simply not paid in some years. Nehemiah found many Levites and singers who had had to leave the temple service in order to survive (Neh 13:10). He ordered that the regular tithes of grain, wine, and oil be brought to the temple storehouses. The responsibility for distribution of these commodities was then given to a committee of trustworthy priests and Levites (Neh 13:12–14).

I also found out that the portions of the Levites had not been given to them; so that the Levites and the singers, who had conducted the service, had gone back to their fields. — Neh 13:10

C. WORSHIP IN THE SECOND TEMPLE

Two factors direct much of the worship in the exile and second temple period. They are the emphasis on proper action and the enhanced role of the priesthood in directing this proper action by the people. The "Holiness Code" of Leviticus 17–26 set the standard for worship, ensuring ritual purity and orderly religious activities. Under this code of law, all worship was to be conducted with the proper solemnity by the priests. When sacrifices were made, care was to be taken to guarantee that they were performed at the proper time, using the prescribed rituals and prayers appropriate to the type of sacrifice involved (Lev 23:10–13). Special attention was to be given to every detail to assure that the ritual in no way resembled that of the idolatrous religions of Canaan or Mesopotamia (Lev 18:1–5).

Sacrifice also served as a link with the past for the returned exiles. By reinstituting the major forms of sacrifice, which had not been performed during the exile, the covenant was renewed and the temple worship of the monarchy period was reenacted. Those sacrifices tied to the religious calendar required pilgrimages to the temple for the major festivals (Neh 8:17–18). This allowed the priests to reinforce their authority while at the same time strengthening the practice of the Yahweh cult. Individual sacrifices and guilt offerings involved the use of priests and further established a tie between the community and the priesthood.

Within the laws of the sacrificial cult, proper observance of the Sabbath was of particular importance because it was one of those religious activities of the Jews which was unparalleled by any other people of the ancient Near East. It set them apart just as it set the day apart in recognition of Yahweh's role as the creator. The Sabbath served both as a weekly reminder of the covenant with God and as the basis for calculation of all religious festivals (Lev 23:1–42).

Speak to the people of Israel and say to them: These are the appointed festivals of the LORD that you shall proclaim as holy convocations, my appointed festivals.
—Lev 23:2

The major religious festivals were celebrated on the first day of each lunar month. The most important were Passover and the Feast of Unleavened Bread in the first month (Lev 23:5–8), the Feast of Trumpets in the seventh month (23:23–25), the Feast of Weeks at the beginning of the wheat harvest (23:15–21), and the Feast of Booths at the end of the harvest (23:4–35). They comprised general convocations of the people to mark the yearly harvests and to remember the

		THE SACRED CALENDAR AND MAJOR FEASTS OF JUDAISM AND CHRISTIANITY			
JEWISH MONTH NAMES	CANNANITE MONTH NAMES	BABYLONIAN MONTH NAMES	JULIAN MONTH NAMES	JEWISH FEASTS	CHRISTIAN COUNTERPART
Nisan	Abib	Nisanu	March-April	Passover (14th) Unleavened Bread (15th, 7 days)	Easter
Iyyar	Ziv	Ayaru	April-May		
Sivan		Simanu	May-June	Feast of Weeks	Pentecost
Tammuz		Du-uzu	June-July		
Ab		Abu	July-August		
Elul		Elulu	August-September		
Tishri	Ethanim	Tehsritu	September-October	Rosh Hashanah (1st) Yom Kippur (10th) Feast of Booths (15th, 7 days)	
Marcheshvan	Bul	Arah-samma	October-November		
Chislev		Kislimu	November-December	Hanukkah	Christmas
Tebeth		Tebitu	December-January	(25th, 8 days)	
Shebat		Shabatu	January-February		
Adar		Adaru	February-March	Feast of Purim (14th, 15th)	

major events in the history of the people. The feasts also promoted an ingathering of the Jews from throughout the Near East to Jerusalem.

During the exilic and post-exilic periods, several new feasts were instituted and others made more elaborate. For instance, Purim was a festival created as a celebration of Esther's deliverance of the Jews from destruction in the Persian period. Another feast included in the religious calendar of this period was the Day of Atonement (Lev 23:27 – 32). It is not mentioned in any pre-exilic text or in Nehemiah, but, like many feasts, it may have its origin in the settlement period. The Day of Atonement eventually became one of the most solemn rituals in the Jewish calendar. This yearly ritual (described in Leviticus 16, including the earlier ritual of the "scapegoat"), observed on the 10th day of the seventh month, was designed to atone for the sins of the people in the previous year. Blood from the sacrifice of a bull and a goat then were rubbed and sprinkled on the altar and within the Holy of Holies by the high priest. This double expiation restored the ritual purity of the sanctuary and of the nation.

Within the strict system of laws developed in the period after the exile, attention was also given to protecting the individual and the community from all forms of contamination. Thus, just as the animal or cereal offering had to meet the requirements for sacrifice, associations (business and social) also had to be scrupulously correct. Every attempt had to be made to avoid the taint of the unclean and the foreign. In this regard, the genealogical system became extremely important as a means of determining membership in the priesthood (Ezr 2:1–63; Neh 12:1–26), as well as proper or correct lineage for the rest of the people.

According to these statutes, lepers (all those with discolorations or "eruptions of the skin"), their dwellings, and clothing were to be examined by the priests. They were expelled from the community if no signs of healing were noted within seven days (Lev 13–14). Similarly, menstruating women and men defiled by sexual or other body emissions were to be avoided until they had been cleansed through ritual purification and bathing (Lev 15:16–18).

When a person has on the skin of his body a swelling or an eruption or a spot, and it turns into a leprous disease on the skin of his body, he shall be brought to Aaron the priest or to one of his sons the priests.
—Lev 13:2

The degree of ritual purity required of individual members of the community was based on their family background and occupation. The high priest was thus required to guard himself against contamination even more strictly than the lay member of the community (Lev 21:10–15). As the only member of the nation who could enter the Holy of Holies (Lev 16:2), it was imperative that he stand apart as a symbol of ritual purity. To a lesser degree, the other priests also practiced rites that kept them ritually pure. For instance, bathing of the body and clothing were required of priests after performing sacrifices (Num 19:7–8).

To determine those who could freely participate in the ritual activities of the temple, the entire nation was divided according to the pattern set in the genealogical list in Neh 7:7–60. The population of Judah was therefore made up of the following classifications: priests, Levites, laypersons, converted Jews, men of uncertain descent, eunuchs, and non-Jews. To participate fully in the religious activities of the community, a person had to be able to provide proof of pure lineage (Ezr 2:59–63).

The increased influence of the priesthood in the life of the returned exiled is reflected in the amount of religious activity it generated. In addition to the reestablishment of the sacrificial practices, the use of the Psalms became even more formalized in Jewish worship. As part of the process of creating the canon of sacred texts, the Psalter was organized into the song book of the second temple. Thus the Chronicler's description of the musical guilds established in David's time (1 Chr 25) probably reflects the situation in the period after the exile.

David and the officers of the army also set apart for the service the sons of Asaph, and of Heman, and of Jeduthun, who should prophesy with lyres, harps, and cymbals. The list of those who did the work and of their duties was: . . .

—1 Chr 25:1

There was also an integration of new cultic practices and religious festivals into the service of worship in this period. Continuity with past practices was a goal, but there were some changes in the types of sacrifices offered. For example, holocausts (burnt offerings) became more frequent in the post-exilic period. In general, it can be said that the increased sophistication of temple activities was due to the enhanced role of the priestly class. The role of the priests continued to grow in importance during the Hellenistic and Roman periods. However, they had to cope with the political ambitions of their rulers, as well as competing philosophies and mystery religions introduced by the Greeks.

5

INTERTESTAMENTAL AND NEW TESTAMENT PERIOD

Jerash forum. Photo by V. Matthews. 5-1

HISTORICAL INTRODUCTION

In this final chapter on the manners and customs of Bible times, the focus will be on the transformations in Palestine during the Hellenistic and Roman periods. Attention will also be given to the origins of the Christian movement within its social context. The primary factors responsible for these events are the introduction of Hellenistic culture after the conquest of the Near East by Alexander the Great of Macedon (336–323 BC), and the emergence of the Roman world empire in the period from about 150 BC to AD 150. Jewish resistance to these forces of change briefly allowed for the formation of an independent Jewish state. The Hasmonean (Maccabean) kingdom, however, soon succumbed to the petty ambitions of its rulers and was easily absorbed into the Roman domain.

Syro-Palestine had long been the victim of the ambitions of the Near Eastern superpowers. The Jews, though, were able to maintain a basic continuity of belief and worship despite the syncretistic influences of the Assyrian, Babylonian, and Persian cultures. This can be seen in Daniel 1–7. Although this was written in the time of the Maccabean revolt (168–165 BC), the model of courage exemplified by its four young heroes speaks of resistance to oppression in earlier periods as well.

Hellenistic philosophies and urban-based administrative policies of the Greeks succeeded in doing what earlier civilizations could not — spark a new set of priorities in Judaism. The sense of world culture implicit in Hellenism contributed to the creation of a new, Hellenized Judaism in Palestine and throughout the Diaspora. Thus, when the Romans came, the Jews were more ready to deal with the cosmopolitan attitudes of a world empire. They became a part of its commercial and social life and contributed in their own way to its blend of many cultures.

The success of the Christian movement can also be attributed to the general social atmosphere first created by the Greeks and then perpetuated by the Romans. Popular philosophies such as Stoicism and Epicureanism were very attractive in the period from the first century BC to the third century AD. Mystery religions like Mithradism were readily adopted by the Roman legionnaires, and were spread by the soldiers, merchants, and traveling philosophers. In a world where the only requirement was loyalty to Rome, new ideas could take root with little hindrance. They were particularly attractive to the disenchanted, the disadvantaged, and the seeker of fresh knowledge. Safe and well-constructed travel routes were a final ingredient in the phenomenal growth of Christianity, as well as many other new religions during this time.

A. BACKGROUND TO HELLENISM: THE PERSIAN PERIOD

While they were under the rule of the Persians, the Jews of Palestine enjoyed a period of nearly 200 years of relative peace. This allowed them to rebuild their destroyed cities and reestablish economic stability within their province. Agricultural lands were returned to cultivation; industrial activity resumed after being dormant during the Babylonian exile.

A greater emphasis on urbanization also began in the Persian period. Jerusalem, with its
walls rebuilt and the temple once again functioning as a center of religious activity, provided a
focal point for life and a model of urbanism for
the other cities and towns of Judah. The strength
of Persian authority throughout the empire also
assured a continuous stream of foreign businessmen into Palestine and the creation of a more cosmopolitan culture there. A greater acceptance of
the outside world made the transition to Hellenistic domination easier for many Jews.

The second major factor influencing the formation of Jewish culture during the period of Persian rule was the elimination of the civil office of
the king of Judah. One direct result of this policy
was the enhancement of the position of the high
priest in Jerusalem. He became the titular religious and civic head of the Jewish community,
bowing only to the authority of the Persian king
and his governor. The high priest's position was
confirmed by the Persian government (Ezr 7:11–
26), and further solidified by his control of the
sacrificial cult in Jerusalem.

According to tradition, the office was to be
held by a member of the Zadokite priestly family
(Ezr 7:1–6). The continuity this family tie had to
temple worship during the pre-exilic period provided legitimacy to the position of high priest.
It also was a reassurance to the people that, at
least in matters of religion, nothing had changed.
Because of the influence wielded by this office,
however, it became increasingly secularized. As
a result, to serve as high priest or to be able to
choose who would hold that post became a political prize that was contested for throughout the period of Hasmonean rule (165–63 BC).

A third important development during the Persian period was the initiation of the canonization
process. This also was related to the growth in importance of the priestly community. Among its

*This Ezra went up from Baby-
lonia. He was a scribe skilled in
the law of Moses that the LORD
the God of Israel had given; and
the king granted him all that he
asked, for the hand of the LORD
his God was upon him.*
—Ezra 7:6

concerns was that the oral as well as written traditions of the people of Israel be compiled. After
the traumatic experience of the exile, the priests
wanted to be certain that sacrifice and other cultic acts were performed regularly and correctly.
They hoped to ensure God's continued good will
by a strict conformity to the law. Thus it had
to be written down and canonized into an authoritative document, the Torah, which could be
consulted to prevent future mistakes or misunder-
standings of what was expected of the people.

Once this was done, the entire body of traditional writings was edited again into what eventually became the "Hebrew Canon" of scriptures.
This compilation and editing process, which took
several centuries to complete, also sparked increased study of the text and the development of
a group known as scribes or rabbis (teachers).
They became authorities on the law and its interpretation and were consulted on these matters by
the religious community.

A final development that can be ascribed to
the Persian period is the separation between the
Jews of Judah and the Samaritans. This break
has its roots both in the political conflicts between these two Persian provinces and in their
individual religious differences. The returning exiles excluded the Samaritans from participation
in the rebuilding of the Jerusalem temple (Ezr
4:1–3). Later, Nehemiah also stood up to Samaritan pressure against the rebuilding of the city's
walls and literally threw their representatives out
of the temple precincts (Neh 13:4–9). With the
Jews denying them participation in the cult in
Jerusalem and calling them unfit because of their
mixed cultural heritage, it is no wonder that the
Samaritans rejected Jerusalem as the true temple
site and place of God's presence. Instead they declared Mt. Gerizim near Shechem as their place
of worship and took advantage of Alexander's
political good will to construct an alternative
temple there in 325 BC (*Ant.* 11.346–347).

But Zerubbabel, Jeshua, and the rest of the heads of families in Israel said to them, "You shall have no part with us in building a house to our God; but we alone will build to the LORD, the God of Israel, as King Cyrus of Persia has commanded us."
— Ezra 4:3

B. THE COMING OF HELLENISM:
ALEXANDER AND THE DIADOCHOI

Alexander of Macedon burned the Persian capital of Persepolis and in the years from 330 to 323 BC broke their control over the Near East. He thereby set the stage for the introduction of an entirely new period in that area's history. Alexander believed in the creation of a "world culture" based on Greek philosophy, law, and political administration. Hellenistic, Greek-like, culture was then eventually formed from the blend of Greek ideas and the customs and traditions of the areas into which it was introduced.

One sign of Alexander's determination to create such a synthesis of cultures can be seen in his inclusion of Greek scholars and scientists with his army. They introduced the use of Greek as the principal language in conquered regions. These scholars also studied local languages and customs, popularizing some of them among the Greeks and thereby speeding the process of cultural blending. Another, and even more far reaching contribution to the spread of Greek culture, was the founding of many new cities, such as the Egyptian port city of Alexandria. The Greeks had founded their society upon the polis, the political community of the city-state. New immigrants to the areas of the Near East expected their lives to continue to revolve around the polis. It would thus become the major vehicle for the transmission of their culture to the rest of the ancient world.

The speed with which Alexander conquered the Near East reflected his own genius as a military commander as well as the general discontent, especially in Egypt and Syro-Palestine, with Persian rule. Pacification of these conquered regions was made even easier by retention of the old administrative structure. To maintain political stability, Alexander and his successors retained those officials who proved loyal to the new regime. The local economy was then stimulated by the introduction of Greek marketing techniques and fresh operating capital.

Following Alexander's death in 323, his generals divided up his empire among themselves. These successors, or Diadochoi, completed the process of pacifying conquered regions and introducing Hellenistic culture. In the areas of the former Persian empire, two of these generals eventually held sway. Ptolemy ruled Egypt and Syro-Palestine, while Seleucus gained control over the provinces of Asia and Asia Minor. Their successors introduced typical forms of Greek culture: the gymnasium, the theater, and the social associations for professional, cultural, and religious groups. At the same time, these foreign rulers and their Greek subjects acclimated themselves to the patterns and traditions of their new home, forming the Hellenized culture that would dominate the area until the coming of Islam.

During the early years of Greek rule, Palestine saw no drastic cultural changes. The Ptolemies introduced new coinage and exploited the economic resources of that region, but they did not attempt to impose Hellenistic ideas on the Jews. Temple worship continued unhindered and the office of high priest still exercised great authority on matters of religion. Hellenization was most popular among the new generation after the conquest and among those Jews who had contact with Jews outside of Palestine, such as the large communities in Antioch and Damascus. There were also obvious advantages for merchants and administrators who adopted Greek language and manners.

Competition between the Ptolemies and Seleucids for control of Syro-Palestine heated up during the mid-third century BC. Continual intrigue occurred with both sides trying to create or maintain support for their rule. When the high priest Onias II took a pro-Seleucid position,

Inscription of Alexander's generals. Photo by Ralph Harris.   5-2

refusing to pay tribute to the Ptolemaic government in 245, the battle for Palestine was begun. Even members of the high priest's family chose sides; his nephew Joseph, the son of Tobias, remained loyal to the Egyptians and served as chief tax collector of Syria and Palestine. Joseph's economic success is heralded by Josephus (*Ant.* 12.160–195), and the Tobiads became the chief advocates of Hellenization as a result.

The Tobiads' political loyalties, however, shifted after 200 BC when Antiochus III won the battle of Panion and gained control over Palestine and Jerusalem. This battle changed the political balance, leaving the Ptolemies bottled up in Egypt, and requiring a quick transference of allegiance by the new high priest Simon II to Antiochus' camp. Simon was the leader of the group which advocated strict adherence to Jewish tradition and as little Hellenization as possible. To obtain its support, Antiochus made a series of concessions to the leaders in Jerusalem. His decree forbade Gentiles from entering the precincts of the Jewish temple. He also made grants of financial assistance to the Jerusalem temple, and authorized an exemption from taxes for members of the priesthood and the council of elders, the Sanhedrin (*Ant.* 12.145–153).

These concessions and promises of religious freedom quickly evaporated as Antiochus became embroiled in the international disputes of the Romans. He helped the Carthaginian general Hannibal and tried to aid the embattled Greeks of Asia Minor. Roman territorial ambitions and military prowess were too much for both the Greeks and Antiochus. He was forced to sign a treaty in 188 deeding his territories in Europe and Asia Minor to Rome. His nephew Demetrius was also sent to Rome as a hostage, an action that eventually destabilized the Seleucid monarchy. The loss of revenues from these areas forced him to increase taxes and caused him to seek additional revenues by plundering the temple of Bel in the Persian city of Susa. He was killed during this expedition in 187. A brief struggle then ensued for the throne; it ended when Antiochus IV Epiphanes took power in 175 by usurping the rights of Demetrius and other rightful claimants.

The weakened position of the Seleucids sparked a new wave of political shifts. Onias III, Simon's successor, once again began to suggest a pro-Ptolemaic policy, although the Tobiads, at least outwardly, continued to support Antiochus. Eventually, the Tobiads took advantage of Antiochus' desire for allies (and additional revenues).

They purchased the office of high priest by offering to pay higher tribute to the Seleucid ruler. Antiochus then ousted Onias and replaced him with his pro-Seleucid brother Jason (2 Macc 4:7– 10). Onias apparently fled to Transjordan, but his proximity to Jerusalem and his vocal opposition to the actions of the high priest led to his murder in 171 (2 Macc 4:33–34).

Coin with the bust of Antiochus IV Epiphanes. Photo courtesy of the British Museum.

5-3

As high priest Jason hoped to further his own political position with Antiochus IV by transforming Jerusalem and the rest of Palestine into a Hellenized state. His model for this was the capital of the Seleucid kingdom, Antioch. First Maccabees 1:11–15 describes Jason's role in carrying out Antiochus' policy of Hellenization. The text describes a group of "lawless men" (Hellenizers) who willingly violated the covenant in order to please the Greek king. Opposition became increasingly vocal to the construction of gymnasia and the neglect of sacrifices (2 Macc 4:10–15). Jason, however, was deposed after three years when a fellow Tobiad ally, Menelaus, outbid him for his office by 300 talents of silver (2 Macc 4:24).

This new high priest only made matters worse, embezzling funds and stealing sacred vessels from the temple treasury to pay his debts to Antiochus (2 Macc 4:27–32). When Onias denounced him for doing this, Menelaus ordered his murder (2 Macc 4:33–34). A struggle then ensued for control of the office of high priest between Jason

Not content with this, Antiochus dared to enter the most holy temple in all the world, guided by Menelaus, who had become a traitor both to the laws and to his country. — 2 Macc 5:15

and Menelaus. At one point Jason captured the city of Jerusalem and drove out the Seleucid officials (2 Macc 5:5 – 7).

These chaotic conditions were interpreted by Antiochus as open rebellion, and he sent in troops to pacify the province. This resulted in a brutal loss of life (2 Macc 5:11 – 14). In 169, with Menelaus' aid, he defiled the temple, and looted its treasury (2 Macc 5:15 – 16). Antiochus then began an anti-Jewish campaign designed, according to 1 Macc 1:41 – 42, to make all of the people of the Seleucid realm "one people" and have them renounce their old traditions and religion. His anger may have been increased by continued pressure on his kingdom by the Romans. However, the stipulations of his decree all suggest that his plan was to completely Hellenize the Jews. Their shrines and altars were to be defiled and swine were to be sacrificed in the temple. Other ritual acts, like circumcision, were no longer to be performed (1 Macc 1:45 – 48).

C. Temporary Independence: The Hasmonean Kingdom

Antiochus' policies culminated in the construction of an altar to the Greek god Zeus Olympios in the Jerusalem temple (Dan 11:31; 1 Macc 1:54; Mk 13:14). This "abomination of desolation," combined with his other anti-Jewish measures, sparked a revolt led by the priest Mattathias of the house of Hasmon. The revolt, reflecting the more conservative attitudes of the rural areas of Palestine, began in the village of Modin, northwest of Jerusalem. Mattathias refused to obey the decree to sacrifice to idols and went so far as to kill the first Jew who attempted to obey this command. His justification for the killing was the precedent set by Aaron's grandson Phinehas, who killed an Israelite for marrying outside the congregation (Num 25:6 – 8). In both cases the principle involved obedience to the covenant and the purity of the nation.

Following his act of defiance, Mattathias led his five sons into the hill country where they began to wage a guerrilla war against the Seleucids and their Hellenized supporters. The rebels, joined by the traditionalists called the Hasidim (holy ones), saw this war as both a national struggle and a cultural one. Their adherence to the law, however, led at least in one instance to a massacre when a group of 1,000 Jews refused to defend themselves when attacked on the Sabbath (1 Macc 2:29–38). This reluctance was eventually overcome as the idea of holy war made it possible to temporarily set aside legal restraints.

By 165, Judas, Mattathias' oldest son, had recaptured most of Jerusalem (1 Macc 3:1–9) and justified his title Maccabaeus (the hammer) by his exploits. This title then became the name for the revolt as well as for the rest of Judas' family. The temple was rededicated and restrictions on the practice of Judaism were removed, an event still celebrated today as the feast of Hanukkah. However, the Seleucids had erected a fortress named the Akra just to the south of the temple mount. This bastion of Seleucid control (*Ant.* 12.252–253) remained a "thorn in the side" of the Maccabees until 141 when it was finally captured by Judas' brother Simon (1 Macc 13:49–51). It was then totally demolished to prevent its standing higher than the temple and to guarantee that it could never again be used against the people (*Ant.* 13.215–217).

Final victory was made possible by the disputes within the Seleucid royal house. Since the death of Antiochus IV in 164, rival claimants had attempted to outbid each other for the support of the provincial leaders. The Maccabees were also approached by some of these aspiring kings and received legitimization of their position as secular leaders. This process went a step

Then his son Judas, who was called Maccabeus, took command in his place. All his brothers and all who had joined his father helped him; they gladly fought for Israel. —1 Macc 3:1–2

The Jews and their priests have resolved that Simon should be their leader and high priest forever, until a trustworthy prophet should arise. —1 Macc 14:41

further in 153 when Judas' successor, Jonathan, was appointed high priest by the Seleucid pretender Alexander Balas (1 Macc 10:20).

After Jonathan's death, the people proclaimed his brother Simon to be "their leader and high priest forever, until a faithful prophet should arise" (1 Macc 4:46; 14:41; *Ant.* 13.213). This appointment was particularly important since Simon was not of the Zadokite line and thus was not, according to tradition, entitled to hold the office of high priest. Josephus (*Ant.* 16.163) describes John Hyrcanus, the successor of Simon, as the high priest of "God Most High." The implication is that the Maccabees were attempting to justify their position as priest and civil leader through a comparison with the Old Testament figure of Melchizedek, who was described as a king of Salem and priest of "God Most High" (Gen 14:18).

Political developments and a shift in expectation by the people in favor of a return of prophetic direction had made Simon's appointment possible; the Hasmoneans, as they now called themselves, took full advantage of the situation. Indications are, however, that there were a significant number of dissenters to Maccabean claims to the high priesthood. Documents associated with the Essene community (Manual of Discipline and the so-called Damascus Document from the Cairo geniza) seem to point to this period as the time when the Essenes ceased to support the Hasmoneans and created their separatist group. The *Assumption of Moses* (6:1), most likely a pharisaic document dating to about 100 BC, also contains a statement of discontent with the Hasmonean claims to both civil and religious authority.

Simon and his son John Hyrcanus continued to use the unsettled political situation in the Seleucid empire to their advantage. Simon also obtained official recognition of his position from the Roman Senate in 138 to add a further dimen-

sion of support. The Seleucids did attempt to re-
assert their power at the beginning of Hyrcanus'
reign. However, according to Josephus (*Ant.*
7.393), when Antiochus VII besieged Jerusalem,
Hyrcanus succeeded in bribing him to leave after
taking spoil from David's tomb. Hyrcanus, during his long reign (135–104), expanded his area
of control. Moving north, he conquered Samaria
and destroyed the temple on Mt. Gerizim. In the
south, he forced the Idumeans, living in the area
once known as Edom, to convert to Judaism and
be circumcised.

Despite these accomplishments, Hyrcanus was
not popular with all segments of his people. His
Hellenized court and lifestyle were offensive to
the stricter elements of Jewish society. One group,
known as the Pharisees, demanded that he renounce the office of high priest and in one instance accused him of uncertain parentage, saying
his mother had been a captive of Antiochus IV
(*Ant.* 13.288–292). This did not prove to be a particularly damaging accusation, however, since
Hyrcanus was able to rely on the support of the
wealthier landowners and merchants. This group,
known as the Sadducees, also controlled membership in the priesthood (*Ant.* 13.293–296). Both of
these groups eventually emerged as important elements in the political and religious history of the
nation.

Hyrcanus' son, Aristobulus I, was the first to
bear the title of king of Judea (*Ant.* 13.301). He
continued his father's expansion policies in the
north, but was deposed after only one year in 103
by his brother Alexander Jannaeus. This particularly ambitious and cruel ruler used the support
of the Sadducees and a company of mercenary
troops to impose his rule on the people. The Pharisees, however, were ardently opposed to his position as high priest, ridiculing him as he officiated
at sacrifices (*Ant.* 13.372) and allying themselves
with the Seleucid king Demetrius III, in an ef-

Now when their father Hyrcanus was dead, the eldest son Aristobulus, intending to change the government into a kingdom, for so he resolved to do, first of all put a diadem on his head, four hundred and eighty-one years and three months after the people had been delivered from the Babylonish slavery, and were returned to their own country again.
—Josephus, *Ant.* 13.301

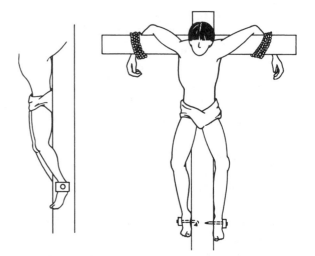

Artist's conception of a crucified man. After a model by Joseph Zias. Courtesy of the Israel Department of Antiquities and Museums. 5-A

fort to depose him. Jannaeus managed to gain his revenge after withstanding the Seleucid invasion. He systematically exterminated the leading Pharisee families, crucifying 800 of them and killing their wives and children during a banquet for his supporters (*Ant.* 13.380).

The potential problems of continuing this internal struggle against his own people took their toll on Jannaeus. On his deathbed he advised his wife and successor, Salome Alexandra (76–67), to make peace with the Pharisees. Jannaeus' older son Hyrcanus II was appointed high priest by his mother. His more energetic brother Aristobulus II was not satisfied with this arrangement, however, and precipitated a civil war in 67 after their mother's death.

During this period of political chaos, two new elements began to powerfully influence Judean politics. The first was Antipater of Idumea. Seizing the opportunity to gain influence in Judean affairs, he advised Hyrcanus to seek refuge with the Nabatean ruler Aretas in Petra while he sought help in his struggle against Aristobulus. The other major new influence, and the really decisive element in the dispute between the brothers was the escalating civil war in Rome and the arrival in Jerusalem of Pompey, the Roman general. Romans had made alliances with the leaders of Judah as far back as Jonathan and Simon. Their interests in the Near East had brought them into conflict with the Armenian king Mithridates. In 63, Pompey was sent to unseat him and protect the new Roman province of Syria. His success in this mission made Rome the emerging power in the area.

Thus when Pompey arrived in Damascus he was met by representatives of many of the small kingdoms of the Near East, including both Hyrcanus II and Aristobulus II of Judea. Pompey sided with Hyrcanus; Aristobulus then fortified the temple mount and his followers held out against the assaults of the Roman forces for three months. When their position was finally overrun, a general slaughter, luridly described in Josephus, took place. Aristobulus was saved so that he could be taken as a captive to Rome as part of Pompey's triumphal procession (*Ant.* 14.69–79). Jewish reaction to these events may be found in the pharisaic document, the *Psalms of Solomon* 2:30–33 (dating about 40–30 BC), which is apparently referring to Pompey when it triumphantly describes the death in Egypt of one who placed himself before God. What may be implied here is Pompey's reported desecration of the temple by entering the Holy of Holies (*Ant.* 14.72).

As a result of Pompey's intervention, Judea was added to the Roman province of Syria and was administered by Pompey's chief lieutenant Gabinius. The country itself was divided into five districts, each centered on a major population center: Jerusalem, Jericho, Sepphoris in Galilee, Amathus (east of the Jordan River), and Gazara (Gezer). The Romans also claimed all the cities in the north and in Transjordan which had been ruled by the Hasmoneans, but which did not have large Jewish populations. Hyrcanus was

For Pompey went into it, and not a few of those that were with him also, and saw all that which it was unlawful for any other men to see, but only for the high priests. There were in that temple the golden table, the holy candlestick, and the pouring vessels, and a great quantity of spices; and besides these there were among the treasures two thousand talents of sacred money; yet did Pompey touch nothing of all this, on account of his regard to religion; and in this point also he acted in a manner that was worthy of his virtue.
—Josephus, *Ant.* 14.72

reappointed as high priest, but with no claims of civil authority (*Ant.* 14.73 – 76).

For the next 20 years Judea was plagued by popular uprisings led by Aristobulus, who escaped from Rome in 56, or by his sons. Hyrcanus and his Idumean adviser Antipater managed to survive these threats to their authority while playing a dangerous game of shifting allegiances with the Roman generals who were locked in bloody civil war with one another. In 55 or 54, Hyrcanus' lack of real power was demonstrated when Rome's proconsul for Syria, Marcus Licinius Crassus, plundered the temple treasury. He was hoping to show that his abilities as a general matched those of his fellow triumvirate members, Julius Caesar and Pompey, by campaigning against the Parthians (successors of the Persians). His theft of sacred items from the temple helped fund this expedition, but all he accomplished was a major defeat and his own death.

Crassus' death helped to increase the tensions between Caesar and Pompey that eventually led to the height of the Roman civil war. Antipater, son of the governor of Idumea under Alexander Jannaeus, and Hyrcanus supported Caesar, and after Pompey's death they helped marshall support for him among the Jews in Egypt. As a reward, Hyrcanus was appointed in 47 as ethnarch of Judea, becoming once again both a civil as well as a religious leader. In addition, Caesar permitted the rebuilding of the walls of Jerusalem and promised the Jews free exercise of their religion. Antipater received Roman citizenship and was named procurator of Judea by the Senate.

Antipater's and Hyrcanus' good fortune was once again upset when Caesar was murdered in 44 BC. Seizing what they saw was an opportunity for more independence, they supported one of the conspirators, Cassius, and helped him gather an army and funds by extorting new taxes from the people. During this time Antipater's son

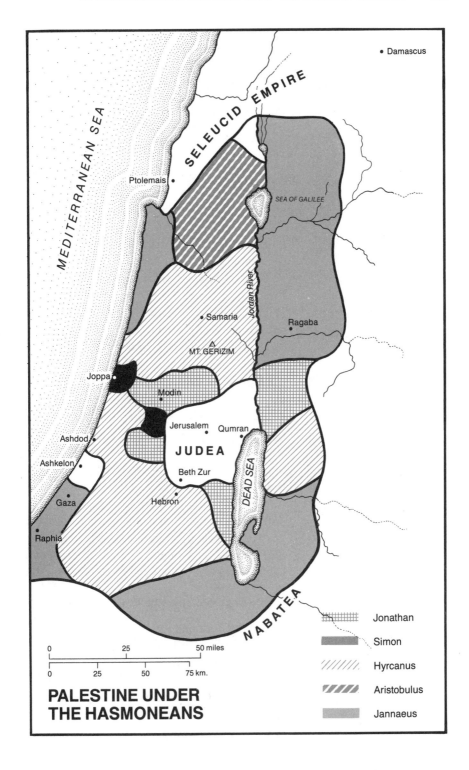

Damascus

SELEUCID EMPIRE

MEDITERRANEAN SEA

Ptolemais

SEA OF GALILEE

Jordan River

Samaria

Ragaba

MT. GERIZIM

Joppa

Modin

Jerusalem   Qumran

Ashdod

JUDEA

Ashkelon

Beth Zur

DEAD SEA

Gaza

Hebron

Raphia

NABATEA

	Jonathan
	Simon
	Hyrcanus
	Aristobulus
	Jannaeus

0   25   50 miles

0   25   50   75 km.

**PALESTINE UNDER
THE HASMONEANS**

Herod emerged as a leader. He was appointed governor of Syria and became the head of the family after 43 when his father was murdered.

The emergence of Mark Anthony as the new Roman power and his triumph over Cassius simply meant a change of masters for Herod and his brother Phasael. They were appointed tetrarchs of Judea in 41. Hyrcanus, however, was once again stripped of his civil powers and restricted to control of the temple worship. Even with these changes, the maneuverings for control of Syro-Palestine were not yet over. The Parthians now took advantage of Anthony's delaying in Egypt to invade Syria and install Antigonus, the son of Aristobulus II, on the throne in Jerusalem. Phasael committed suicide while in prison and Hyrcanus II was mutilated (his ears were cut off) so that he could no longer serve as high priest (according to the proscriptions of Lev 21:16–23).

Speak to Aaron and say: No one of your offspring throughout their generations who has a blemish may approach to offer the food of his God. — Lev 21:17

Herod escaped by fleeing with his family to the fortress of Masada in the Judean desert. He then went to Rome where his arguments and his bribes convinced the Roman Senate to declare him king of Judea in 40. It would take three years and another Roman siege of Jerusalem before Antigonus and his Parthian supporters were defeated. At Herod's request, Antigonus was beheaded by the Roman general Sosius in Antioch. His death and the murder of his cousin Aristobulus III in 35 ended the Hasmonean line, and left the door open for a new ruling dynasty led by Herod.

D. Last Glimpses of Power: The Herods

Having obtained the rulership of Judea, Herod now plotted to legitimize his position and obtain the support of the people. This would not be easy since he was an Idumean, and his family had converted to Judaism at sword's point. Herod's first steps to overcome these problems included tying himself to the Hasmoneans. Like David (1 Sam

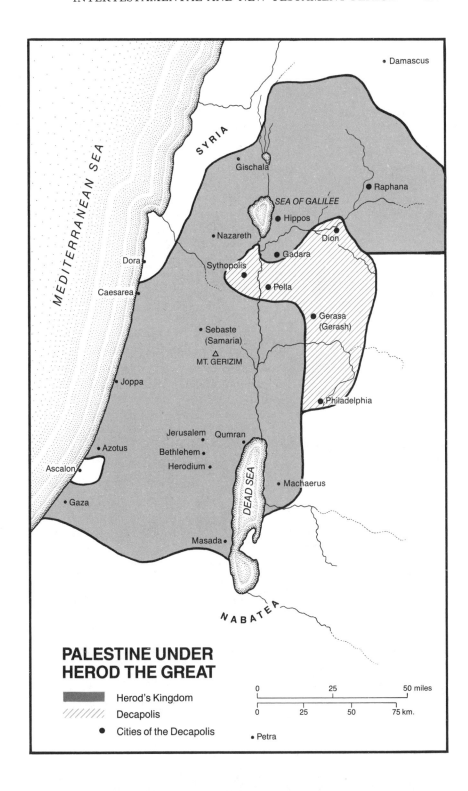

PALESTINE UNDER HEROD THE GREAT

▓ Herod's Kingdom

/////// Decapolis

● Cities of the Decapolis

0   25   50 miles

0   25   50   75 km.

For that Herod was ill-natured, and severe in his punishments, and had no mercy on them that he hated; and everyone perceived that he was more friendly to the Greeks than to the Jews; for he adorned foreign cities with large presents in money; with building them baths and theatres besides: nay, in some of those places, he erected temples, and porticoes in others; but he did not vouchsafe to raise one of the least edifices in any Jewish city, or make them any donation that was worth mentioning.
—Josephus, *Ant.* 19.329

Herodium, Herod's desert citadel near Bethlehem. Photo by Ralph Harris.   5-4

18:22 – 27), he allied himself to the family of the previous ruler, marrying Mariamme, the granddaughter of Aristobulus II. He also appointed her 17-year-old brother Aristobulus III as high priest, but quickly found it necessary to arrange his drowning when the young man's popularity began to grow (*Ant.* 15.31 – 56). Herod's paranoia also claimed the life of Hyrcanus, now in his 80s.

Violent acts such as these characterized Herod's entire reign (37 – 4 BC). Despite the continued good will of the Roman emperors and the expansion of his kingdom, the reign of terror continued to spread. Eventually it claimed the lives of several of Herod's wives and sons, and many others whom he suspected of plotting against him (Mt 2:16 – 18; *Ant.* 15.80 – 87, 222 – 239). Despite the tragedy of his personal life, Herod achieved real diplomatic triumphs, obtaining Octavian's (later named Augustus) support for his rule and reacquiring territory around Jericho and in Transjordan that had been lost to Cleopatra and Mark Anthony.

Herod's lasting accomplishments came in his building program. He styled himself as a Hellenistic prince who was obligated by his position to rule as a benefactor to his people. With this in mind, he constructed Judea's first port (Caesarea Maritima) and restored old cities (Samaria, renamed Sebaste) with all the items considered necessary in a Hellenistic urban center: temples, theaters, and stadia. While he flattered Augustus Caesar with the names of these cities, Herod strengthened his own position by reequipping the strategic hilltop fortresses, including Masada, Herodium, and Alexandrium.

The crowning architectural achievement of Herod's career was the rebuilding of the temple in Jerusalem (*Ant.* 15.380–425). Its gold inlaid columns and massive construction (using blocks of stone weighing over 450 tons in the supporting platform of the temple complex) were designed to impress the Jews, but it never won their affection. He destroyed any credibility he might have had as a pious Jew by erecting temples to the Roman gods and by staging athletic games in Caesar's honor (*Ant.* 19.329; 15.268).

On Herod's death, riots erupted throughout Judea that had to be suppressed by the Roman legate of Syria, Varus. Herod's will divided the kingdom among three of his sons, Archelaus, Antipas, and Philip. The Roman Senate ratified Herod's will and named Archelaus ethnarch (not king) of Judea, while his brothers were appointed tetrarchs of Galilee and Perea respectively. Archelaus ruled 10 years, relying on Varus' backing to control the office of high priest and continue the building projects of his father. In AD 6, a delegation sent by both Jews and Samaritans convinced Augustus to exile him to Gaul (France), and Judea was annexed to the Roman province of Syria. A procurator was then appointed to serve as local administrator.

From AD 6 until AD 41 six Roman procura-

> *For, in the first place, he appointed solemn games to be celebrated every fifth year, in honor of Caesar, and built a theatre at Jerusalem, as also a very great amphitheatre in the plain. Both of them were indeed costly works, but opposite to the Jewish customs; for we have had no such shows delivered down to us as fit to be used or exhibited by us.*
> —Josephus, *Ant.* 15.268

An inscription bearing the name of the Roman procurator Pontius Pilate. Photo courtesy of Southwest Missouri State University.   5-5

tors ruled Judea. Their administrative offices were in Caesarea Maritima on the coast, but they were required to attend major festivals in Jerusalem when the influx of pilgrims created a dangerous situation for the Romans. The first of these procurators was P. Sulpicius Quirinius. He began his administration by ordering a census (*Ant.* 18.1), an action which led to armed rebellion throughout the province by people fearing higher taxes and labor service (cf. 2 Sam 24:1–9). He and his successors also controlled the appointment of the high priest. Quirinius placed Ananus (Annas in Lk 3:2) in the office, while Valerius Gratus deposed Ananus in AD 14 and later appointed and deposed three other high priests.

The best known of the procurators was Pontius Pilate, who succeeded Gratus in AD 26. Like his predecessors, he gave little attention to the traditions of the people he was ruling (Lk 13:1). Josephus mentions two examples of this lack of respect for the Jews. Early in his reign Pilate ordered that the Roman legionary standards be brought into Jerusalem. These standards and an accompanying bust of Caesar (*Ant.* 15.55–59) represented the military occupation of the country and were also extremely offensive to the Jews, who forbade the worship of images. Some Jews demonstrated their disgust for what Pilate had done by laying down with their necks bared before the soldiers. They challenged the Romans to kill them since they would rather die than live in a city defiled by the presence of the standards (*War* 2.169–174).

Perhaps in the hope of restoring the people's confidence in his rule, Pilate proposed to build an aqueduct that would transport water to the growing population of Jerusalem. This backfired when he financed the aqueduct with funds (*Qorban*) from the temple treasury that were restricted to religious projects (*War* 2.175–177). His dealing with the case of Jesus (Lk 23:1–25) played into the hands of the Sanhedrin council, but also failed to gain him any more respect with the Jews. For instance, his placement of the inscription over the crucified Jesus, "This is the King of the Jews" (Lk 23:38), was a too obvious attempt to humiliate them rather than Jesus. He was eventually ousted from his position in 37 after massacring a crowd assembled to hear a Samaritan prophet speak.

Then Pilate asked him, "Are you the king of the Jews?" He answered, "You say so."
    —Luke 23:3

While these events were occurring in Judea, Herod Antipas continued to rule in Galilee. He had strengthened his position by marrying the daughter of Aretas IV, the king of the Nabateans. He later divorced her in order to marry Herodias, the wife of his deceased, half brother Philip (Mk 6:17–28). John the Baptist was one of the many voices raised against this illegal marriage (see Lev 20:21). It was Antipas' fear of John's popularity (*Ant.* 18.118) and his desire to silence the voice of dissent that led to John's eventual execution (Mk 6:27). Antipas also showed his disdain for his Jewish subjects by constructing his new capital city of Tiberias on the site of an

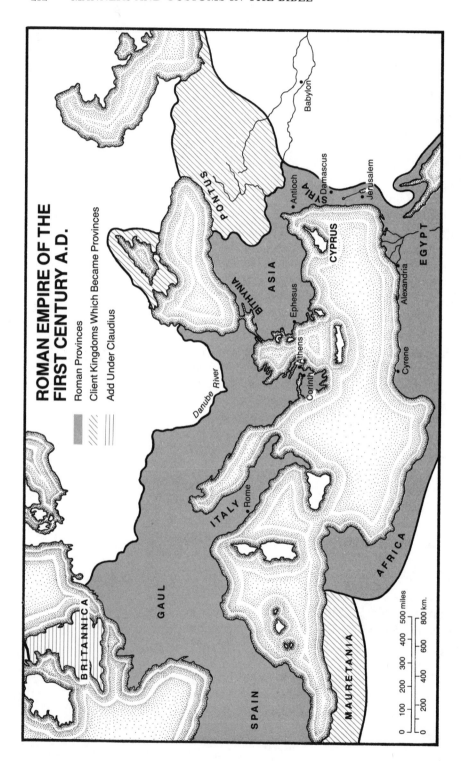

ROMAN EMPIRE OF THE
FIRST CENTURY A.D.

Roman Provinces

Client Kingdoms Which Became Provinces

Add Under Claudius

ancient cemetery, at the southern end of the Sea of Galilee. This violated the Jewish law against contact with the dead and the burial of dead within city walls.

A change came in the Judean political situation in AD 39 when the mentally unstable Roman emperor, Caligula, exiled Antipas to Gaul. Caligula had given Philip's lands to Herod Agrippa (a grandson of Herod I), as well as the title of king. When Antipas also asked for the title of king, he was exiled, and Agrippa was awarded his lands. He was also given Judea in 41 by Emperor Claudius (*Ant.* 19.274–275). Thus he controlled all the lands that his grandfather had ruled 45 years earlier.

Herod Agrippa attempted to build support for his rule through strict adherence to the Torah. He also gave several gifts to the temple treasury, including the golden chain he had worn while a prisoner in Rome. Perhaps as another way of currying favor with the Pharisees, Agrippa persecuted the disciples of Jesus. James the brother of John was executed and Peter was imprisoned (Acts 12:1–3). Shortly after this the king was stricken with an illness. Tradition suggests that this was a result of his being proclaimed a god. He subsequently died while officiating at games held in the emperor's honor at Caesarea in 44 (Acts 12:22–23; *Ant.* 19.350).

And immediately, because he had not given the glory to God, an angel of the Lord struck him down, and he was eaten by worms and died.
　　　　　　　　—Acts 12:23

E. ROMAN RULE AND JEWISH PROTEST: THE FIRST JEWISH REVOLT

Following Agrippa's death, the Emperor Claudius once again placed Judea under the rule of a Roman procurator, Agrippa's son. Agrippa II was given the rule over Galilee, but he was thoroughly loyal to the Romans and became one more source of irritation for the Jewish rebels. Each of the men who held the position of procurator between AD 44 and 66 faced a difficult administrative task. They were continually re-

Coin from the First Jewish Revolt. Photo courtesy of the British Museum. 5-6

quired to quell small rebellions and put down street riots caused by the people's desire to end Roman rule and presence in Palestine. The volatile situation was worsened by periodic famines, the provocative and insensitive actions of some of the Roman soldiers, and the teachings of a series of messiah figures who offered the people hope of independence and restored greatness (*Ant.* 20.97 – 112; Acts 21:38).

One of principal measures used by the procurators was to divide the Jews, get them fighting among themselves, and thus be able to provide a common front against the Romans. In one case described by Josephus, Felix (procurator 52 – 60) arranged the murder of the high priest Jonathan, hiring assassins (*sicarii,* so named for the short, curved sword they carried) to mingle with the crowd during worship and kill him (*Ant.* 20.163 – 164). This act created an even more dangerous situation; an Egyptian prophet called for rebellion and promised to arrange the miraculous destruction of the walls of Jerusalem (*Ant.* 20.169 – 172).

These insurrections brought swift and bloody reprisal on the Jews. They also painted every other nontraditional speaker with the brush of sedition, as the apostle Paul discovered (Acts 21:38). He was subsequently brought before Felix by the Jewish high priest Ananias, but at that point Felix was disposed to delay the trial (Acts 24). Paul was not sent to Rome for his hearing before Caesar until Felix was succeeded by Festus in 60

(Acts 25:1–12). Acts 25:9 suggests that this was done, again, as a part of the political maneuvering of the procurator who "wished to do the Jews a favor."

Festus died while in office in 62. His death and the delay in the arrival of his replacement, Albinus, led to an anarchic period in which the high priest Ananus took the opportunity to execute several of his political and religious enemies. Among his victims was James, the brother of Jesus and the head of the Christian community in Jerusalem (*Ant.* 20.200–201). Matters did not improve substantially when Albinus arrived. In exchange for bribes he allowed the tithes of food from the threshing floor that were earmarked for the poor to be stolen. Albinus was also forced to submit to extortion by the *sicarii*, who kidnapped his servants and then demanded the release of their imprisoned fellows in exchange (*Ant.* 20.208–210).

Gessius Florus succeeded Albinus in 64. He acquired this position as a result of his wife Cleopatra's friendship with Nero's wife (*Ant.* 20.252). Desiring to make the most financial gain he could from the procuratorship, Florus allowed the plundering of whole villages and took bribes from his political favorites (*War* 2.278–279). Feeding upon the climate of discontent which Florus had created, the political situation then worsened as religious riots broke out in Caesarea over the obstruction of the Jews' right to worship in the local synagogue (*War* 2.284–292). When it became clear that justice could not be obtained from Florus and that Nero had no intention of sending a replacement for him, revolt became inevitable.

The First Jewish Revolt began in 66 with two acts of defiance by those hoping to oust the Romans from Judea. Eleazar, the son of Ananias the high priest, called on the sacrificial priests to no longer accept gifts or offerings from foreign-

When, therefore, Ananus was of this disposition, he thought he had now a proper opportunity [to exercise his authority]. Festus was now dead, and Albinus was but upon the road; so he assembled the sanhedrin of judges, and brought before them the brother of Jesus, who was called Christ, whose name was James, and some others [or, some of his companions]; and when he had formed an accusation against them as breakers of the law, he delivered them to be stoned; but as for those who seemed the most equitable of the citizens, and such as were the most uneasy at the breach of the laws, they disliked what was done; they also sent to the king [Agrippa], desiring him to send to Ananus that he should act so no more, for that what he had already done was not to be justified.
—Josephus, *Ant.* 20.200–1

ers. This virtually ended the practice of sacrificing in honor of the emperor (*War* 2.409). Many of the chief priests and Pharisees argued against this action (*War* 2.410 – 416), fearing Roman reprisals against the temple and the people. The inflammatory actions of both Florus and Eleazar's radical followers helped initiate the final confrontation with Rome.

The other act precipitating the war was the capture of the fortress of Masada by the rebel leader Menahem ben Hezekiah. The Roman garrison was massacred and arms were distributed to the people with a call for a general insurrection (*War* 2.433 – 434). What occurred, however, was not a united effort to throw off Roman rule, but rather a confused period in which debtors and instigators of the rebellion rushed to burn contracts (*War* 2.426 – 427); various Jewish factions claimed the leadership. There were also some massacres of the Jewish populations in the predominantly Gentile cities of Caesarea, Scythopolis, and the cities in Transjordan known as the Decapolis (*War* 2.457 – 480).

After the Roman forces under Cestius experienced some initial reverses, Nero appointed Vespasian and his son Titus to command the Roman legions in charge of quelling the Jewish revolt.

Masada, the ancient fortress where 960 Jews committed suicide rather than fall into the hands of their Roman enemies. Photo by Ralph Harris.   5-7

Cave IV at Qumran. Photo by LaMoine DeVries. 5-8

Their more organized efforts led to the surrender of several towns, although some like Jotapata were besieged and most of their defenders were killed (*War* 3.127–339). Josephus himself was one of the Jewish commanders at Jotapata. He escaped the final fall of the city, but was subsequently captured and became an advisor and seer for the Roman generals (*War* 3.344–354).

Gradually all of the Judean countryside and the rebel fortresses (Tiberias, Gamala, Gischala) fell to the Romans. One group of Jews, led by Rabbi Johanan ben Zakkai, made a separate peace with the Romans in 68 and moved to the town of Jamnia. They established a scholarly and commercial community there that served as a center of revived Judaism after the revolt. Others, like the Essenes of the desert community of Qumran were scattered and their villages destroyed. They did manage to hide their sacred books in mountain caves near their settlement. These "Dead Sea Scrolls" were discovered in 1947 and serve as one of the most important modern tools for studying the biblical text.

Jerusalem, overcrowded with refugees from all over Judea and divided into warring factions, finally came under siege in 70. Vespasian had returned to Rome to become emperor after the death of Nero, which left Titus to complete the war. His efforts were made easier by the fighting between the Jewish leaders John of Gischala, Simon bar Giora, and Eleazar (*War* 5.248 – 274, 527 – 540). Five months of fighting and starvation gradually wore down the defenders. The end of the fighting came in September, AD 70 (*War* 6.435). Herod's temple as well as large portions of the city and its defenses were torn down at Titus' command, and a great slaughter of the population followed the siege. An encampment was constructed for the occupying Tenth Roman legion, but the city per se ceased to be a major Jewish population center (*War* 7.1 – 12). All that remained of the revolt were some hill top fortresses, and the last of these, Masada, fell in 74 after the

The Habakkuk Scroll taken from Qumran Cave I. Photo by LaMoine DeVries.   5-9

960 defenders committed mass suicide rather than be captured by the Romans (*War* 7.252 – 406).

F. A FINAL CHAPTER:
BAR KOCHBA AND DIASPORA

The fall of Jerusalem and the destruction of the temple ended the power of the Sanhedrin and the high priesthood (*Ant.* 20.224 – 251). Separate centers of learning and worship, such as that at Jamnia, represented post – 70 Judaism — a non-sacrificial cult, devoted to study of the law and the development of community religious standards. The Roman emperors attempted to encourage this more peaceful form of Judaism while doing everything they could to destroy nationalism and messiah figures. An indication of their efforts is found in the writings of the early church historian Eusebius (*Eccl Hist* 3.12, 19 – 20), who describes attempts by Vespasian and Domitian to hunt down members of the house of David.

A further step in this policy of preventing nationalism from recurring among the Jews was the rebuilding of Jerusalem by Emperor Hadrian in 130. He constructed a Roman-style city and renamed it Aelia Capitolina. Other construction projects were also ordered at Caesarea and Sepphoris (now renamed Diocaesarea). Instead of quieting the Jews, however, this attempt to extinguish the traditional religious and political heritage of Jerusalem sparked the Second Jewish Revolt in 132. Sources for this revolt and its primary causes are fragmentary, but they all seem to indicate that Jerusalem and Jewish traditions, including circumcision, were still rallying points for rebellion.

The leader of the revolt was a messianic figure who took the name of Bar Kochba, "son of the star" (Num 24:17 – 19). He drew support from those, like the famous Rabbi Akiba, who believed that Yahweh would use this man to rid their land of the hated Romans. For a brief time

I see him, but not now; I behold him, but not near — a star shall come out of Jacob, and a scepter shall rise out of Israel; it shall crush the borderlands of Moab, and the territory of all the Shethites. — Num 24:17

Silver tetradrachma of Bar Kochba. Photo courtesy of the British Museum. 5-10

the rebels were successful. They reoccupied Jerusalem, set up a bureaucracy to govern the affairs of the state, and reestablished the religious calendar of festivals. Coins minted during this period by the revolutionary government have the inscription "Year One of the Liberty of Israel."

Such high hopes were soon dashed as Rome marshalled its forces from all over the empire to put down yet another Jewish war. Coins found in excavations dated to this period come from as far away as Britain and Germany where the legionnaires were paid before they were shipped to the Near East. The Roman general Sextus Julius Severus recaptured Jerusalem in 134 and drove the rebels into the mountainous areas of the Judean wilderness. Guerrilla warfare continued for another year until the fall of the last rebel stronghold of Bethar in 135.

Rabbinic tradition contends that Jerusalem fell on the same day, 9th of Ab, in both the first and second revolt. True or not, this became the traditional day for ritually mourning these events. Jews were expelled from the restored Aelia Capitolina and from Judea in general. The expulsions also applied to Jewish Christians, thus leaving the Gentile population to lead the church in that area. Hadrian continued his rebuilding of Aelia Capitolina and the other cities of the province, now renamed Palestina ("land of the Philistines"). His plans included the construction of a temple to his personal god Jupiter over the site of Solomon's temple as well as on the site of the Samaritan shrine on Mt. Gerizim.

With the exile of a large portion of the Jews from Palestine came a shift in the history of the people to the communities of the Diaspora. Jews were scattered throughout the Roman empire and their synagogues became focal points for worship and for the study of the canon of scriptures that was developed by the rabbis at Jamnia between AD 90 and 100. These communities in Antioch, Corinth, and throughout Asia Minor proved to be both fertile ground for converts and a source of contention for Paul and the other missionaries of the Christian faith (Acts 14:1–2; 17:1–8; 18:1–4).

The same thing occurred in Iconium, where Paul and Barnabas went into the Jewish synagogue and spoke in such a way that a great number of both Jews and Greeks became believers.
—Acts 14:1

I. SOCIAL LIFE

What were the basic aspects of the social life of the people during the Hellenistic and Roman periods?

Alexander's conquests brought a new and vibrant culture to the Near East. Gradually it mixed with local customs and traditions creating a Hellenistic culture. In general, this synthesis was beneficial for both. For the Jews, however, the introduction of Hellenism became a major source of controversy, dividing the people between the Hellenizers and the traditionalists. The resulting cultural conflict spilled over into economic, political, and religious areas. What will be explored below are those developments in everyday life which changed or became more focused as a result of the introduction of Hellenistic culture.

A. CITIES AND CITY PLANNING

At the center of Greek culture was the city-state. When Alexander's armies conquered the Near East they established many new cities and rebuilt others. In part, this was a way of consolidating their control over the conquered areas, but it also was what the new Greek immigrants to these areas expected. Urban centers with gymnasia, theaters, and the agora were the basis of life wherever Greeks settled. A further sense of order was created in the Hellenistic cities by the imposition of the gridiron pattern of streets and buildings. The agora then served as the heart of the business district of the city with a variety of buildings and shops located on all four sides of a public square. Sometimes another agora was constructed within a quieter district of the city where temples were its focal point. This arrangement was not always possible in the older cities, but where destruction or mass rebuilding had taken place (as in Herod's Jerusalem and Samaria), the new pattern was employed.

In new cities, such as Herod's administrative center and port, Caesarea Maritima (founded between 12 and 10 BC), the full range of Hellenistic construction and civic planning took place. The port, a vital strategic and economic link for shipping-poor Palestine, had a breakwater, docks, and quarters for sailors on leave. To satisfy his Hellenistic tastes and please his Roman masters, Herod built a temple to the deified Caesar in the unwalled city as well as a theater and amphitheater. Some of the sanitation needs of the people were handled by an underground sewage system, and transportation was facilitated by an arrangement of parallel streets (*Ant.* 15.331–341).

Other than the palaces of kings and Roman officials, and the homes of the wealthy, the majority of housing within the cities of Palestine was overcrowded and not well constructed. Evidence at Capernaum, for example, suggests that private houses, set in blocks of four around a central courtyard, often consisted of one story, with a staircase on the outside wall leading up to living area on the roof. They were crudely constructed of uneven blocks of basalt and mortar.

Because of a lack of large wooden beams, the rooms tended to be less than 18 feet wide and the ceilings were quite low. There were small windows allowing some ventilation and providing a relatively cool dwelling in the often hot and humid climate of the Upper Galilee region. The floor was made of uneven basalt slabs, which could easily cause a stumble or the loss of some item, like a coin, between its cracks (Lk 15:8).

These new and expanded urban centers were designed to accommodate relatively large populations (perhaps as many as 50,000 to 100,000 in Jerusalem). Such a large number of people (increasing dramatically during festivals like Passover) meant increased demands for water and food supplies. To meet this former need Herod initiated public works projects to construct new water channels and to stimulate a periodically stagnant economy. Pontius Pilate went a step further constructing an aqueduct capable of supplying a continuous supply of fresh water to Jeru-

Roman aqueduct. Photo courtesy of Southwest Missouri State University. 5-11

salem's inhabitants. Even with these measures, however, it was standard for every home to have one or more rain-catching cisterns or pools.

The supplies of food and other farm products consumed by the people of the cities were supplied by the agricultural villages that ringed the urban centers. Jerusalem was surrounded by concentric circles of smaller communities which produced the grains, meat, and oil which were the staple of the Jewish diet. There was continuous contact between these two different population areas, but there were some very large differences between them.

B. URBAN-BASED BUREAUCRACY

Helping to administer both the cities and the surrounding villages was a new group of bureaucrats whose positions were owed to the rulers of Palestine. Thus their loyalties belonged to the dominating culture of the Greeks and Romans. In like manner the Hasmoneans and the Herods also employed a civil service to collect taxes and enforce order. This service gave many Jews the opportunity to move up socially, and in some cases they became quite wealthy and powerful. For instance, Zacchaeus, the chief tax official in the Jericho region, is said to have been very rich (Lk 19:2). He, like John, the port official at Caesarea, mentioned in Josephus (*War* 2.287), had taken advantage of the Roman system of tax farming. Under this system the tax collector was assigned a certain amount to collect and then was allowed to collect as much more as he could to cover administrative expenses.

A man was there named Zacchaeus; he was a chief tax collector and was rich.
— Luke 19:2

In fact, by Jesus' time nearly all tax collectors, civil officials, and local judges in Palestine were Jews. Like the stewards who manipulated the day laborers and tenant farmers (Lk 16:1–8), these middle and lower level government employees considered themselves socially above the masses and were despised for this (Lk 19:7; Mt

11:19). The tensions between these officials, necessarily loyal to Rome, and other Jews (Lk 18:10 – 14) were very real. Jesus used them to preach nonviolence (as when he diffused the question of whether to pay tribute to Caesar in Lk 20:22 – 25), and love of enemies (even tax collectors, as in Mt 5:44 – 46).

C. VILLAGE LIFE

Despite the growth of urban centers and the incentives offered by jobs and occasionally better housing (see Herod Antipas' inducements to new settlers in Tiberias, *Ant.* 18.36 – 38), the majority of Palestinian Jews in Jesus' time still lived in small towns and villages. Josephus wrote of the many villages in Galilee that were aided by the richness of the soil in that region (*War* 3.43). A conservative estimate of 200 villages with populations of about 500 each would total 100,000 peasant villagers inhabiting that area. The effects of Hellenism were less pronounced here than in the cities. Counsels of elders continued to decide local matters, although tax collectors and other government officials would have added another level of authority to their lives. Aramaic remained the common language in the villages, while Greek was the principal tongue in the cities. The basic conservatism of the peasants in these small settlements meant a retention of older traditions and values that tied them more closely to the Old Testament era.

Those social activities which existed in the rural areas centered around family ties and seasonal religious festivals. Marriages were celebrated with a wedding feast. The ritual included having the bride brought to the wedding by the groomsman (Jn 3:29) while the bridegroom was accompanied to the celebration by the bridesmaids (Mt 25:1 – 10). A steward was placed in charge of the arrangements for the feast, orchestrating the festivities and parceling out the wine

He who has the bride is the bridegroom. The friend of the bridegroom, who stands and hears him, rejoices greatly at the bridegroom's voice. For this reason my joy has been fulfilled.
—John 3:29

and other refreshments (Jn 2:8–10). To separate these activities from other gatherings, a special wedding garment was required for admission to the feast (Mt 22:11–13).

Pilgrimages to Jerusalem to attend the Passover (Lk 2:41), the Feast of Tabernacles (Jn 7:2), and other major religious events (Jn 10:22, Hanukkah celebration) were the social highlight of the villager's year. Religious obligations could be fulfilled while leaving enough time to shop, see family and old friends, and pass on to the young the importance of their cultural heritage. After the destruction of the temple in AD 70, the law of the Torah and the synagogue took the place of the Jerusalem cult community. Villagers retained the memory and image of that holy place, but had to be content with local celebrations and an occasional trip to a nearby market center to break the monotony of village life.

D. LEISURE

Leisure was a major pursuit in the urban centers. The Greeks and later the Romans demanded the opportunities and pleasures of the gymnasium and stadium. In the gymnasium a person could engage in a private workout and then bathe either to begin or end a work day. This facility also provided a place to make social contacts, conduct clubs meetings, or participate in the activities of professional or private associations. This latter activity was another innovation of the Greek culture, which was very dependent on the development of social relationships. Businessmen, skilled workers, and even the poor formed these associations of social equals to aid each other in commercial activity, as a social outlet, and even to provide funds to ensure proper burial.

The stadium provided facilities for public athletic contests. For instance, the amphitheater constructed by Herod in Jerusalem was the regular site of games including some in honor of Caesar. Both wrestling matches and chariot races were staged here. The winners of these contests received rich prizes and public recognition (*Ant.* 15.268–271).

There are frequent references in Josephus (*Ant.* 12.241; 15.267–283; and 19.343–345) and in the intertestamental literature to the use of these public facilities by the Hellenizers (1 Macc 1:14; 2 Macc 4:9, 12). This group, which wished to adopt Greek culture and practice, were stronger in the cities. They freely attended dramatic events and participated in games such as foot races, wrestling, and other Olympian events. By the New Testament period, Paul could freely use the analogy of running a race in 1 Cor 9:24–27 in describing his ministry. He further compares it to "fighting a good fight" in 2 Tim 4:7. In these passages, however, he is speaking primarily to Gentiles and Hellenized Jewish Christians. Jews in Palestine were still offended by the excesses of Herod in staging Greek games in Jerusalem. The naked performers and the gold and silver statuettes given to the winners caused a great uproar (*Ant.* 15.277–283).

So they built a gymnasium in Jerusalem, according to Gentile custom, . . .   —1 Macc 1:14

Drama combined the study of Greek literature with live entertainment to enhance the cultural life of the Hellenistic city. Regular performances of the Greek playwrights were held in the theaters (like that at Sepphoris) all over the Near East further educating the people in Greek values and philosophy. Paul's use of quotations from Greek plays, reflects the great familiarity these dramas had in the Hellenized cities. Examples of this are found in 1 Cor 15:33, "Bad company ruins good morals" (a phrase from Menander), and Ti 1:12, "Cretans are always liars, evil beasts, lazy gluttons" (quoted from Epimenides).

Public baths were also constructed to provide city dwellers with a familiar place to socialize, transact business informally, and engage in the hygienic pleasures of alternating hot and cold baths (*Ant.* 19.329). The recently excavated baths at

*Theater. Photo by Ralph
Harris.*   5-12

Capernaum include large pools as well as smaller
rooms where private conversations could take
place within the cleansing steam. A separate bath
facility was also uncovered there for the use of
the Roman garrison. Despite the mixed population of this site on the Sea of Galilee, it was probably best to separate Roman troops from the local
inhabitants. There were also separate bathing facilities (*Miqva'ot*) for ritual cleansing (Lev 15:5–11)
used by the Jews, such as those associated with
the Essenes in Jerusalem and at Qumran. These,
however, were not designed to be used for social
gatherings, but rather as a way of purifying the
body before entering the temple or after it had
been made impure by sexual activity or contact
with the dead.

E. EDUCATION AND SCHOLARSHIP

Throughout the period from 350 BC to AD 70,
traditional Jewish education in Hebrew and Aramaic continued to be conducted in the home, the
temple in Jerusalem (Lk 2:46), and in the local
synagogues. Jewish tradition states that local
schools for young children were created by the
high priest in the 1st century AD (Bab. Talm.
Baba Bathra 21a). There is no scriptural evidence

of this, however, except Jesus' demonstrated knowledge of the law (Lk 2:41–51) and his ability to read Hebrew even though he was just the son of a carpenter (Lk 4:16–17).

In the Diaspora, education for some Jews and most of the Greek residents of the Hellenistic cities took place in the gymnasium. Here students studied Greek language and literature using the same writing exercises and handbooks on rhetoric which were used all over the Greco-Roman world. As the writings of Philo of Alexandria reflect, the mixture of Greek literature with the study of the Hebrew scriptures produced some new schools of thought on Jewish traditions.

During this period priests and scholars in Palestine and the Diaspora gradually came to a consensus on those books which were considered as scripture. This process can be seen in the "Prologue" to Sirach, an apocryphal book written by Jesus ben Sirach about 180 BC, which

A ritual bathing pool called a miqvah. Photo courtesy of Southwest Missouri State University. 5-13

Temple Scroll from Qumran. 5-E

lists the traditional division of the canon into Law, the Prophets, and the Writings. Eventually, it became conventional to close the canon of prophetic speech with the time of Ezra. However, new books continued to be authored as late as the 2nd century AD. One group of 15 books from this period formed the additional set of writings known as the Apocrypha. Some of these manuscripts were written during the Hellenistic period and dealt with the events surrounding the Maccabean revolt, or provided traditional material related to books already included in the canon, such as the Rest of Esther and First and Second Esdras (4 Ezra).

Long before the fall of the temple, the communities of the Diaspora made an accommodation with Hellenistic culture that produced the first translation of the Hebrew text of the Bible. The Septuagint (abbreviated LXX), a Greek version of the Old Testament books, was produced in Alexandria, Egypt some time after 200 BC. It was made necessary when Greek became the common language of the Jewish people outside of Palestine. Being a product of Hellenistic culture, the Septuagint, unlike the Hebrew canon, incorporated some contemporary literature into its collection of writings. Thus the 15 books of the Apocrypha were included in the finalized Alexandrian canon of the Septuagint. By the first century AD, the Septuagint was the Bible version used by most of the New Testament writers.

After the destruction of the temple in AD 70, the burden of Jewish education and the preservation of the Hebrew canon fell on the community of scholars at Jamnia and their successors in synagogues wherever Jews lived. The Jamnia rabbis, in the period from about AD 90–100, compiled manuscripts and in an exhaustive process of deliberations determined which books would be included in this canon of scripture. Fourth Ezra 14:37–48 describes the recreation of the traditional canon of 24 books and an additional 70 volumes of apocryphal wisdom.

The books of the Apocrypha were not accepted into the Hebrew canon by the rabbis at Jamnia for a variety of reasons; neither was another body of literature known as the Pseudepigrapha. These 65 books, many produced during this time of Hellenistic synthesis, date well into the Roman era, and some (Testaments of the Twelve Patriarchs) were influenced by the early Christian community. They contain folk stories, additions to canonical books, and the meditations of scholars and scribes in Palestine and the Diaspora. Examples of these works include 1 Enoch, Jubilees, and the Testament of Job. Their worth was considered secondary to the text of the original body of scripture. Their authorship was often uncertain, and, significantly, most were written in Greek.

Eventually, a dispute arose among the Jews over the importance of these writings in relation to the canonical material. Religious parties arose as a consequence of this issue. Some pious Jews advocated the free use of the interpretive material as the equal of the canonical (Pharisees). Another (Sadducees) argued for strict and exclusive use of the biblical text to answer religious questions.

After AD 200 more emphasis was placed by the rabbis on the study and reiteration of the legal pronouncements in the scriptures. Local communities of scholars taught young men the Torah and expounded on its meaning. This resulted in the creation of the Mishnah under the direction of Rabbi Judah the Prince. It consists of 63 tractates or treatises comprising the consensus of rabbinic opinion on how the laws of the Pentateuch related to aspects of everyday life (agriculture, marriage, ritual purity) in their time. Additional commentary on these legal treatises is contained in the Babylonian and Palestinian Talmuds, dating to the period of the mid-4th through mid-6th centuries AD. Commentary or Midrash on nonlegal material, including legendary narratives of the lives of the major biblical figures in the Hebrew canon, is also contained in the Talmud.

F. LAW AND THE ADMINISTRATION OF JUSTICE

There were several shifts of authority in the enforcement of the law during the Hellenistic and Roman periods. During portions of this era foreign governments and their representatives imposed order, imprisoning offenders, and carrying out capital punishment. At other times the Hasmonean government and the Sanhedrin council had primary responsibility for the administration of justice. In many cases there was little distinction made between civil and religious law since the Torah imposed penalties for crimes against person (theft, murder, adultery) as well as crimes against God (blasphemy, pagan worship). Thus to speak of the administration of justice in this period requires some mental juggling.

Basically, local civil and criminal cases were handled by local courts, whether they were appointed by the Greeks, the Hasmoneans, the Herodians, or the Romans. If it was a matter of land or property ownership, the services of a scribe or lawyer might be employed (Lk 11:45 – 46). Capital crimes, and cases of treason or civil unrest brought the higher authorities based in Jerusalem or Caesarea to bear on the problem (Mt 26:57 – 27:49). Clear cut religious crimes were handled by the leaders of the local synagogue or by the high priest and the Sanhedrin. For instance, some Sadducean members of the Sanhedrin had Peter and John arrested and tried for preaching, in Jesus' name, the resurrection of the dead (Acts 4:1 – 22).

The Roman officials throughout the empire had jurisdiction to overrule local courts or to intervene in any case in which they were interested. Thus, when the members of the Sanhedrin

While Peter and John were speaking to the people, the priests, the captain of the temple, and the Sadducees came to them, much annoyed because they were teaching the people and proclaiming that in Jesus there is the resurrection of the dead.

—Acts 4:1–2

and their followers nearly came to blows over Paul's case, the Roman tribune had him taken to the local army barracks for safekeeping (Acts 22:6–10). Roman citizenship, which had been acquired by some of the people of the provinces, also figured in the process of justice. As a Roman citizen of Cilicia, Paul successfully avoided further prosecution by the Jewish leadership by appealing his case to Caesar. Despite his desire to do a favor for the Jews, Festus, the Roman procurator, was obliged by law to grant Paul's request (Acts 25:9–12).

G. CLOTHING AND PERSONAL ADORNMENT

The wealthy and those involved in the government during the Persian period and on through the Roman era commonly adopted foreign clothing styles. Among those items of Persian clothing most often adopted were riding trousers with boots and leggings and a high felt cap. Zephaniah's admonitions (1:8) against the wearing of "strange apparel" suggest that these fashions had become fairly widespread. Persian garb was displaced, however, with the coming of the Greeks.

And on the day of the LORD's sacrifice I will punish the officials and the king's sons and all who dress themselves in foreign attire. —Zeph 1:8

At first there was some resistance among the Jews to Hellenistic fashions. For instance, one charge made against Jason, the high priest in the time of Antiochus IV, was that he forced the nobility of Jerusalem to wear a broad-brimmed hat associated with the cult of the Greek god Hermes (2 Macc 3:12). It was not until the mid-Hasmonean period that Greek costume became common among the general population in Palestine. Rejection of the new fashions was less common in the Diaspora communities like Alexandria. There the Jews quickly adopted the Greek styles of dress.

By the time of Jesus there was no stigma attached to wearing the *colobium,* a long seamless tunic (Jn 19:23), with a cloak (*pallium,* Mt 27:31), and tassels (*tsitsith*) on the four corners of the hem

(Mt 9:20; Mk 6:56). There were often decorative bands on the *colobium* which ran from the shoulder to the hem. Foot coverings included both the sandal as well as the Roman *calceus,* a shoe that covered the entire foot. There was no formal headgear for men, except for the embroidered cap of the high priest (*Ant.* 3.172), in this period. Women were required to cover their long hair with a veil while praying or prophesying, a Roman style (1 Cor 11:4 – 7), but no generalization about this practice in other contexts is possible.

While specific items of jewelry are seldom mentioned in the New Testament, archaeological discoveries have shown that the jeweler's art continued to flourish. Gold bracelets and clothes clasps encrusted with jewels, colored glass, and pearls have been uncovered, adding credence to the description of the woman in Rev 17:4. Greek and Roman styles of jewelry were also borrowed along with female hairstyles. First Timothy 2:9 contains Paul's admonition that women in the Christian community not adopt unseemly apparel, which he describes as "braided hair or gold or pearls or costly attire" (cf., Juvenal's *Satire* 6; T Reuben 5:1 – 5). Enscribed seals and rings, used to stamp documents or possessions or as adornment on fingers and toes, are also common finds in the excavation of Roman occupation levels.

Although not specifically for adornment purposes, *tephillin* or phylacteries were commonly worn by devout men in the time of Jesus. Found in the excavations of the Qumran community, they were black leather boxes, each containing four passages of scripture. Based on injunctions in Ex 13:9 and Dt 6:8 to keep the law constantly in the mind and heart, they were attached to the forehead and the left arm by leather straps. The phylacteries also became a source of excessive pride, according to Mt 23:5, for some literally wore their religion on their sleeves.

The woman was clothed in purple and scarlet, and adorned with gold and jewels and pearls, holding in her hand a golden cup full of abominations and the impurities of her fornication; . . .

— Rev 17:4

H. WEAPONS AND WARFARE

The methods and instruments of warfare continued to become more sophisticated during the Hellenistic and Roman eras. This was due in large part to the introduction of new weapons (catapults and ballistae) and siege engines by the Greek and Roman armies that conquered the area (*War* 3.80). Acquiring skill with these new weapons and methods took time for the Jews. Their basic lack of military experience lead to a terrible massacre during the early part of the Maccabean revolt. Being attacked on the Sabbath and refusing to break the Sabbath law, over 1,000 were killed (*Ant.* 12.274–275). Subsequently, they learned to put this law aside temporarily in times of national crisis.

Open warfare against Antiochus IV's army of experienced soldiers, horsemen, and elephants (*War* 1.41) was clearly impossible for the under-equipped Jews. It was the guerrilla tactics of Judas Maccabeus and his brothers Jonathan and Simon that finally outlasted the Seleucid forces. Even after the Greek armies were expelled from most of Palestine, the Jews' lack of skills in siege warfare meant that the Seleucid citadel in Jerusalem, the Akra, was not captured until 142 BC (1 Macc 13:49–52; *Ant.* 13.215–217).

In the Roman period there were numerous Jewish uprisings in addition to the two principal revolts of AD 69–70 and 132. Weaponry for infantry in these conflicts generally consisted of the Greek or Roman short sword and javelin, a breastplate, shield, and helmet (Eph 6:13–17; *War* 7.94–95). Daggers or short swords were often concealed under the garments of rebels and those, like the *sicarii*, who sought to instigate civil unrest (*War* 7.409–412; 20.164–165; Mt 26:51). The Roman cavalry carried pikes, shields, and a quiver of throwing darts. Their horses were also partially armored (*War* 7.96–97).

Throughout the New Testament period the

So this Antiochus got together fifty thousand footmen, and five thousand horsemen, and fourscore elephants, and marched through Judea into the mountainous parts. He then took Bethsura, which was a small city; but at a place called Bethzacharias, where the passage was narrow, Judas met him with his army.
—Josephus, *War* 1.41

Romans were the unprecedented masters of warfare. The effects of their unparalleled organizational skills and expertise in siege warfare could only be delayed, not overcome (*War* 7.70–101). Josephus' description of the siege of Jerusalem is a case in point. Although the Jews managed to burn the Roman siege works and battering rams, famine and lost of life during the many skirmishes eventually led to the fall of the city (*War* 5.466–490).

I. DISEASE AND MEDICAL TREATMENT

Ben Sira, during the early 2nd century BC, described the physician as a partner with Yahweh in the healing process. He was to be given "his place," because his skill came from God. The patient was to pray to God, but "there is a time when success lies in the hands of physicians, for they too pray to the Lord" to aid with the diagnosis (Sir 38:12–14). In contrast, the New Testament does not give such a positive endorsement of physicians or the practice of medicine (Lk 4:23 and 5:31 mention them proverbially) because of its emphasis on the healing character of God's Spirit. Luke is the most prominently mentioned (Col 4:14), but of course he is a Greek.

He said to them, "Doubtless you will quote to me this proverb, 'Doctor, cure yourself!' And you will say, 'Do here also in your hometown the things that we have heard you did at Capernaum.'"
— Luke 4:23

Jewish physicians might well have had the same training as Luke, but it is likely that most of their medical knowledge had Egyptian origin. The Egyptians were the most advanced physicians in the ancient Near East. They performed intricate surgeries including trepaning, boring through a skull to relieve the pressure of fluid built up after a concussion or as a result of a tumor, and the lancing of boils. Their medical treatises display a general knowledge of herbal medicines for the relief of certain ailments such as indigestion, constipation, and sleeplessness. These cures, as Ben Sira notes (Sir 38:1–15), were also many times accompanied with sacrifices, prayers, and incantations to invoke God's aid along with the medicines.

In Palestine and elsewhere there were groups of doctors seeing patients whom they could not heal. The primitive (by modern medical standards) instruments they used to diagnose and treat illness simply could not cope with many diseases. This is graphically seen in Mk 5:25 – 26 (paralleled in Lk 8:43 – 44), which tells of a woman who had suffered from a chronic form of hemorrhaging for 12 years and had spent all her savings paying for useless cures from physicians. With hope running out, she sought out Jesus, whose reputation as a healer had been growing throughout the country. This sort of desperation to find a cure is of course still a part of the medical scene today with people traveling great distances in hopes of a wonder drug or a miracle at the hands of a faith healer.

It had also been standard procedure since the earliest periods of Jewish history to consult priests (Lev 13:2 – 8) or prophets (1 Kgs 14:1 – 3; 2 Kgs 5:3) to diagnose and cure disease. Although Jesus was not a priest, his stature as a prophet was accepted by many (Mt 16:13 – 14) and this attracted those looking for the traditional curative abilities of the man of God (Lk 9:37 – 40; Acts 5:16).

This seems to be especially the case in instances of demon possession. These individuals were afflicted with both physical (blindness, Mt 12:22; epilepsy, Lk 9:39) and severe mental disorders (Mk 5:2 – 5), and thus were beyond the abilities of normal medical practitioners. The dialogue Jesus has with the possessing spirits in Mk 5:7 – 10 provides a recognition by these beings of his power, just as Jesus' explanation in Mt 12:25 – 32 differentiates his actions and his realm from that of Satan. There is no modern explanation for Jesus' casting out of demons. The mental distress these people manifest in the Gospels may be purely psychological or they may represent the Gospel writ-

Now there was a woman who had been suffering from hemorrhages for twelve years. She had endured much under many physicians, and had spent all that she had; and she was no better, but rather grew worse.

— Mark 5:25 – 26

Pool of Siloam. Photo by Ralph Harris.   5-14

ers' attempt to emphasize the messianic qualities of Jesus.

The other major source of cures in ancient Palestine was the hot spring, such as that near Tiberias, or a pool in which the afflicted dipped themselves (cf. also Na'aman's cleansing in the Jordan in 2 Kgs 5:10–14). Among the best known of these pools was that at Bethesda (or Bethzatha) near the Sheep Gate in Jerusalem. In Jn 5:2–7, this pool was said to be surrounded by the sick and the crippled who believed that the first to enter the water when its surface became troubled would be instantly cured. The movement of the water was probably due to the actions of an intermittent spring, but in antiquity this was attributed to the touch of an angel or other divine being.

Modern scholars have attempted to identify Bethesda through excavation as well as the use of ancient literary sources. The Copper Scroll from the Qumran community as well as Eusebius mention two rain-fed pools frequented by the sick. Although the number of ancient churches and other structures built over this area prevent a full tracing of the cisterns in question, it seems likely that those uncovered just north of the temple are the pools of Bethesda.

J. BURIAL CUSTOMS

The poor and the stranger were buried in unmarked, shallow graves (Lk 11:44) or in a "potter's field" (Mt 27:1–10). The remains of these burials have long since disappeared. Therefore, our knowledge of burial customs in the Hellenistic and Roman periods is primarily based on the tombs of the more affluent or those who belonged to associations which provided proper burial for their members. Most of these individuals were interred in caves (Jn 11:38) or rock-cut tombs located outside the city walls, such as those in the Kidron Valley on the western slope of the Mount of Olives.

Then Jesus, again greatly disturbed, came to the tomb. It was a cave, and a stone was lying against it. —John 11:38

After death the body was washed, its eyes were closed and its mouth and other orifices were bound shut (Jn 11:44). A mixture of spices was applied to the body, perhaps as a preservation or perhaps to ward off the smell of decomposition for those who visited the tomb later (Jn 11:39; 19:39–40). It was then dressed in its own clothes or placed in a linen shroud (Mt 27:59). Next, a procession, including musicians, family, and (if the family could afford it) professional mourners followed the corpse to the tomb (Mt 9:23). It was customary for mourners to continue to visit the tomb for 30 days, to reanoint the body (Mk 16:1) or to check to be sure the person had not been buried prematurely (Jn 11:31).

Tombs varied in size and design. The very elaborate tomb of Jason, dated to the 1st century BC, contains four outer chambers separated by stone doors, and a burial chamber with radiating loculi (individual interment chambers). There is

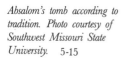
Absalom's tomb according to tradition. Photo courtesy of Southwest Missouri State University. 5-15

also a communal charnel, designed to hold the bones of earlier burials that had been displaced by more recent ones. This seems particularly elaborate compared to the description of Joseph of Arimathea's garden, rock-cut tomb, with its sealing stone, in which the body of Jesus was laid (Jn 19:41; Mt 27:59–60).

Some of the Herodian era and early 1st century tombs show the wealth expended in the building of tombs. Most contain carved limestone ossuaries in which the bones of several people were placed. The condition of some of the skeletal remains from this period also show the unrest and conflict of the times. Some clearly reveal sword cuts and one case of death by crucifixion has been discovered in a tomb at Givat ha-Mivtar. In this instance an iron nail was driven through one of the victim's heel bones and twisted as it struck a knot in the cross.

Among the most spectacular of those Herodian era tombs in the Kidron Valley are Zechariah's Tomb, dated to period of the fall of the temple, and Absalom's monument, dated to the period just before AD 70. They both include a *nefesh,* a pyramidal-shaped monument, considered a habitation for the soul of the deceased in Egyptian and other cultures, but simply as a memorial among the Jews (1 Macc 13:27 – 30). The outsides of these tombs may have been whitewashed to note a recent burial and thus warn Jews from contaminating contact with the dead (Mt 23:27).

II. ECONOMIC LIFE

What were the basic elements of economic life during the Hellenistic and Roman periods of domination?

A. TRADE ROUTES AND THE MEANS OF TRAVEL

The international character of the Greek and Roman empires required reliable and well-kept travel routes. Since ancient times Palestine had relied on the Via Maris, the King's Highway,

The sophisticated Roman road system was one reason for the rapid spread of Christianity. Photo courtesy of Southwest Missouri State University. 5-16

and a system of roads that had expanded with the fortunes of the Israelite monarchy. With the coming of the Greeks and Romans, however, the network of roads throughout the Near East markedly expanded and improved. There were still dangers along these roads (Lk 10:30) from robbers, but a real attempt was made by the Romans to keep them open. For instance, Pompey's swift rise to political power and notoriety in Rome came after ridding the Mediterranean Sea of pirates. With travel to distant places becoming more feasible for large numbers of people (Acts 18:2, 16:4; 1 Cor 1:12), a general upsurge in commercial activity took place. Along with this was an increase in cultural exchange as these improved trade routes were travelled by eager merchants carrying goods, gossip, and religious beliefs.

There he found a Jew named Aquila, a native of Pontus, who had recently come from Italy with his wife Priscilla, because Claudius had ordered all Jews to leave Rome. Paul went to see them,
—Acts 18:2

Wherever the Greek, Roman, or Jewish merchant went, he took with him his goods as well as his culture. Thus, in every commercial center (Antioch, Corinth, Ephesus), there were ethnic communities established. For the Jews this meant a synagogue with its governing body of elders, a school, and a network of families in whose houses travelers could stay without encountering the dangers of public inns or taverns. These communities of Jews, in turn, provided the first stop for Paul and the other early Christian missionaries (Acts 13:15–48).

Means of travel included the traditional pack animals, the donkey and camel, as well as two- and four-wheel carts. These latter vehicles, pulled by teams of oxen, were used to transport grain to market from the farming villages and trade goods throughout the Near East. Chariots were also used by wealthy travelers and government officials. One example of this is found in Acts 8:26–29 where Philip meets the Ethiopian eunuch, who is riding in his chariot on the desert road between Gaza and Jerusalem.

Wheeled vehicles needed wider paths and broader,

paved city gate complexes. In heavy traffic zones, more than one lane would have been required to facilitate movement and prevent disputes between teamsters. Because these vehicles and traveling officials needed well-kept roads (Prov 15:19), governments and perhaps even local authorities must have regularly sent work gangs along the more traveled routes to clear away stones and other obstructions (Isa 62:10). Where river crossings had to be made, fords were identified, and in the Roman period flat stones were laid in the river bed to smooth the way for the wagon wheels.

The Persians introduced a system of way stations every 10 to 15 miles along the roadways throughout their vast empire. This practice was continued by the Hellenistic rulers as well as the Romans. One way that archaeologists are able to identify ancient roads today is through the discovery of Roman mile markers that were set up by the rulers who ordered the roads to be built or repaired. These markers not only indicate the route but, based on the name of the Roman emperor in the inscription, when it was constructed.

Travel by sea, although generally only during certain seasons of the year, was also quite common. Paul's journey described in Acts 27 provides a great deal of information on accommodation of prisoners and passengers on commercial ships. Their voyage, despite ending in shipwreck, is an excellent portrayal of the type of difficulties faced by an often overloaded vessel whose only means of forward motion was its sails. Their first ship is described as being one that made calls at the ports of Asia, presumably transporting cargo and making deliveries along the way. At Myra, in Lysia, they transferred to an open sea vessel from Alexandria. During this leg of the voyage, mention is made of sailing leeward of islands to avoid contrary winds; baggage, tackle, and finally cargo (wheat) are thrown overboard to lighten the ship when it had to run before a storm. The cupidity

Embarking on a ship of Adramyttium that was about to set sail to the ports along the coast of Asia, we put to sea, accompanied by Aristarchus, a Macedonian from Thessalonica.
—Acts 27:2

An ancient Roman milestone.
Photo courtesy of Southwest
Missouri State University.
5-17

of the ship's owner, captain, and crew are also displayed in their insistence on sailing in the stormy winter season (vv 9–11), and their attempt to abandon the ship during the storm, leaving the passengers to fend for themselves (v 30).

The very circuitous route of Paul's ship from Caesarea to Rome was typical of trading vessels. The war galleys of Rome of course took a more direct path and had rows of oars to supplement the sails. They were used to support and transport land troops and to carry messages quickly to the farther corners of the empires. Paul, whose status as a prisoner did not warrant transport on a galley, had to rely on lesser and slower accommodations (Acts 28:11–13).

B. WEIGHTS AND MEASURES

The commercial advantages of a standardized system of weights and measures was recognized very early in Israelite history. The standard shekel weight (8.75 grams), which became the primary measuring unit, was borrowed from the Canaanites, who had borrowed it from Mesopotamia. As trade expanded into the Egyptian sphere of influence adjustments had to be made to provide equivalencies to their system. Weights uncovered by archaeologists at Israelite sites (dated to the 8th and 7th centuries BC) show this development with Egyptian hieratic symbols inscribed on metal balance weights.

Although somewhat cumbersome compared to modern western standards of weights and measures, the 8-shekel weight as the basic module, when used consistently, provided a reasonably sound system for commerce. Multiples or fractions of this weight allowed for transference of goods and commodities with a reasonable expectation that a shekel's weight in one area would be a shekel's weight in another. Discrepancies did occur of course since some areas relied on a so-called heavy shekel while others used a "light" or "royal standard" shekel. Corruption was also a problem, as the numerous references to the use of "false balances" show (Hos 12:7; Amos 8:5).

Volume measures again varied because of the differences between the Jewish system and the overlapping Greek and Roman systems. According to the terminology of Ezk 45:11–14, it seems the basic unit of dry measure was the homer (variously equated with 6.5 to 14 bushels). The cor was equal to the homer, and could be used for liquid measure as well. Its volume varies, with some sources describing it as equal to between 35

A trader, in whose hands are false balances, he loves to oppress. — Hos 12:7

Bronze "lion weights." Photo courtesy of the British Museum.

5-18

and 95 gallons. This unit was then broken down with 10 baths equal to one cor. The bath was then used to determine many smaller measures (1 Kgs 7:26), although the log (2/3 pint) is the smallest unit mentioned (Lev 14:10). The approximate nature of this system of measurement can be seen by examining storage jars found at Tell Beit Mirsim which are inscribed with the word bath. They have been shown to have the liquid capacity of about 5.5 gallons.

Roman measures used in the New Testament period include the pint (sextarius), the quart (choinix) in Rev 6:6, and the jar (metrete), which is said in Jn 2:6 to hold about 10.6 gallons. The pound of costly ointment which Mary, the sister of Martha, used to anoint Jesus's feet probably weighed 12 ounces (Jn 12:3).

Measurements of distance in Israel were based on the cubit (17.5 inches = the length of a man's forearm), the span (about 9 inches), and the finger (about 3/4 inch). These units, like all others in antiquity, varied from place to place and over time (cf., the larger cubit of Ezk 40:5 = 20.6 inches). The Roman cubit was approximately 17 inches in length and was used to measure distances (Jn 21:8) and height (Rev 21:17). A mile (Mt 5:41) in Roman measure equaled 5,000 feet. This was broken down into smaller measures: the stadium (Lk 24:13 has 7 miles = 60 stadia or 650 feet/per stadium), and the fathom, mentioned in Acts 27:28 as a depth guide used by sailors = 6 feet.

C. Coins

Since the time of the Persians, the Near East had become reliant on a money economy (1 Chr 29:7 and Neh 7:70 mention the Persian daric). Minted coinage had been introduced by the Lydians in the 7th century BC and became widespread by the time of Alexander the Great. Standardization of weights and the certification of coinage size and weight with the royal Persian and later Alexandrian seal speeded commerce and facilitated trade between regions.

Now some of the heads of ancestral houses contributed to the work. The governor gave to the treasury one thousand darics of gold, fifty basins, and five hundred thirty priestly robes.
— Neh 7:70

The fact that the Jews were allowed to coin money during the Persian period (4th century BC) is attested by the discovery of a number of small silver coins bearing the inscription "Yehud" (Judah). For large transactions and donations to the temple, the mina (727 grams) and the talent (43,620 grams) continued to be used (Ezr 2:69; 8:26), but the smaller shekel weight (8.75 grams) was more common in the marketplace.

The Greek rulers of Palestine restricted the coining of money to their own mints. However, after the Maccabean revolt (as they will during the Jewish revolts of AD 70 and 135), the Jews once again began minting their own bronze and lead coins to proclaim their independence and to supplement the silver and gold coinage of the Hellenistic kingdoms. Greek inscriptions on these Jewish coins mention the Hasmonean kings Alexander Jannaeus and Jonathan, and contain inscribed anchors and flowers.

Herod's mints in Tiberias and Jerusalem issued dated coins based on the Roman standard weights. The Roman procurators in Palestine used imperial coinage supplemented with locally minted coins, which bore nonreligious symbols to prevent having problems with the scrupulously monotheistic Jews. The silver denarius from Antioch or Caesarea and the didrachma of Tyre were commonly used to pay the annual temple tax. One of these was probably the coin mentioned in Mk 12:16 which is said to bear the likeness of Caesar.

By New Testament times a remarkable variety of Greek, Roman, and foreign coins circulated in Palestine. This was due in part to the longevity of coins and the introduction of the coins of Roman soldiers brought to Palestine from all over the empire. Larger currency contained the image of the reigning emperor who had ordered it to be minted (Mk 12:15; Lk 20:24). These dated coins help archaeologists determine the chronology of levels within their excavations. When they are found embedded in them, they can aid in the determination of when walls or floors were built.

"Show me a denarius. Whose head and whose title does it bear?" They said, "The emperor's." — Luke 20:24

The range of common coinage sizes and types runs from the Greek copper lepton, worth half a penny (Mk 12:42; Mt 5:26), to the shekel weight Greek silver stater (Mt 17:27) and the Roman silver denarius (Mt 22:20). The denarius in Mt 20:2, however, was a smaller coin (worth about 20 cents), which apparently was the standard wage for day laborers. There was also a gold shekel worth 15 silver shekels, the larger weight currency, the pound (Lk 19:16) and the talent mentioned in Mt 25:15 (worth 3,000 shekels).

Despite the free use of many different currencies, money changers did exist to exchange foreign coins for the silver didrachma of Tyre which was used to pay the temple tax. A fee was charged for this service of between 4 and 8 percent. They also served as bankers, paying interest on money left in their charge (Mt 25:37). These commercial transactions and the sale of sacrificial animals within the outer precincts of this holiest of places led the angered Jesus to "cleanse the temple" (Mt 21:12–13; Mk 11:15; Lk 19:45–46).

D. URBAN INDUSTRY AND PROFESSIONS

Skilled and service industries dominated the work force in the cities of Palestine and the Greco-Roman world. Royal and administrative patrons spent great sums on public works projects, employing large numbers of masons and other workmen. For example, in Corinth a Latin inscription states "Erastus laid this pavement at his own expense, in appreciation of his appointment as aedile." This may be the same man mentioned in Rom 16:23 as city treasurer of Corinth.

The idea of patronage, of leaving a permanent monument to one's service to the people, and the honor to be gained from beautifying the city, motivated many such individual acts by the wealthy and powerful. The Herods were no exception, with Herod the Great almost rebuilding Jerusalem and endowing temples and other buildings throughout Palestine and the Near East. Josephus, following this line of reasoning, described Herod Agrippa as being:

> by nature generous in his gifts, and made it a point of honour to be highminded towards gentiles; and by expending massive sums he raised himself to high fame. He took pleasure in conferring favours and rejoiced in popularity. . . . (*Ant.* 19.328)

The remains of a glass oven.
Photo by Ralph Harris. 5-19

The Herods did produce a remarkable number of beautiful public buildings. However, the large numbers of workmen attracted to these projects were eventually left without employment when the building boom ended. Their discontent and lack of hope contributed to the passions that exploded in the Jewish revolt of AD 70.

While cottage industry was the pattern in the villages, in the cities larger scale finishing and manufacturing took place. Woolen thread, spun by village women, was woven into cloth on the looms in the garment district of Jerusalem, near the Dung Gate. Tailors were also available to cut and sew this cloth into finished garments (Mt 11:8), and fullers could dye or bleach them (Mk 9:3). Pottery, metal utensils, and weapons were all made and sold in the shops of Jerusalem.

Leather goods were produced as well, although the tanning process was conducted outside the walls because of the smells and resulting residue. Paul had learned the trade of tentmaking and leather work as a young man in Tarsus and continued to earn his living at it during his missionary journeys (1 Thes 2:9; 1 Cor 9:6). It also gave him the opportunity to associate with other urban craftsmen and thus make contacts wherever he went (Acts 18:3).

And, because he was of the same trade, he stayed with them, and they worked together — by trade they were tentmakers.
—Acts 18:3

The grain brought in from the surrounding villages was baked into bread for the city's inhabitants (*Ant.* 15.309 – 310), and there were butchers who provided freshly slaughtered meat. The large number of olive trees growing in the vicinity of the city of Jerusalem (Acts 1:12) provided enough oil that it could be exported. Spices and ointments to anoint the body were commonly available (Mk 14:3 – 5, 16:1) and may have either been refined or prepared in Jerusalem.

E. VILLAGE ECONOMY

Rural life and economic activity were still based on the small family land holding. Jesus frequently drew from simple agricultural activity to make his point in telling parables (the sower in Mt 13:3–9 and the winnower in Lk 3:15). Produce from plots of land, often on terraced hillsides, fed the family, the village, and the nearby urban centers. A portion also went for taxes (*Ant.* 14.202–206), thereby impoverishing some farmers in bad years. Some villages, like those on the Sea of Galilee around Capernaum, supplemented their income and their diet with fishing (Lk 5:2–11).

Due to economic hardship and political changes, a growing proportion of the better land came into the hands of absentee landlords. On several occasions they gained ownership through the patronage of the Herods (Mk 3:6; *Ant.* 15.2) or the Romans. They used tenant farmers Mk 12:2) or day laborers to work the land (Mt 20:1), and employed stewards to manage the affairs of their estates (Lk 16:1). These landless peasants in turn became discontented with their lot and their economic helplessness (Mt 20:1–16; Mk 12:2–9), and formed a portion of the rebel forces during the First Jewish Revolt.

Depending upon the size of the village, some goods would have been produced by local craftsmen. Tiny, insignificant Nazareth (Jn 1:46) was probably pleased to have the services of the carpenter Joseph and his son (Mk 6:3). They probably produced baskets, chests, and furniture, and they would have been responsible for transporting and installing ceiling beams in most of the village homes (Mt 7:4–5). Local potters undoubtedly worked in these villages as well, although the finer ware and that which was imported from Greece and Cappadocia would have been purchased in the cities.

Then Jesus said to the disciples, "There was a rich man who had a manager, and charges were brought to him that this man was squandering his property."
—Luke 16:1

III. RELIGIOUS LIFE

What were the basic aspects of religious life in the period from Alexander to the fall of Jerusalem in AD 70?

The rebuilding of the temple in Jerusalem in 515 BC had once again provided the Jews with a focus for their religion. Although temple worship and religious life was not perfect (Isa 58:1–9), a symbol of unity was recreated that served all of the communities of Jews throughout the Near East and elsewhere. The physical aspect of their devotion to the temple, aside from sacrifice, is found in regular pilgrimages and in the payment of the annual temple tax by all adult males (Mt 17:24). Religious rites and instruction were in the hands of the priests. The power of the priesthood grew to new heights since there was no restoration of the monarchy. Also in this period, however, a growing number of Jewish sects were born out of the discontent with the priestly monopoly over the temple and over theological disagreements.

For as the lightning flashes and lights up the sky from one side to the other, so will the Son of Man be in his day.
— Matt 17:24

A. PRIESTS AND TEMPLE

Worship in the post-exilic temple in Jerusalem was formalized with the Zadokite priesthood in strict control. Their role in the Second Temple period was one of responsibility and regulation. They were responsible for reinitiating and maintaining the sacrificial cult, and the religious calendar of festivals. The orchestration of temple music and other lesser rites would have also been in their hands. Levites who returned from the exile or who had remained in Palestine during the Babylonian Captivity were given some responsibilities for the maintenance of the temple complex, but were not allowed to participate in sacrificial activities. In addition to performing their cultic duties, the priests also regulated certain aspects of life, such as marriage (Ezr 9–10) and the types of work activities which could be carried out on the Sabbath (Neh 13:15–22).

In the Second Temple period it once again became customary to make pilgrimages to Jerusalem to attend the three major religious festivals: Passover, the Feast of Weeks, and the Feast of Tabernacles. The temple treasury grew with the donations of these pilgrims and the annual temple tax, making it the wealthiest institution in the country. Its wealth also became a target during the period of Seleucid control when Antiochus IV plundered the temple (1 Macc 1:21–23; 2 Macc 5:15–21). With so much cash coming into its coffers, the temple must have served as a bank, lending out sums to help finance business and to stimulate the economy by increasing the amount of money in circulation.

The power and prestige of the temple and the priestly community eventually led to involvement in politics. It was the high priest Jason who helped precipitate the Maccabean revolt in 169 BC with his introduction of Greek customs and acceptance of Antiochus IV's tribute demands (2 Macc 4:7–17). Following the revolt, the Hasmoneans gained control of both the office of high priest (1 Macc 14:17) as well as secular leadership (1 Macc 14:41–45). Their control of these offices continued until Herod obtained the kingship from the Romans and thereafter handpicked the high priest (*Ant.* 15.39–41).

Herod's attempt to control the priests and the people also included his construction of a newly designed and expanded temple over the one built by Zerubbabel. Construction began in Herod's 18th year as king and continued for 46 years (Jn 2:20). Josephus, who had seen this temple before its destruction, provides a detailed description of its construction and appearance (*Ant.* 15.380–425). A large area was cleared around the temple and a huge, walled platform (approximately 1,440 feet long and 960 feet wide) was constructed as a base for the temple and its adjoining structures. The slope was enclosed with massive blocks of limestone and the Antonia Tower was constructed on the northwest corner to house the Roman garrison and serve as the residence of the Roman procurator when he was in Jerusalem. Gates were

The Jews then said, "This temple has been under construction for forty-six years, and will you raise it up in three days?"
—John 2:20

built in all four walls, with a huge staircase leading up to those on the south side.

The older structure of the shrine was preserved until the walls of the new building enclosed it. It was then dismantled by priests trained as stone masons. Although the new sanctuary was patterned after Solomon's temple, its Greco-Roman colonnades and lavish use of gold decorated roofs and columns demonstrated that it was a product of the Hellenistic age. The holy site had been preserved and fortified, but the new temple was as much a testament to Herod's power and wealth as it was to the people's devotion to Yahweh.

Despite Herod's political motives in rebuilding the temple, the structure itself was accepted by the Jews and it is described as a central feature in the religious life of the people in the New Testament. Its precincts included several distinct enclosures leading inward to the Holy of Holies. Only priests could enter the inner areas, but ritually pure Jews and their wives could enter the outer temple or porch. Women, however, were not allowed in the area immediately outside the temple proper where sacrifices were conducted on the altar.

Thus was the first enclosure. In the midst of which, and not far from it, was the second, to be gone up to by a few steps; this was encompassed by a stone wall for a partition, with an inscription, which forbade any foreigner to go in, under pain of death.
—Josephus, *Ant.* 15.417

Gentiles were restricted to the outermost part of the temple's enclosures. An inscription was set into the wall near the gate leading inward which warned non-Jews, on pain of death, to proceed no further (*Ant.* 15.417). Excavators have discovered such an inscription dating to c. 20 BC, written in Greek, which forbids Gentiles from entering the temple. It was probably from Solomon's Porch (Jn 9:22), on the eastern side of this outer zone, from which Jesus drove the money changers in Mt 21:12.

B. JEWISH RELIGIOUS FACTIONS

While there were many religious and political factions in Palestine during the period from 200 BC until the 1st century AD, the four "philosophies"

singled out by Josephus as the most influential were the Sadducees, the Pharisees, the Essenes, and the Zealots. Drawing most of their support from the wealthy and influential families of the community, Sadducees sat on the Sanhedrin council and generally supported the policies of the Romans as a way of preventing conflict that could further ravage the nation (Jn 11:49–50). Although they were Hellenized in some of their manners of dress and custom, they rejected the use of anything other than the Pentateuch in matters of law and favored harsher punishments than the other factions (*Ant.* 13.293–295). The Sadducees also rejected the idea of a resurrection of the dead, saying that the soul died with the body and that man had complete free will to determine his own fate during life (*Ant.* 18.16; Mk 12:18).

Originating as a distinct group during the Hasmonean period, the Pharisees appear to have had a broader base of support among the people than the Sadducees. This may have been due to their advocation of more lenient punishments for crimes

Inscription warning Gentiles against entry into temple. Photo courtesy of Southwest Missouri State University. 5-20

(*Ant.* 13.294), their belief in a resurrection of the dead, and their belief in an eternal punishment of the wicked (*Ant.* 18.14–15; Rev 21:6–8). One indication that this latter belief was fairly widespread among the people may be Martha's statement to Jesus that Lazarus would "rise again in the resurrection at the last day" (Jn 11:24). Jesus also uses the theme of the resurrection of the dead in a statement dealing with the judgment of the righteous and the unreigheous in Jn 5:28–29.

The Pharisees also differed philosophically from the Sadducees by their acceptance of both free will and fate as factors influencing human lives (*Ant.* 18.13). Perhaps the most fundamental difference, however, between Pharisee and Sadducee was in the former's equal acceptance of oral tradition and the Torah to interpret the law (*Ant.* 13. 297 – 298). Jesus seems to take a similar position in Mt 5:21 – 48 where he quotes several of the commandments from the Sinai code and then expands upon them. What he apparently is doing here is establishing his own oral tradition on these issues of law and personal behavior.

But I say to you, Love your enemies and pray for those who persecute you, . . . — Matt 5:44

In Mk 7:8, however, Jesus tells the Pharisees, "You leave the commandment of God, and hold fast the tradition of men." This seems to be a clear acceptance of the Sadducean position regarding the sanctity of the Torah as the basis of interpretation of the law. His intent, however, was to point out the ways in which they had overburdened the original intent of the law by demanding strict adherence to every aspect of ritual.

The Pharisees are generally portrayed as the opponents of Jesus in the New Testament, but Paul does continue to identify himself as a Pharisee after his conversion (Acts 23:6). Jesus highlights the positive character of the Pharisees' teachings and strict adherence to the law, and in Mt 23:2 – 3 he tells the disciples and the crowd to "practice and observe whatever they tell you." However, he then notes their hypocritical nature in not practicing what they themselves teach.

The Essenes are not mentioned by name in the New Testament and thus our chief sources of information on them are Josephus and the scrolls produced by the Essene community at Qumran near the Dead Sea. Founded in protest to the usurpation of the high priesthood by Jonathan Maccabaeus in 152 BC, the Essenes separated themselves from the temple sacrificial cult. Like the Pharisees, they also believed in the resurrection and rewards for a righteous life. Some chose to found separate settlements like the wilderness community at Qumran. There, according to the scrolls, they were led by the "Teacher of Righteousness" in the proper way of life away from the contaminating influences of the less ritually pure Jews. This all male group lived a strict and regimented life, sharing their wealth with the community and practicing celibacy. Other groups of Essenes continued to live in Jerusalem and other cities where they engaged in their rituals of purification and performed private sacrifices (*Ant.* 18.18–22).

Josephus' "fourth philosophy," the Zealots, was founded in AD 6 by Judas of Galilee (Acts 5:37) in response to the imposition of a census by the Romans (*Ant.* 18:23–25). There were several other rebel groups in Palestine, variously known as Zealots or *sicarii* (*War* 7.262–270), but they had no common agenda and can only be tied to Judas' ideas, not his leadership. It seems that the Zealots were closely affiliated with the Pharisees and their beliefs. However, they were more of an extremist group, violently demonstrating their opposition to Roman taxation and assuring the people that God would come to the aid of his faithful worshippers. Their fanaticism led them to terrorist acts against the Romans and to the formation of opposition Jewish groups. Eventually the conflict culminated in the ill-fated defense of Masada in AD 74.

After him Judas the Galilean rose up at the time of the census and got people to follow him; he also perished, and all who followed him were scattered.

—Acts 5:37

C. SANHEDRIN

In addition to the priestly community and the various religious factions, there was another major religious body which influenced life in Jerusalem. This was the Sanhedrin, a council made up of 71 members, and chaired by the high priest. This group is described in Mk 15:1 and Lk 19:47 as including "the chief priests and the scribes and the principal men of the people." It had been organized during the Hasmonean period and included, at least during the New Testament period, both Sadducees and Pharisees (Acts 23:6). Its duties originally involved hearing criminal cases and imposing the death sentence (*Ant.* 14.167). After Herod became king, however, he killed all but one of its members for putting him on trial for murder, and presumably replaced them with men who could be controlled more easily (*Ant.* 14.175–176).

In the New Testament period the Sanhedrin appears to only have had jurisdiction over religious matters. They deliberated over what to do about

The synagogue at Capernaum. Photo by Ralph Harris. 5-21

Jesus in Jn 11:47, and questioned him before turning him over to Pilate for trial in Mk 14:53–15:1.
Some of the members of the Sanhedrin had Peter
and John arrested for preaching in the temple and
the whole council then questioned them, asking,
"By what power or by what name did you do
this?" (Acts 4:1–22). Their powers to punish the
evangelists were limited by popular opinion, however, since these men had performed confirmed
miraculous healings; thus they simply warned
them not to speak in Jesus' name (v 18). The
Sanhedrin also found it difficult to speak with
a united voice against the teachings of the Christians since some on the council, the Pharisees,
believed in the resurrection of the dead while
the Sadducean members did not (Acts 23:7–9;
Ant. 18.14, 16).

D. SYNAGOGUE WORSHIP AND LEADERSHIP

During the time that the Jerusalem temple
was still in existence, the synagogue served as a
secondary place of worship in Palestine. It originated in the Diaspora communities of Egypt and
Mesopotamia and spread to Palestine with the establishment of the Hasmonean kingdom (*Ant.*
19.300) During the New Testament period a synagogue was apparently built in every Palestinian
village and city of any size.

Jesus began his ministry in the Nazareth synagogue (Lk 4:16–21) and later used the Capernaum
synagogue to open his activities in the Galilee
region (Mk 1:21–28). In the rest of the ancient
world, wherever their was a community of Jews,
the synagogue served as a meeting place as well
as a seat for the study of the scriptures and for
worship. Paul would have received his early training in the Septuagint at the synagogue in Tarsus
before coming to Jerusalem for advanced Hebrew
studies with the scholar Gamaliel (Acts 22:3).
After his conversion he first went to the syna-

When he came to Nazareth, where he had been brought up, he went to the synagogue on the sab-bath day, as was his custom. He stood up to read, . . .
—Luke 4:16

Hear, O Israel: The LORD is our God, the LORD alone.
— Deut 6:4

gogues of the Diaspora before taking his message to the Gentiles (Acts 18:3 – 6).

Sabbath worship in a synagogue varied from place to place, but generally included the reciting of the *shema'* (confession of faith, Dt 6:4 – 9), scripture readings from the Law and the Prophets, prayer, thanksgiving, and individual exhortations (Acts 13:15). Some of the rites associated with temple worship were also transferred to the synagogue after AD 70, although not animal sacrifice. These places of worship were open to all people during services and they did attract some pious Greeks interested in the moral teachings of the Jewish law (*War* 7.45). Some of these people converted to Judaism (Acts 13:43) or were among the group known as the "God-fearers" (Acts 13:16, 26, 43; 14:1). Many of these same people were later converted to Christianity by Paul and the other apostles (Acts 17:4).

The leadership in the synagogues was not in the hands of priests. Lay officials and a council of elders headed by an archon (Mk 5:22, *archisynagōgos*) directed synagogue worship, supervised maintenance of the building, and enforced the rules of the congregation. The head of the synagogue was also sometimes aided by an attendant or deputy head (Lk 4:20). It was their responsibility to discipline members who disobeyed some aspect of the law (Lk 13:14). Paul's statement that he had five times received 39 lashes at the hands of the Jews probably refers to synagogue justice (2 Cor 11:24).

For as in one body we have many members, and not all the members have the same function, . . . — Rom 12:4

It may be presumed that some early converts to Christianity continued their membership in the local synagogue (Jas 1:1). Being Jews as well as Christians, they may have blended into the life of the congregation or perhaps shared the building with the Jews. The antagonism of some Jews against the Christian converts (Acts 13:45; 14:2; 17:5 – 9) suggests, however, that this sort of arrangement could not have lasted long and the

Christians would have been forced to meet in private homes and their own churches (Rom 16:5; Acts 18:5 – 7; 20:20).

These early Christian congregations worshipped according to the pattern set in Acts 2:42, "they devoted themselves to the apostles' teachings and fellowship, to the breaking of bread and the prayers." The various talents of the members were used in worship and in the governance of the community (Rom 12:3 – 8). The letter to Titus describes the qualities needed by elders and other leaders of the church, but all of the adult members were to serve diligently as good examples to each other and the outside community as well.

Map of principal New Testament cities. Mercer Dictionary of the Bible. 5-F

SELECT BIBLIOGRAPHY

PREFACE

Barre, M. L. "The Extrabiblical Literature." *Listening* 19 (1984): 53–72.
Ben-Tor, A. "The Regional Study—A New Approach to Archaeological Investigation." *BAR* 6 (2, 1980): 30–44.
Brandfon, F. R. "Archaeology and the Biblical Text." *BAR* 14 (1, 1988): 54–59.
Dever, W. G. "Archaeological Method in Israel: A Continuing Revolution." *BA* 43 (1980): 41–48.
_____. *Recent Archaeological Discoveries and Biblical Research.* Seattle: University of Washington Press, 1990.
Fishbane, M. "The Earliest Biblical Exegesis Is in the Bible Itself." *Bible Review* 2 (4, 1986): 42–45.
Kenyon, K. M. *Archaeology in the Holy Land.* New York: Praeger, 1960.
King, P. J. "The Contribution of Archaeology to Biblical Studies." *CBQ* 45 (1983): 1–16.
Mazar, A. *Archaeology of the Land of the Bible 10,000–586 B.C.E.* New York: Doubleday, 1990.
Millard, A. R. *The Bible BC: What Can Archaeology Prove?* London: Presbyterian & Reformed, 1982.
Miller, J. M. "Approaches to the Bible Through History and Archaeology: Biblical History as a Discipline." *BA* 45 (1982): 211–16.
_____. *The Old Testament and the Historian.* Philadelphia: Fortress Press, 1976.
_____. "Old Testament History and Archaeology." *BA* 50 (1987): 55–63.
Rogerson, J. W. *Anthropology and the Old Testament.* Sheffield, England: JSOT Press, 1984.
Sauer, J. A. "Syro-Palestinian Archaeology, History, and Biblical Studies." *BA* 45 (1982): 201–9.
Wright, G. E. *Biblical Archaeology,* 2nd ed. Philadelphia: Westminster Press, 1962.

INTRODUCTION

Aharoni, Y. *The Land of the Bible.* Philadelphia: Westminster Press, 1967.
_____. and M. Avi-Yonah. *The Macmillan Bible Atlas.* New York: Macmillan, 1968.
Baly, D. *The Geography of the Bible,* 2nd ed. New York: Harper & Row, 1974.
Beitzel, B. *Moody Atlas of Bible Lands.* Chicago: Moody Press, 1985.
Brodsky, H. "The Shephelah—Guardian of Judea." *Bible Review* 3 (4, 1987): 48–52.
Casson, L. *Travel in the Ancient World.* Toronto: Hakkert, 1974.
Hallo, W. W. and W. K. Simpson. *The Ancient Near East: A History.* New York: Harcourt Brace Jovanovich, Inc., 1971.
Hayes, J. H. and J. M. Miller, eds. *A History of Ancient Israel and Judah.* Philadelphia: Westminster Press, 1986.
_____. *Israelite and Judean History.* Philadelphia: Westminster Press, 1977.
May, H. G., ed. *Oxford Bible Atlas,* 3rd edition. New York: Oxford University Press, 1985.
Pritchard, J. B. *The Harper Atlas of the Bible.* New York: Harper & Row, 1987.
Rasmussen, C. G. *Zondervan NIV Atlas of the Bible.* Grand Rapids, Mich.: Zondervan, 1989.
Rogerson, J. *Atlas of the Bible.* New York: Facts on File, 1985.
Whitelam, K. M. "Recreating the History of Israel." *JSOT* 35 (1986): 45–70.

CHAPTER 1

Barth, F. *A Tribe of the Khamseh Confederacy: The Basseri Nomads of South Persia.* Oslo: Little, Brown and Co., 1961.

Contenau, G. *Everyday Life in Babylon and Assyria.* New York: W. W. Norton Co., 1966.

Frymer-Kensky, T. "Patriarchal Family Relationship and Near Eastern Law." *BA* 44 (1981): 209–14.

Haran, M. "The Religion of the Patriarchs: An Attempt at Synthesis." *ASTI* 4 (1965): 30–55.

Kempinski, A. "Jacob in History." *BAR* 14 (1, 1988): 42–47.

Luke, J. T. "Abraham and the Iron Age: Reflections on the New Patriarchal Studies." *JSOT* 4 (1977): 35–47.

Malamat, A. "Aspects of Tribal Societies in Mari and Israel." *Recontre d'assyriologique internationale* 15 (1967): 129–38.

Matthews, V. H. *Pastoral Nomadism in the Mari Kingdom, ca. 1830–1760 B.C.* Cambridge, Mass.: American Schools of Oriental Research, 1978.

———. "Pastoralists and Patriarchs." *BA* 44 (1981): 215–18.

———. "The Wells of Gerar." *BA* 49 (1986): 118–26.

Matthews, V. H. and Benjamin, D. C. *Old Testament Parallels: Laws and Stories from the Ancient Near East.* Mahwah, N.J.: Paulist, 1991.

McKane, W. *Studies in the Patriarchal Narratives.* Edinburgh: Handsel Press, 1979.

Millard, A. and D. J. Wiseman, eds. *Essays on the Patriarchal Narratives.* Leicester: Inter-Varsity Press, 1980.

Morrison, M. "The Jacob and Laban Narrative in the Light of Near Eastern Sources." *BA* 46 (1983): 155–64.

Ramsey, G. W. *The Quest for the Historical Israel.* Atlanta: John Knox Press, 1981.

Rowton, M. C. "Autonomy and Nomadism in Western Asia." *Or* 42 (1973): 247–58.

———. "Dimorphic Structure and the Parasocial Element." *JNES* 36 (1977): 181–98.

Rubens, A. *A History of Jewish Costume.* New York: Funk & Wagnalls, 1967.

Sarna, N.M. *Understanding Genesis.* New York: Shocken Books, 1966.

Thompson, T. L. *The Historicity of the Patriarchal Narratives.* Berlin: Walter de Gruyter, 1974.

———. "A New Attempt to Date the Patriarchal Narratives." *JAOS* 98 (1978): 76–84.

Tucker, G.M. "The Legal Background of Gen 23." *JBL* 85 (1966): 77–84.

Van Seters, J. *Abraham in History and Tradition.* New Haven, Conn.: Yale University Press, 1975.

Vaux de, R. *Ancient Israel: Social Institutions,* 2 vols. New York: McGraw-Hill, 1965.

Warner, S.M. "The Patriarchs and Extra-Biblical Sources." *JSOT* 2 (1977): 50–61.

Westermann, C. *The Promises to the Fathers: Studies on the Patriarchal Narratives.* Philadelphia: Fortress, 1980.

Yadin, Y. *The Art of Warfare in Biblical Lands in the Light of Archaeological Discoveries.* London: Weidenfeld and Nicolson, 1963.

CHAPTER 2

Beebe, H. K. "Ancient Palestinian Dwellings." *BA* 34 (1971): 38–58.

Ben-Tor, A. "Tell Qiri: A Look at Village Life." *BA* 42 (1979): 105–13.

Bimson, J. J. and D. Livingston. "Redating the Exodus." *BAR* 13 (5, 1987): 40–53, 66–68.

Borowski, O. *Agriculture in Iron Age Israel.* Winona Lake, Ind.: Eisenbrauns, 1987.

Callaway, J. A. "A Visit with Ahilud." *BAR* 9 (5, 1983): 42–53.

Coote, R. B. and K. W. Whitelam. "The Emergence of Israel: Social Transormation and State Formation Following the Decline in Late Bronze Age Trade." *Semeia* 37 (1986): 107–47.

Davey, C. "The Dwellings of Private Citizens." *Buried History* 13 (1977): 21–37.

Dothan, T. "What We Know About the Philistines." *BAR* 8 (4, 1982): 20–44.

Finkelstein, I. *The Archaeology of the Settlement of Israel*. Jerusalem: Israel Exploration Society, 1988.
Fritz, V. "Conquest or Settlement? The Early Iron Age in Palestine." *BA* 50 (1987): 84–100.
de Gens, C. H. L. *The Tribes of Israel*. Assen/Amsterdam: Van Gorcum, 1976.
Gottwald, N. K. *The Tribes of Yahweh: A Sociology of the Religion of Liberated Israel 1250–1050 B.C.E.* Maryknoll, N.Y.: Orbis, 1979.
Halpern, B. "Radical Exodus Redating Fatally Flawed." *BAR* 13 (6, 1987): 56–61.
Hopkins, D. A. *The Highlands of Canaan*. Decatur, Ga: Almond Press, 1985.
_____. "Life on the Land: The Subsistence Struggles of Early Israel." *BA* 50 (1987): 178–91.
Lemche, N. P. *Ancient Israel: A New History of Israelite Society*. Sheffield: JSOT Press, 1988.
Malamat, A. "Mari and the Bible: Some Patterns of Tribal Organization and Institutions." *JAOS* 82 (1962): 143–50.
Mendenhall, G. E. "The Relation of the Individual to Political Society in Ancient Israel." In *Biblical Studies in Memory of H. C. Alleman*. Edited by J. M. Myers, et al. Locust Valley, N.Y.: J. J. Augustin, 1960: 89–108.
Miller, J. M. "The Israelite Occupation of Canaan." In *Israelite and Judean History*. Edited by J. H. Hayes and J. M. Miller. Philadelphia: Westminster Press, 1977: 213–84.
Muhly, J. D. "How Iron Technology Changed the Ancient World — and Gave the Philistines a Military Edge." *BAR* 8 (6, 1982): 40–54.
North, R. "Violence and the Bible: The Girard Connection." *CBQ* 47 (1985): 1–27.
Stager, L. E. "The Archaeology of the Family in Ancient Israel." *BASOR* 260 (1985): 1–35.
Thompson, J. A. "Farming in Ancient Israel." *Buried History* 20 (1984): 53–60.
_____. "The Israelite Village." *Buried History* 19 (1983): 51–58.
Ussishkin, D. "Lachish — Key to the Israelite Conquest of Canaan?" *BAR* 13 (1, 1987): 18–39.
Vaux de, R. *Ancient Israel: Social Institutions*, Vol. 1. New York: McGraw-Hill, 1965: 19–61.
Zohary, M. *Plants of the Bible*. Cambridge: Cambridge University Press, 1982.

CHAPTER 3

Ahlstrom, G. W. "Where Did the Israelites Live?" *JNES* 41 (1982): 133–38.
Alt, A. *Essays in Old Testament History and Religion*. Oxford: Blackwell, 1966.
Beebe, H. K. "Ancient Palestinian Dwellings." *BA* 31 (1968): 38–58.
Benjamin, D. C. *Deuteronomy and City Life*. Lanham, Md.: University Press of America, 1983.
Boecker, H. J. *Law and the Administration of Justice in the Old Testament and Ancient East*. Minneapolis: Augsburg Press, 1980.
Borowski, O. "Five Ways to Defend an Ancient City." *BAR* 9 (2, 1983): 73–76.
Cole, D. P. "How Water Tunnels Worked." *BAR* 6 (2, 1980): 8–29.
DeVries, L. F. "Cult Stands — A Bewildering Variety of Shapes and Sizes." *BAR* 13 (4, 1987): 26–37.
Edelstein, G. and Gibson, S. "Ancient Jerusalem's Rural Food Basket." *BAR* 8 (4, 1982): 46–54.
Frick, F. S. *The City in Ancient Israel*. Missoula, Mont.: Scholars Press, 1977.
_____. *The Formation of the State in Ancient Israel*. Sheffield: Almond Press, 1985.
Fritz, V. "What Can Archaeology Tell Us about Solomon's Temple?" *BAR* 13 (4, 1987): 38–49.
Hanson, P. D. *The People Called, The Growth of Community in the Bible*. San Francisco: Harper & Row, 1986.
Haran, M. *Temples and Temple Service in Ancient Israel*. Oxford: Clarendon Press, 1970.
Hasel, G. F. "Health and Healing in the Old Testament." *AUSS* 21 (1983): 191–202.
Hauer, C. "From Alt to Anthropology: The Rise of the Israelite State." *JSOT* 36 (1986): 3–15.
Heaton, E. W. *Solomon's New Men*. New York: Pica Press, 1974.
Herrmann, S. "King David's State." In *In the Shelter of Elyon, Essays on Ancient Palestinian Life and Literature in Honor of G. W. Ahlstrom*. Edited by W. B. Barrick and J. R. Spencer. Sheffield: JSOT Supplement Series, 31, 1984: 261–75.

Kinnier Wilson, J. V. "Medicine in the Land and Times of the Old Testament." In *Studies in The Period of David and Solomon and other Essays*. Edited by T. Ishida. Winona Lake, Ind.: Eisenbrauns, 1982: 337–65.

Kohler, L. *Hebrew Man*. London: SCM, 1956.

Lang, B. "Afterlife: Ancient Israel's Changing Vision of the World Beyond." *Bible Review* 4 (1, 1988): 12–23.

Lemche, D. "David's Rise." *JSOT* 10 (1978): 2–25.

McCarter, P. K. "The Historical David." *Interp* 40 (1986): 117–29.

MacKenzie, R. A. F. "The City and Israelite Religion." *CBQ* 25 (1963): 60–70.

Matthews, V. H. "Entrance Ways and Threshing Floors: Legally Significant Sites in the Ancient Near East." *FEH* 19 (1987): 25–40.

Milgrom, J. "Of Hems and Tassels." *BAR* 9 (3, 1983): 61–65.

Neufeld, E. "Hygiene Conditions in Ancient Israel (Iron Age)." *BA* 34 (1971): 42–66.

Patrick, D. *Old Testament Law*. Atlanta: John Knox Press, 1984.

Platt, E. E. "Jewelry of Bible Times and the Catalog of Isa 3:18–23." *AUSS* 17 (1979): 71–84, 189–201.

Pritchard, J. *Ancient Near Eastern Texts Relating to the Old Testament*. Princeton: Princeton University Press, 1969. (abbreviated *ANET*).

Rahmani, L. Y. "Ancient Jerusalem's Funerary Customs and Tombs." *BA* 45 (1, 1982): 43–53.

Rubens, A. *A History of Jewish Costume*. New York: Funk and Wagnalls, 1967.

Shiloh, Y. "The Four-Room House: Its Situation and Function in the Israelite City." *IEJ* 20 (1970): 180–90.

Soggin, J. *A History of Ancient Israel*. Philadelphia: Westminster Press, 1985.

Thompson, J. A. "The 'Town' in Old Testament Times." *Buried History* 19 (1983): 35–42.

Ussishkin, D. "King Solomon's Palaces." *BA* 36 (1973): 78–105.

de Vaux, R. *Ancient Israel: Its Life and Institutions*. London: Darton, Longman and Todd, 1973.

Whitelam, K. W. *The Just King: Monarchical Judicial Authority in Ancient Israel*. Sheffield: JSOT Supplement Series, 12, 1979.

———. "The Symbols of Power: Aspects of Royal Propaganda in the United Monarchy." *BA* 49 (1986): 166–73.

Wilkinson, J. "Leprosy and Leviticus: The Problem of Description and Identification." *SJT* 30 (1977): 153–69.

Wilson, R. R. *Prophecy and Society in Ancient Israel*. Philadelphia: Fortress Press, 1980.

Yadin, Y. *The Art of Warfare in Biblical Lands in the Light of Archaeological Discovery*. London: Weidenfeld and Nicolson, 1963.

CHAPTER 4

Ackroyd, P. R. *Exile and Restoration, A Study of Hebrew Thought of the Sixth Century B.C.* Philadelphia: Westminster Press, 1968.

———. "Archaeology, Politics and Religion: The Persian Period." *Iliff Review* 39 (1982): 5–23.

Bossman, D. "Ezra's Marriage Reform: Israel Redefined." *BTB* 9 (1979): 32–38.

Coogan, M. D. "Life in the Diaspora: Jews at Nippur in the Fifth Century B.C." *BA* 37 (1974): 6–12.

Cross, F. M. "A Reconstruction of the Judean Restoration." *JBL* 94 (1975): 4–18.

Dumbrell, W. J. "Kingship and Temple in the Post-Exilic Period." *RTR* 37 (1978): 33–42.

Freedman, D. N. " 'Son of Man, Can These Bones Live?' " *Interp* 29 (1975): 171–86.

Japhet, S. "Sheshbazzar and Zerubbabel: Against the Background of the Historical and Religious Tendencies of Ezra-Nehemiah." *ZAW* 94 (1982): 66–98; 95 (1983): 218–29.

Klein, R. *Israel in Exile*. Philadelphia: Fortress Press, 1979.

Koch, K. "Ezra and the Origins of Judaism." *JSS* 19 (1974): 173–97.

Kuhrt, A. "The Cyrus Cylinder and Achaemenid Imperial Policy." *JSOT* 25 (1983): 83–97.
Malina, B. *The New Testament World: Insights from Cultural Anthropology.* Atlanta: John Knox Press, 1981.
Mazar, B. *The Mountain of the Lord.* Garden City, N.Y.: Doubleday, 1975.
McCullough, W. S. *The History and Literature of the Palestinian Jews from Cyrus to Herod 550 BC to 4 BC.* Toronto: University of Toronto Press, 1975.
McEvenue, S. E. "The Political Structure in Judah from Cyrus to Nehemiah." *CBQ* 43 (1981): 353–64.
Meyers, C. "The Elusive Temple." *BA* 45 (1982): 33–41.
Miller, J. M. and J. H. Hayes. *A History of Ancient Israel and Judah.* Philadelphia: Westminster Press, 1986.
Myers, J. M. "Edom and Judah in the Sixth and Fifth Centuries B.C." In *Near Eastern Studies in Honor of W. F. Albright.* Edited by H. Goedicke. Baltimore: Johns Hopkins Press, 1971: 377–92.
Stern, E. *The Material Culture of the Land of the Bible in the Persian Period 538–332 BC.* Warminster, England: Aris & Phillips, 1982.
Stohlmann, S. "The Judaean Exile after 701 B.C.E." In *Scripture in Context II, More Essays on the Comparative Method.* Edited by W. W. Hallo, J. C. Moyer, and L. G. Perdue. Winona Lake, Ind.: Eisenbrauns, 1983: 147–76.
Vaux de, R. *Ancient Israel: Its Life and Institutions.* New York: McGraw-Hill, 1961.
Widengren, G. "The Persian Period." In *Israelite and Judaean History.* Edited by J. H. Hayes and J. M. Miller. Philadelphia: Westminster Press, 1977: 489–538.
_____. "Yahweh's Gathering of the Dispersed." In *In the Shelter of Elyon, Essays on Ancient Palestinian Life and Literature in Honor of G. W. Ahlstrom.* Edited by W. B. Barrick and J. R. Spencer. Sheffield: JSOT Supplement 31, 1984: 227–45.
Yamauchi, E. M. "Daniel and Contacts between the Aegean and the Near East before Alexander." *EvQ* 53 (1981): 37–47.
_____. *Persia and the Bible.* Grand Rapids, Mich.: Baker Book House, 1990.
Zadok, R. *The Jews in Babylonia during the Chaldean and Achaemenian Periods.* Haifa: University of Haifa Press, 1979.
_____. "Notes on the Early History of the Israelites and Judeans in Mesopotamia." *Or* 51 (1982): 391–93.

CHAPTER 5

Avigad, N. "Jerusalem Flourishing—A Craft Center for Stone, Pottery, and Glass." *BAR* 9 (6, 1983): 48–65.
Avi-Yonah. M. "The Development of the Roman Road System in Palestine." *IEJ* 1 (1950–51): 54–60.
Barker, G. W., W. L. Lane, and J. R. Michaels. *The New Testament Speaks.* New York: Harper & Row, 1969.
Best, T. F. "The Sociological Study of the New Testament: Promise and Peril of a New Discipline." *SJT* 36 (1983): 181–94.
Collins, J. J. *Between Athens and Jerusalem: Jewish Identity in the Hellenistic Diaspora.* New York: Crossroad, 1983.
Court, J. and K. *The New Testament World.* Englewood Cliffs, N.J.: Prentice-Hall, 1990.
Derrett, J. Duncan M. *Law in the New Testament.* London: Darton, Longman & Todd, 1970.
Dowley, T., ed. *Discovering the Bible.* Grand Rapids: Eerdmans, 1986.
Feldman, L. H. "The Omnipresence of the God-Fearers." *BAR* 12 (5, 1986): 58–69.
Finegan, J. *The Archaeology of the New Testament, The Life of Jesus and the Beginning of the Early Church.* Princeton, N.J.: Princeton University Press, 1969.
Gallagher, E. V. "The Social World of St. Paul." *Rel* 14 (1984): 91–99.

Gowan, D. E. *Bridge Between the Testaments.* Pittsburgh: Pickwick Press, 1980.

Gutmann, J., ed. *Ancient Synagogues: The State of Research.* Missoula, Mont.: Scholars Press, 1981.

Harris, O. G. "The Social World of Early Christianity." *LTQ* 19 (3, 1984): 102–14.

Hengel, M. *Judaism and Hellenism.* Philadelphia: Fortress Press, 1981.

Hirschfeld, Y. and G. Solar. "Sumptuous Roman Baths Uncovered Near Sea of Galilee." *BAR* 10 (6, 1984): 22–40.

Jeremias, J. *Jerusalem in the Time of Jesus.* Philadelphia: Fortress Press, 1969.

Koester, H. *Introduction to the New Testament: History, Culture, and Religion of the Hellenistic Age,* 2 vols. Philadelphia: Fortress Press, 1980.

Malherbe, A. J. *Social Aspects of Early Christianity.* Baton Rouge: Louisiana State University Press, 1977.

Malina, B. J. *Christian Origins and Cultural Anthropology.* Atlanta: John Knox Press, 1986.

———. *The New Testament World, Insights from Cultural Anthropology.* Atlanta: John Knox Press, 1981.

Meeks, W. A. *The First Urban Christians: The Social World of the Apostle Paul.* New Haven: Yale University Press, 1983.

Meshorer, Y. *Ancient Jewish Coinage.* New York: Amphora Books, 1982.

Meyers, C. L. "The Elusive Temple." *BA* 45 (1, 1982): 33–41.

Meyers, E. M. "Ancient Synagogues in Galilee: Their Religious and Cultural Setting." *BA* 43 (2, 1980): 97–108.

Murphy-O'Connor, J. "The Corinth that Saint Paul Saw." *BA* 47 (3, 1984): 147–59.

———. "The Essenes in Palestine." *BA* 40 (3, 1977): 100–124.

Neusner, J. *From Politics to Piety: The Emergence of Pharisaic Judaism.* Englewood Cliffs, N.J.: Prentice Hall, 1973.

Osiek, C. *What Are They Saying About the Social Setting of the New Testament?* New York: Paulist Press, 1984.

Peters, F. E. "Hellenism and the Near East." *BA* 46 (1, 1983): 33–39.

———. *Jerusalem.* Princeton: Princeton University Press, 1985.

Rahmani, L. Y. "Ancient Jerusalem's Funerary Customs and Tombs, Part Three." *BA* 45 (1, 1982): 43–53.

Rivkin, E. *A Hidden Revolution: The Pharisee's Search for the Kingdom Within.* Nashville: Abingdon, 1978.

Roetzel, C. J. *The World That Shaped the New Testament.* Atlanta: John Knox Press, 1985.

Scott, R. B. Y. "Weights and Measures of the Bible." *BA* 22 (2, 1959): 22–40.

Smallwood, E. M. *The Jews Under Roman Rule, From Pompey to Diocletian.* Leiden: E. J. Brill, 1976.

Stambaugh, J. E. and D. L. Balch. *The New Testament in Its Social Environment.* Philadelphia: Westminster Press, 1986.

Stieglitz, R. R. "Long-distance Seafaring in the Ancient Near East." *BA* 47 (3, 1984): 134–42.

Tcherikover, V. *Hellenistic Civilization and the Jews.* New York: Atheneum, 1970.

Theissen, G. *Sociology of Early Palestinian Christianity.* Philadelphia: Fortress Press, 1978.

Thompson, J. A. *Life in Bible Times.* Downers Grove, Ill.: Inter-Varsity Press, 1986.

Van Der Woude, A. S., ed. *The World of the Bible.* Grand Rapids, Mich.: Eerdmans, 1986.

Wilkinson, J. *Jerusalem as Jesus Knew It, Archaeology as Evidence.* London: Thames & Hudson Ltd., 1978.

INDEXES

SUBJECT INDEX

INDEX OF PERSONAL NAMES

INDEX OF PLACE NAMES

INDEX OF ANCIENT TEXTS